Postcard History Series

Suffolk

in Vintage Postcards

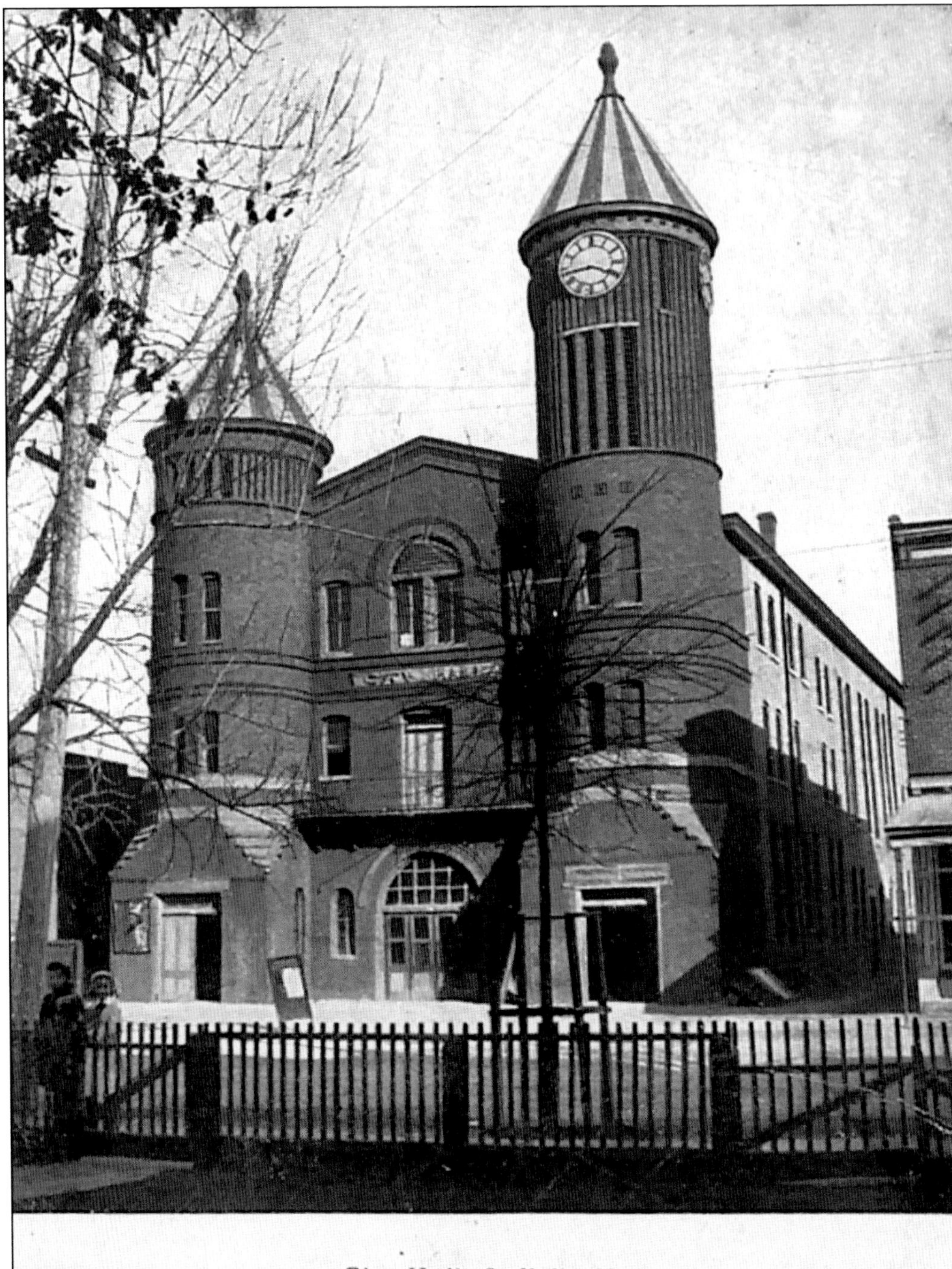

The old City Hall/City Market was the center of community life for more than 50 years. Built in 1891, it took the place of a residence that had been destroyed in the fire of 1888. In 1962 the building shown above was demolished in the name of progress. It was replaced by a cinder-block building, which has since been razed. Part of the courts complex and its adjacent garden now fill this spot.

POSTCARD HISTORY SERIES

Suffolk

IN VINTAGE POSTCARDS

Suffolk-Nansemond Historical Society

ARCADIA PUBLISHING

ISBN 978-0-7385-1535-9

Published by Arcadia Publishing
Charleston, South Carolina

Printed in the United States of America

Library of Congress Catalog Card Number: 2003105089

For all general information contact Arcadia Publishing at:
Telephone 843-853-2070
Fax 843-853-0044
E-Mail sales@arcadiapublishing.com
For customer service and orders:
Toll-Free 1-888-313-2665

Visit us on the Internet at www.arcadiapublishing.com

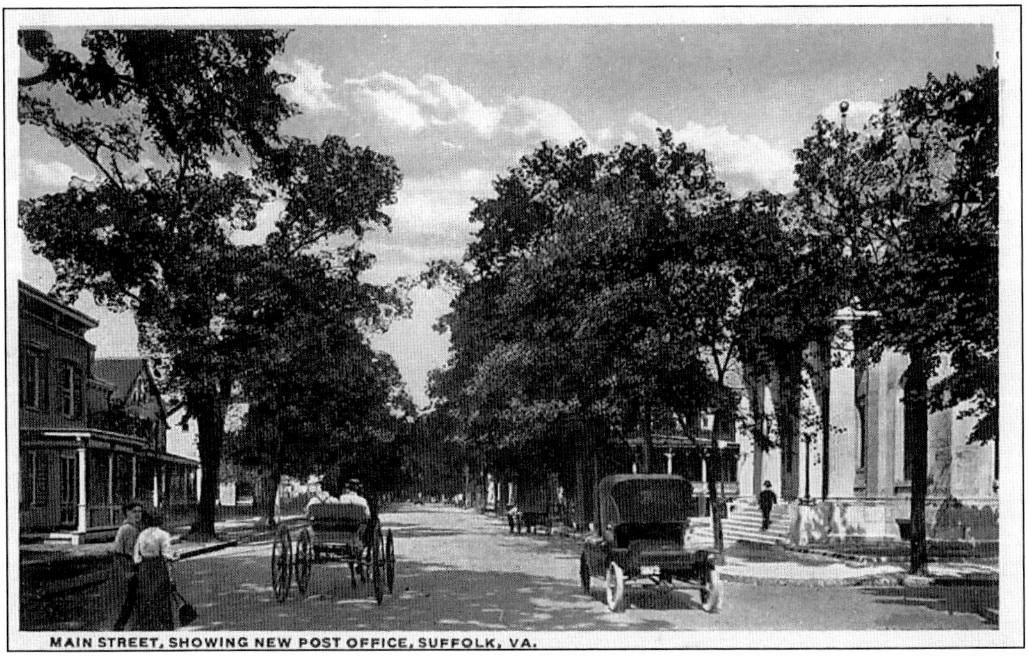

This view of North Main Street around 1913 shows the new post office. On the far left is the postwar home of Confederate general Lawrence Baker. The building formerly housed Maj. William McClenny's store. Trees were essential for keeping the neighborhood cool in the summer, and brick streets kept the dust down.

Contents

ACKNOWLEDGMENTS

It must have been Henry Frazier's interest in his hometown that led him to start collecting Suffolk postcards nearly three decades ago. It was at his suggestion that this postcard book was undertaken. Tommy O'Connor kindly agreed to make his extensive collection available as well. Lynn Rose, Mary Ainslie Latimer, Pret Pretlow, and Joe Ward also provided cards. The Suffolk Nansemond Historical Society is grateful to these two gentlemen and to the many other people who have assisted with this book particularly Hunter Duggan, Kermit Hobbs, Lynn Rose, and Sue Woodward. Tommy Arthur and Charles Sledge also helped, as did numerous other people from all over the City of Suffolk. Information came from many sources but especially from *Suffolk: A Pictorial History* by Kermit Hobbs and William Pacquette and from the special October 27, 1942 edition of the *Suffolk News Herald*. Another source was *Pen and Picture Sketches: Year 1915* reprinted by our organization.

In spite of interest and assistance on all sides, this book would not have been attempted without Henry Frazier and to him we are very grateful.

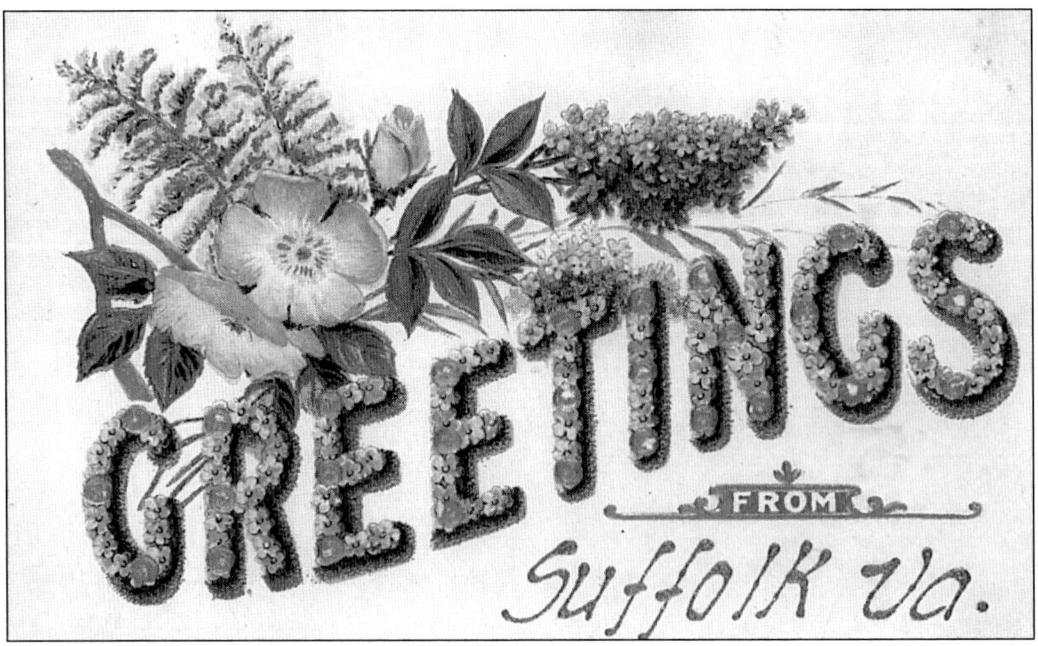

Introduction

When the town of Suffolk was chartered in 1742, a brisk trade had been taking place at that spot on the Nansemond River for about 20 years. The area had been called Constant's Wharf, in honor of John Constant, who operated the trading center there.

During the Revolutionary War, three Nansemond County towns were burned by the British. They were South Quay on the Blackwater River, Milner on the Western Branch of the Nansemond River, and, in 1779, Suffolk. Only Chuckatuck and Somerton were untouched.

The town set about rebuilding aided, perhaps, by the coming of the first railroad—the Portsmouth and Roanoke—in 1834. Before long, disaster struck again in 1837 when a fire, started in a cabinet shop, burned the most densely populated part of town from Second Cross (Mahan) Street to the river.

During the War between the States, Suffolk was held by the Union Army from 1862 to 1863. Part of Suffolk's attraction for the Union commanders was the railroad. By this time there was a second one as well—the Norfolk and Western. The war left Suffolk and Nansemond County devastated. But we were determined to persevere.

By the end of the 19th century there were six first-class railroads, as well as numerous narrow-gauge lumber lines. New towns and villages grew along the railroads—Driver, Holland, and Whaleyville, as well as smaller settlements. The rails moved lumber, farm produce, coal, and of course, people. Around the turn of the century the Old Dominion Steamship line made regular stops in Suffolk as well. Establishments like the Nansemond Hotel and the Elliot Hotel were kept especially busy with business travelers.

A large hall was built in the middle of the bustling downtown in the late 1800s. First called the Academy of Music, it later became the City Hall and City Market, and it was a real center of activity through the mid-20th century. In the 1890s the first public school building, the clerk's office, the Christian Church, and the Episcopal Church were constructed.

The peanut, which had hardly been noticed before the Civil War, became a money crop of importance after the war. The first successful peanut processing business, Suffolk Peanut Company, was started in 1897. Many others would soon follow. In 1911, Amedeo Obici came from Pennsylvania looking for a site to establish his Planters Peanut Company. He wanted to be close to the source for peanuts and soon made his home in Suffolk. Planters Nut and Chocolate Company employed many townspeople, and the Planters symbol, the monocled Mr. Peanut, was based on an idea from a Suffolk school boy.

By the 1940s, Suffolk was known as the World's Largest Peanut Market. Peanuts, lumber, and general agriculture brought prosperity to Suffolk, which became the trading center for a large agricultural region. New streets opened rapidly after the Civil War—Franklin and Pinner Streets, Brewer Avenue, and Broad Street.

Two hospitals, Lakeview and Virginia Hospitals, opened early in the 20th century. They closed in 1951 when Louise Obici Memorial Hospital opened. The hospital was built with funds left by the peanut man, Amedeo Obici, as a memorial to his wife.

The middle of the 20th century brought many changes to Suffolk. Highways improved and railroads declined in popularity. The old hotels gave way to motels outside town. Gas stations appeared on every corner. New buildings, such as the original Morgan Memorial Library on Bosley Avenue, Birdsong Recreation Center, and the new post office, took a boxier, more modern form.

The Great Dismal Swamp has fascinated visitors to the area from the earliest time of human habitation. It was a source of lumber, especially cypress, for hundreds of years and is also a playground for sportsmen and a popular tourist destination. In the midst of change, a few things remain constant.

In the 18th and 19th centuries, Suffolk was a town in Nansemond County. In 1910 it became a city with a separate government. In 1974 the old two-square-mile city merged with what had been the 430-square-mile Nansemond County to form the very large city that Suffolk is today.

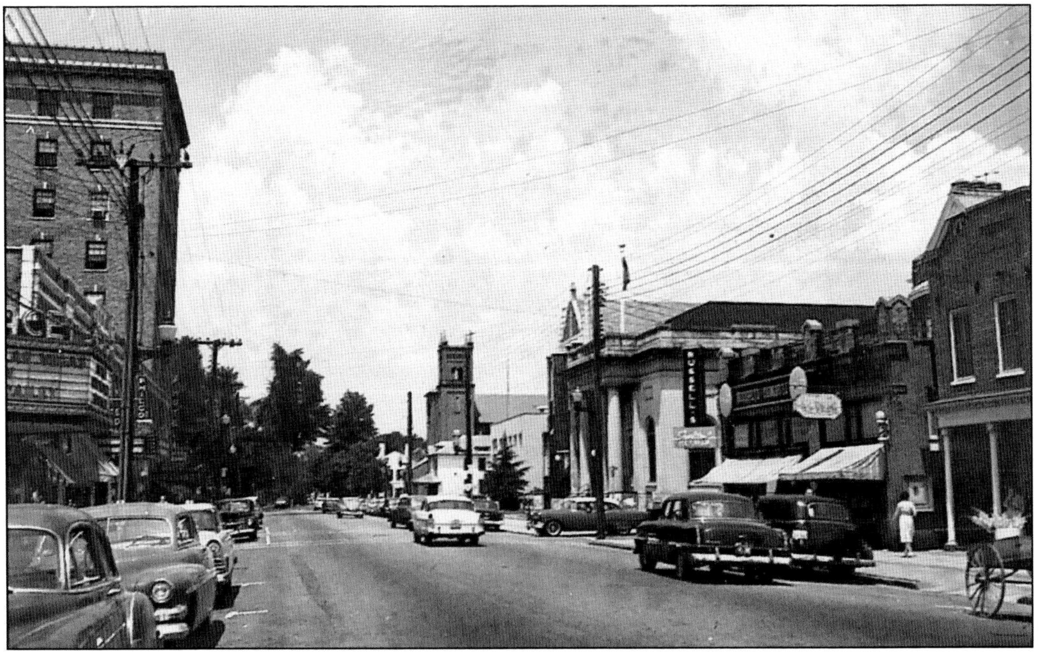

For Baby Boomers—and their parents before them—this was the place to have fun. The Palace Theater is at the far left and the Chadwick Theater is on the same side of the street. Across the street is Russell's Drugstore, a great place to drink a Coke and people-watch. At the right corner is a flower cart at the market.

One

Nurturing Influences

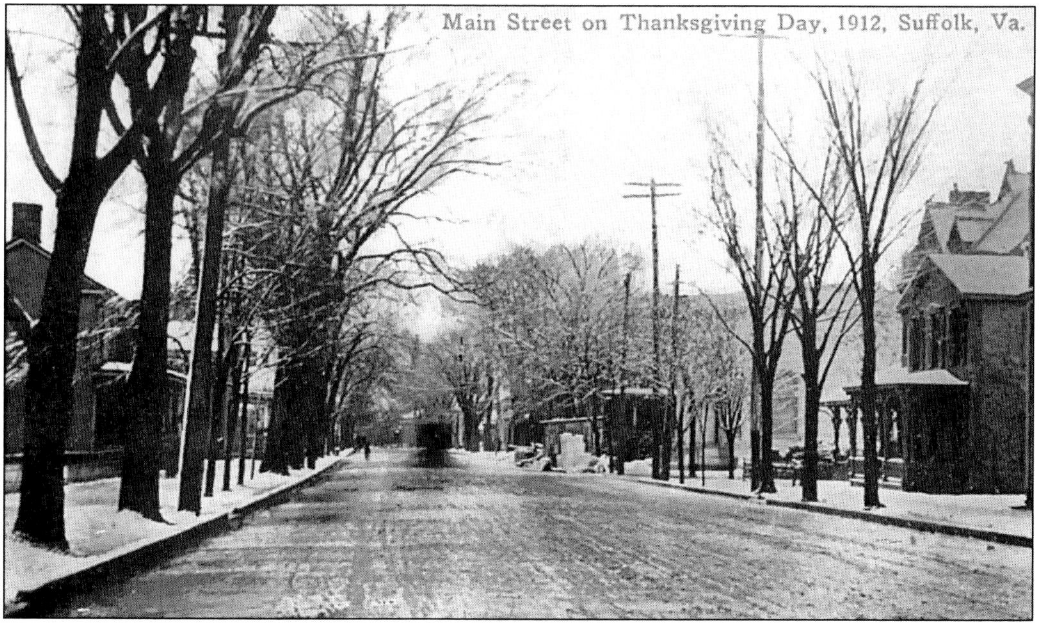

Snow on Thanksgiving in Suffolk is certainly a remarkable occurrence. In 1912 the residential area was as close as possible to the business district to allow residents the ability to walk to work. The second house from the right edge of the picture would become first Ruden's, then Russell's Drug Store. The new post office is under construction.

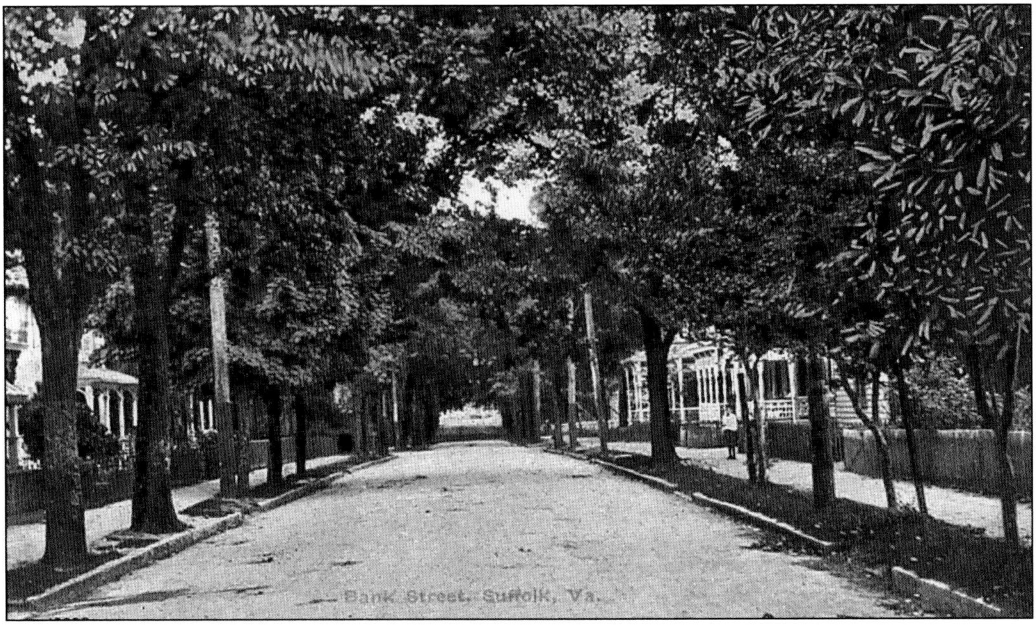

Bank Street was so named because it ran east from Main Street in front of Suffolk's first successful bank. The street was the first new one opened in Suffolk after the Civil War. Many up-and-coming young people who came to Suffolk between the 1870s and the 1890s lived on Bank Street.

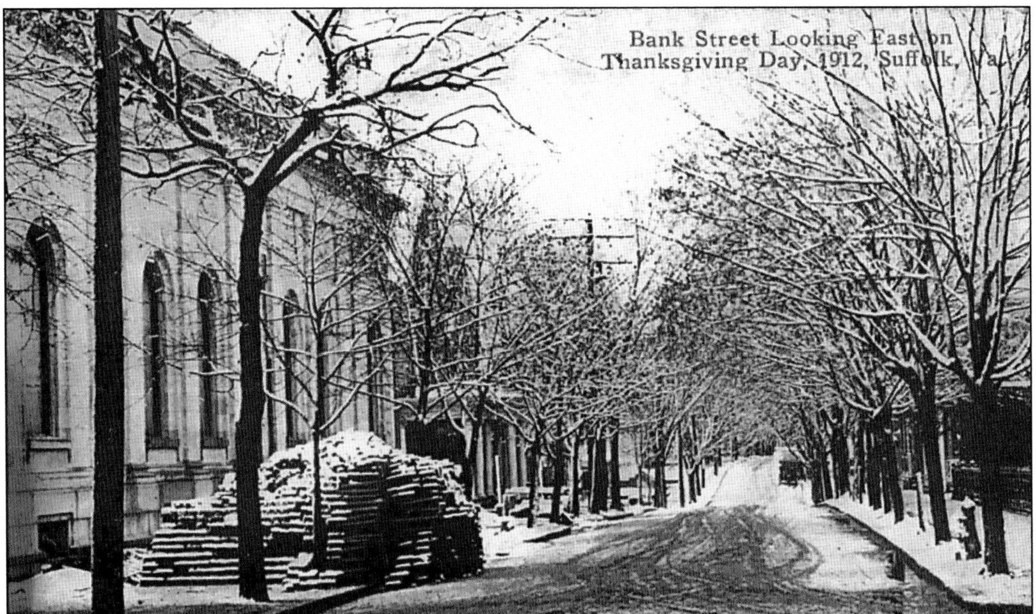

Snow on Thanksgiving Day in 1912 brought out the photographers. This photograph was taken as the new post office was being constructed. The S.R. Dunn house was already on the opposite corner. This fantastic house (of which we can see a small portion here) would soon become a commercial establishment.

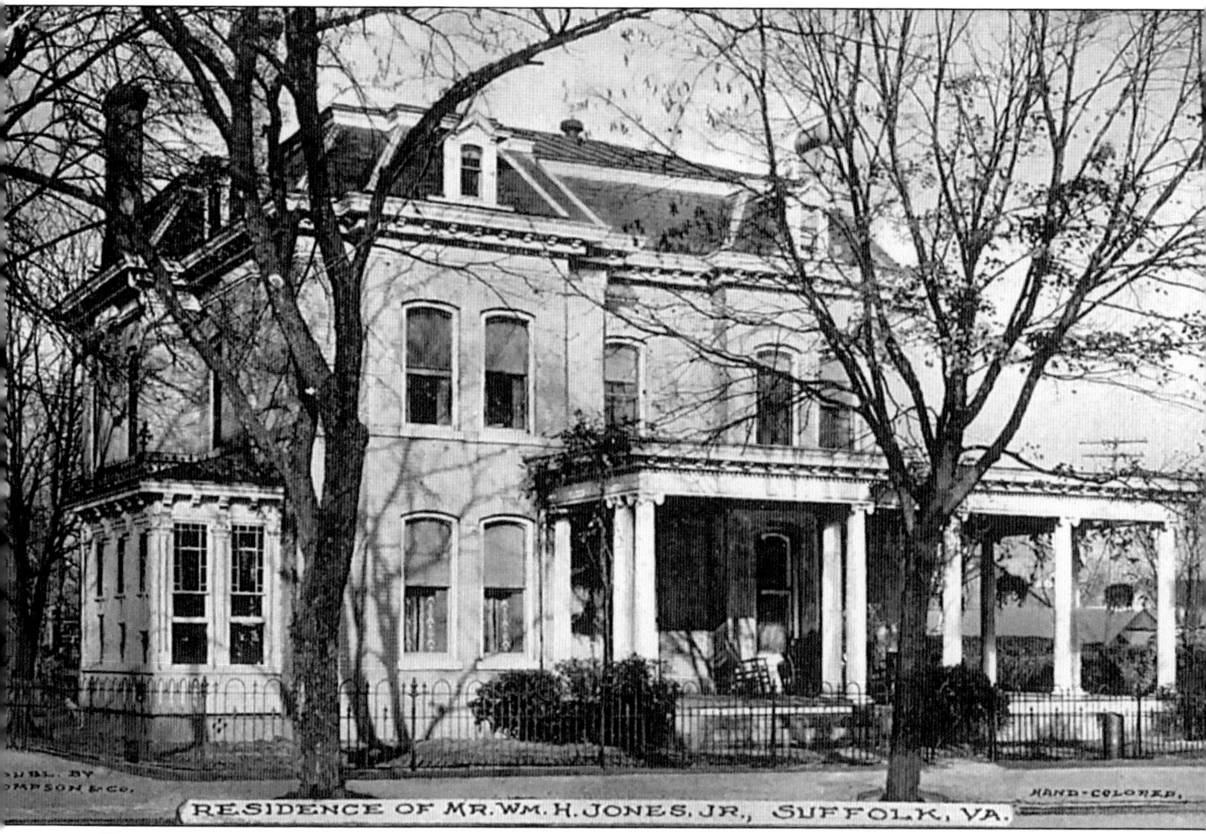

William H. Jones came to Suffolk from the Holy Neck section of Nansemond County and went to work in banking. He was engaged in several business endeavors but gained national acclaim as cashier of the Farmer's Bank. Jones and his wife Sally built this house *c.* 1880 at the corner of Bank and Pinner Streets, where it still stands today.

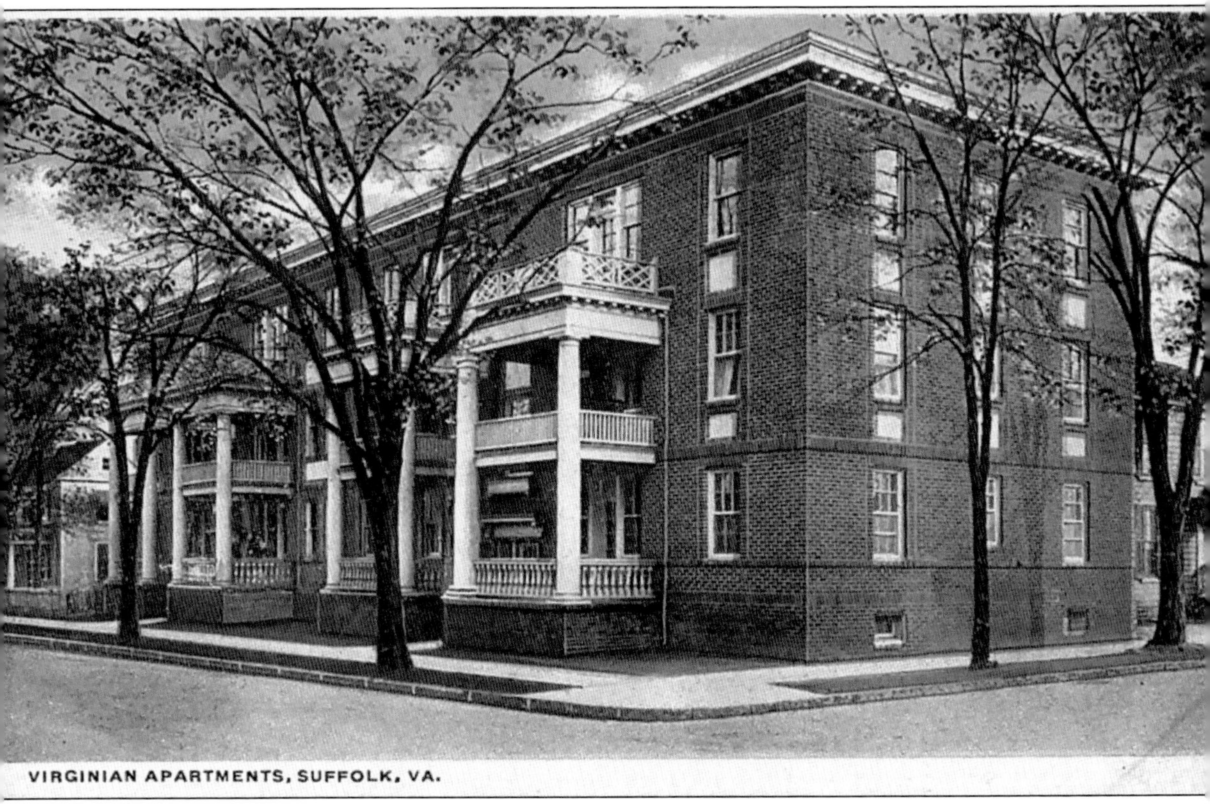

The Virginian Apartments were built on the southeast corner of Bank and Pinner Streets in 1915 by the Virginian Apartment Corporation with J.T. Withers as trustee. The apartments were a fashionable residence for young couples and single ladies of a certain age for much of the 20th century. Several older houses were demolished for the construction of these apartments.

This was the Bank Street home of successful businessman, C.A. Shoop. Shoop, in partnership with N.R. Withers, owned a brick company, the Standard Peanut Company, Benthall Machinery, and other businesses. The brick street visible in this picture was paved over but has been uncovered in the last few years. The house was demolished for a parking lot.

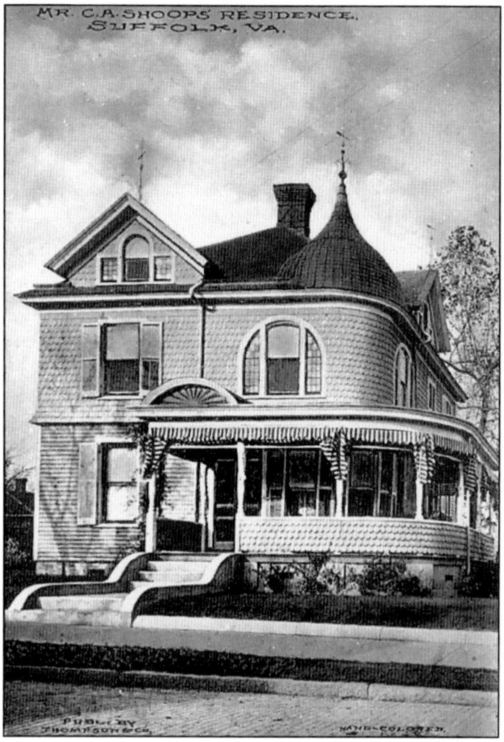

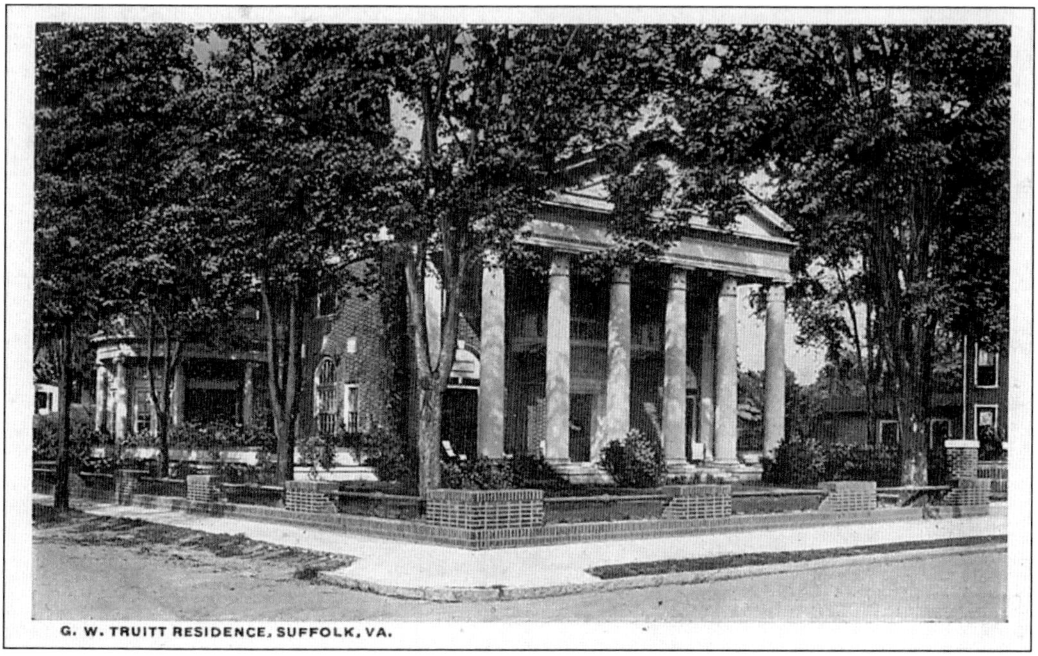

G.W. Truitt demolished an earlier house to build this mansion on the corner of Bank and Grace Streets. A lumber man, Truitt used very fine and unusual woods to build the house, which boasts a gallery for musicians and a third floor ballroom. The house was bought by Bank Street native William Crumpler in the mid-20th century and still belongs to his family.

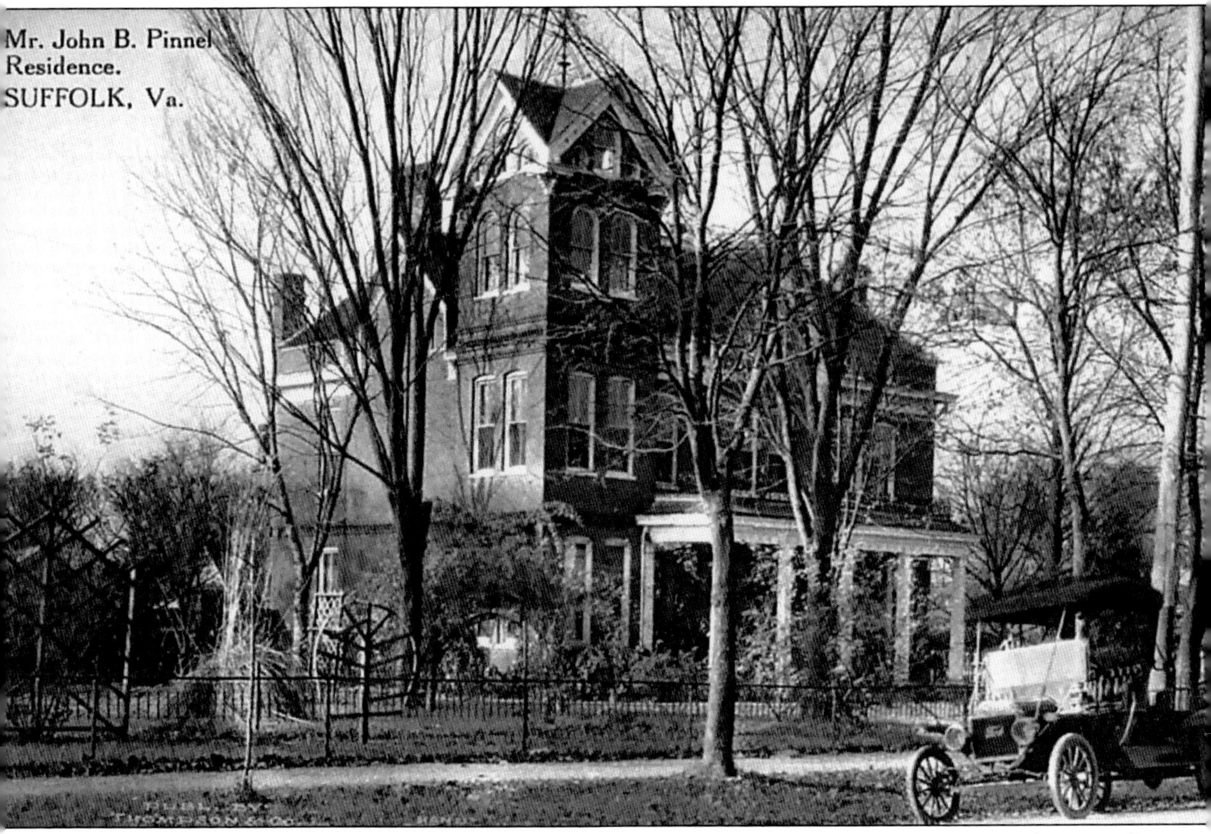

Pinner Street was opened by the Pinner family in the late 1800s. The John B. Pinner home still stands, but in the early 20th century, the façade underwent a radical change. The Pinners were Suffolk's biggest cheerleaders and were great supporters of the Presbyterian Church, as well. The Woman's Club was born as a result of a gathering that Mrs. Pinner held here.

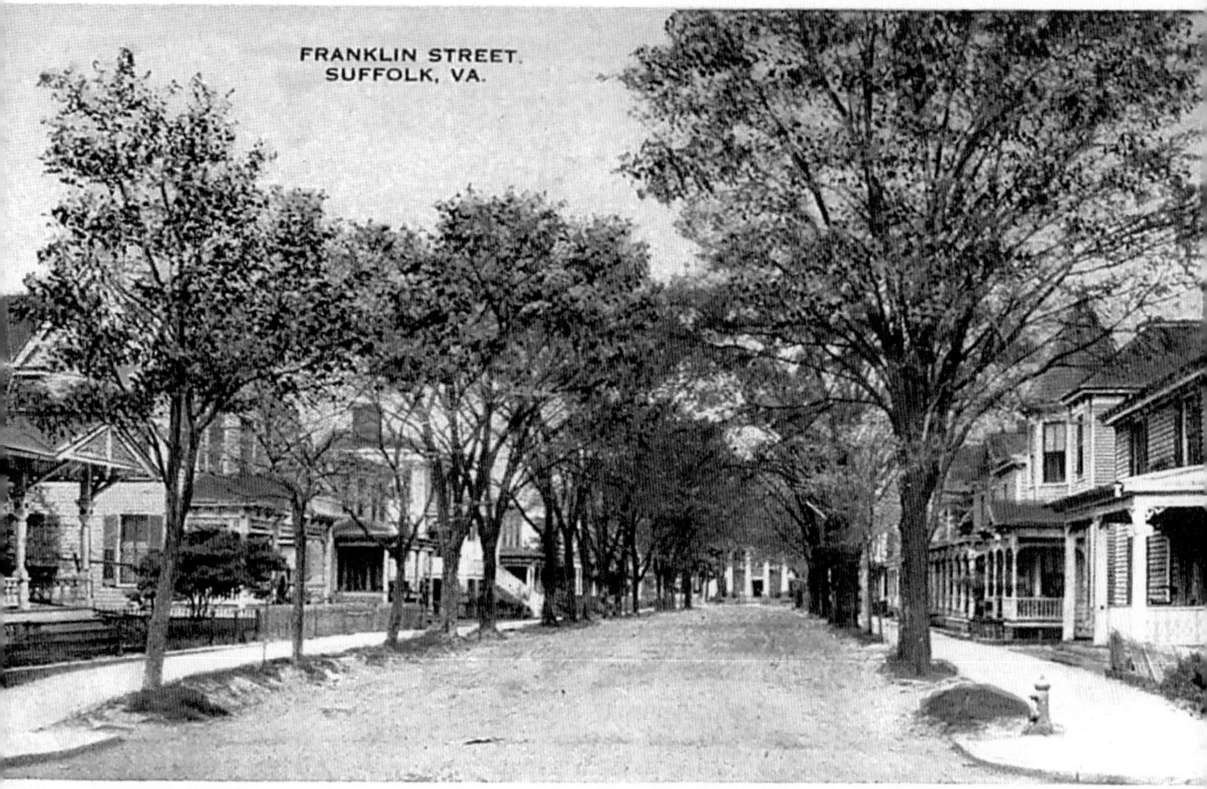

Franklin Street, only one block long, was opened about 1870 between Bank and East Washington Streets. It was reportedly named for John Franklin Pinner, a developer. This view looks north from East Washington to Bank Street and the Truitt mansion. Tom Smith, who gave the Confederate monument, lived on the west side of the street (approximately the third house from the left.)

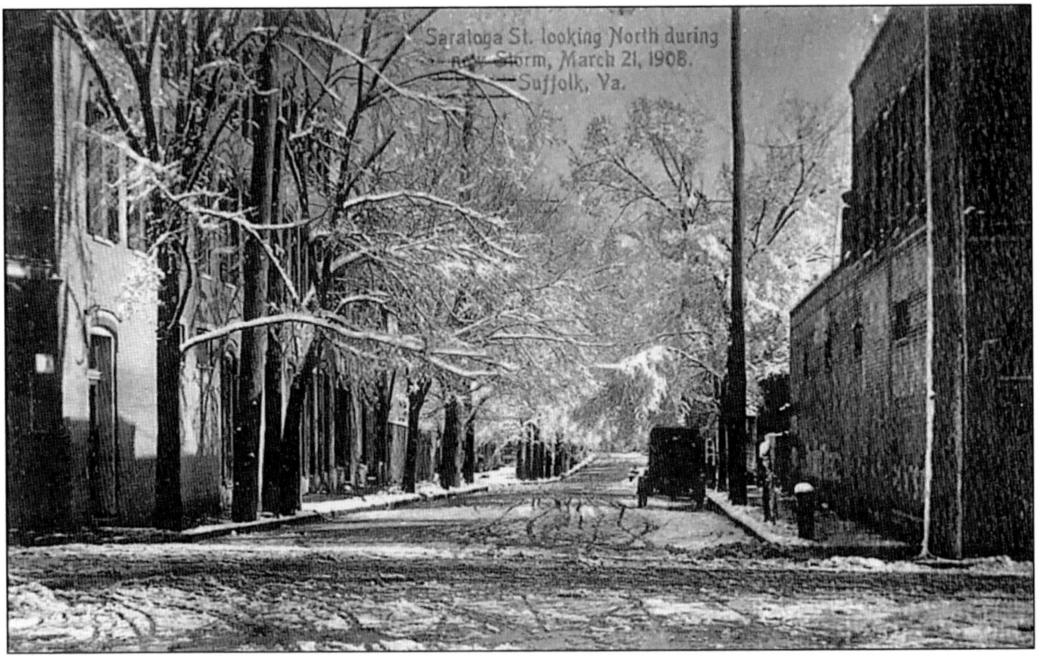

Saratoga Street was first called Sycamore Street. It seems that most of Saratoga Street was originally residential but gradually South Saratoga, near the Norfolk and Western Railroad, and the 100 block of North Saratoga have become primarily commercial. This snowy view in March of 1908 is taken from Washington Street looking north. The Nansemond Hotel is on the left.

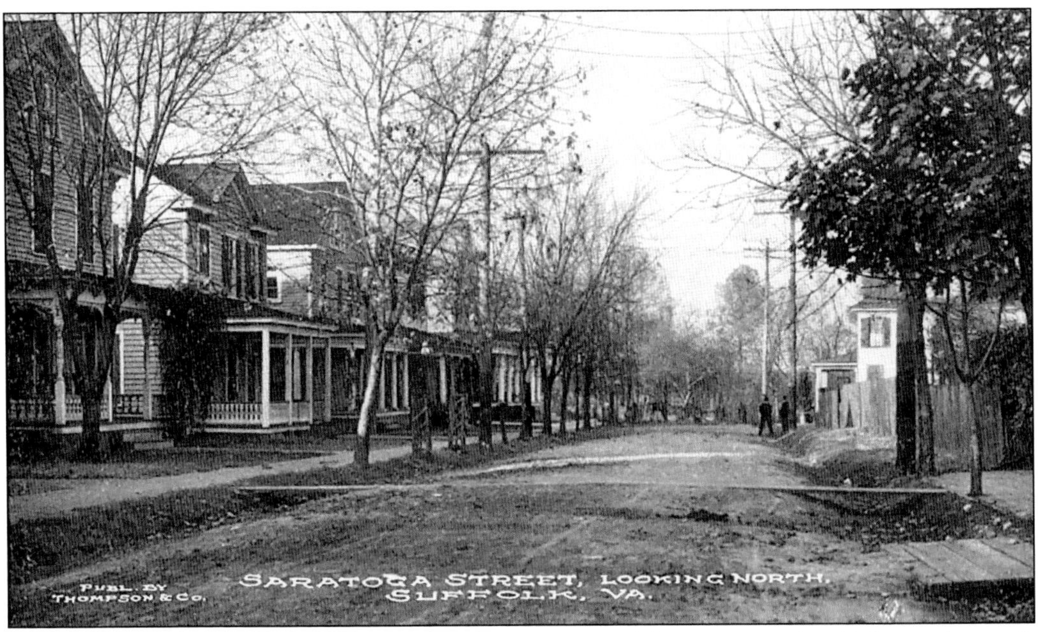

The north end of Saratoga Street opened around the turn of the century. The thicket at the north end of the street would eventually be cleared with the opening of Suffolk High School and, later, Freemason Street. The house on the east side of the street has been replaced by a playground. The west side of this block has seen few changes.

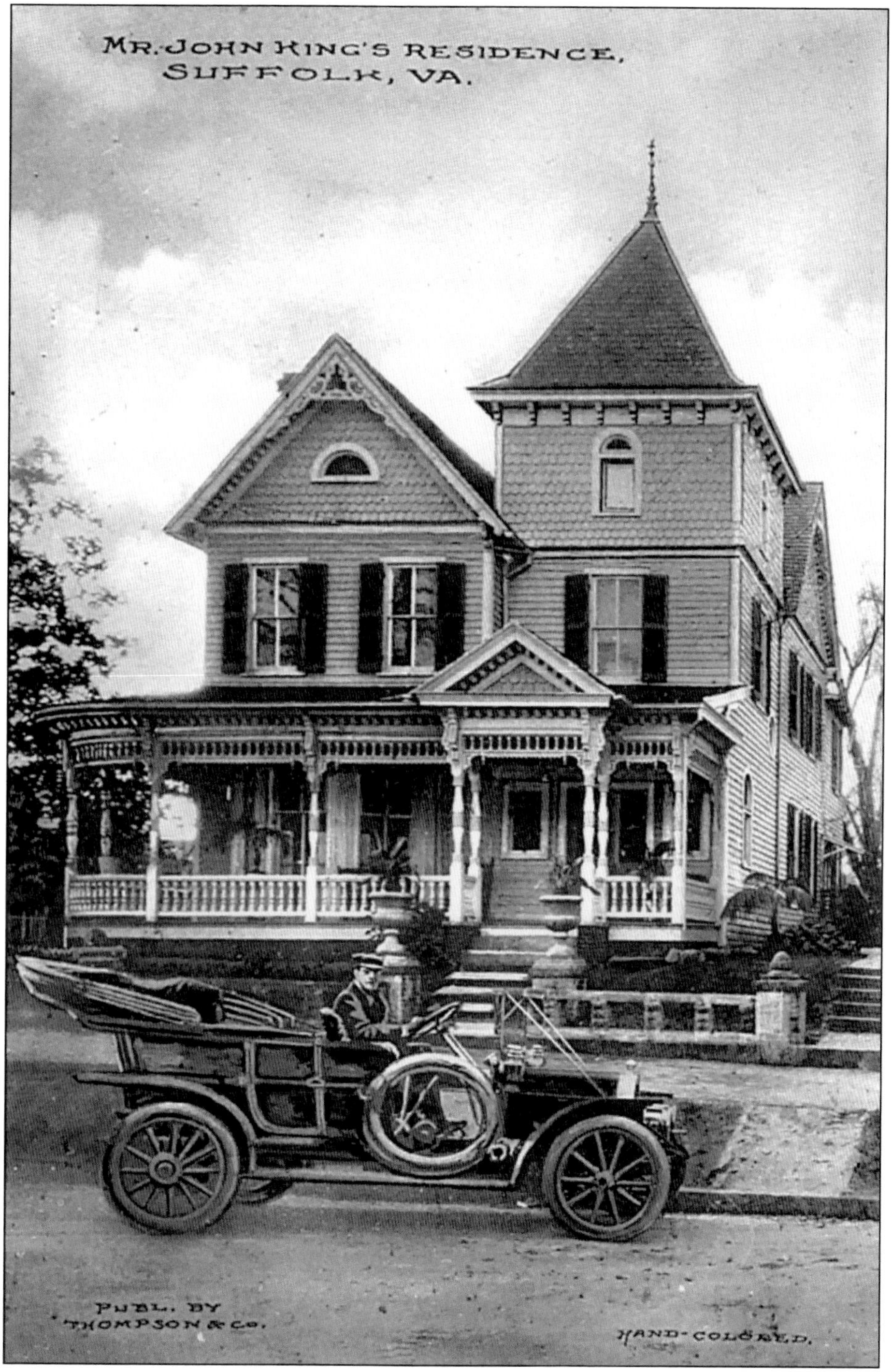

Back on Main Street, the oldest street in town, the late 19th-century Walter Ferguson house was a modern intrusion. It was once the home of John King who, with John Pinner, started the first successful peanut processing business in Suffolk. The house was demolished in the 1950s prior to the construction of Birdsong Recreation Center.

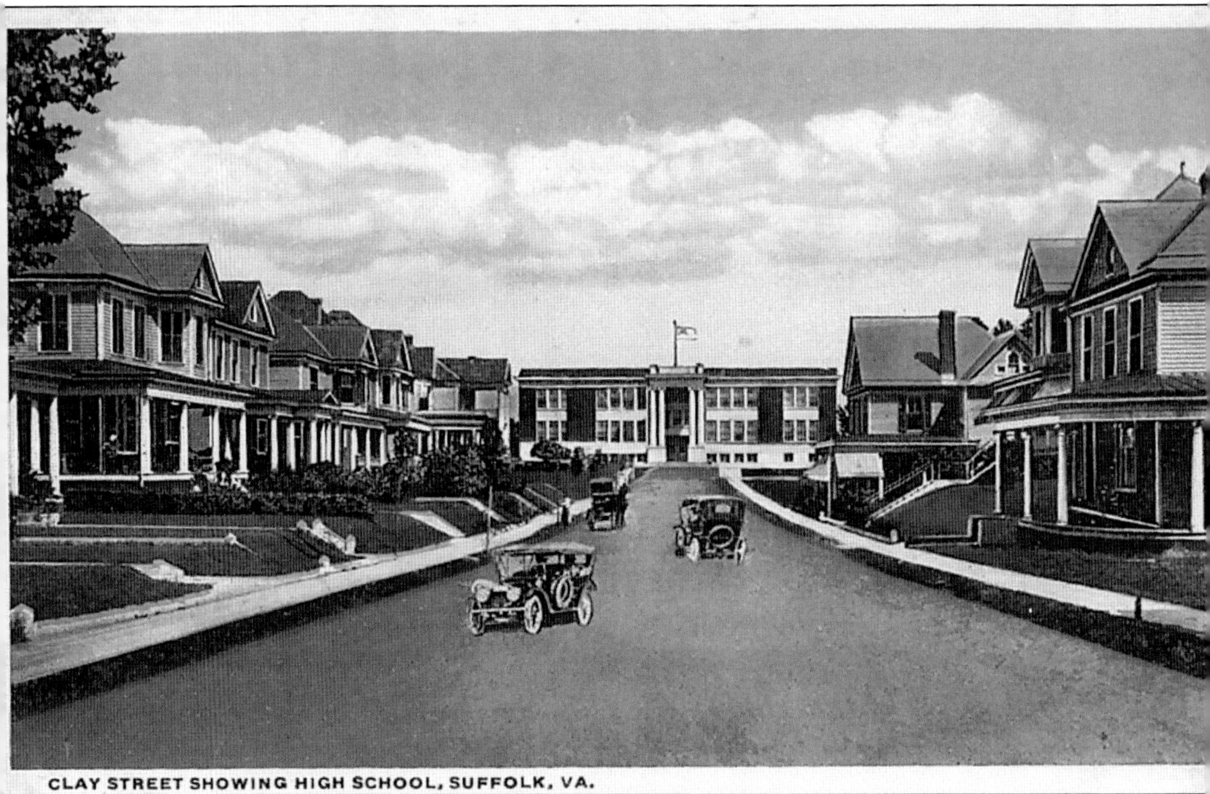

Clay Street was opened by George Nurney in 1890.The 200 block, shown here, furnished a fine approach to Thomas Jefferson School when it was built in 1911. The street is now one way and seems narrow because traffic was more of the pedestrian variety in those days. Part of this end of the street has been filled in, having once been portion of Church Branch, a tributary of the Nansemond River. Mother Nature doesn't like change. Even in the late 20th century, the low end of the street flooded in heavy rains.

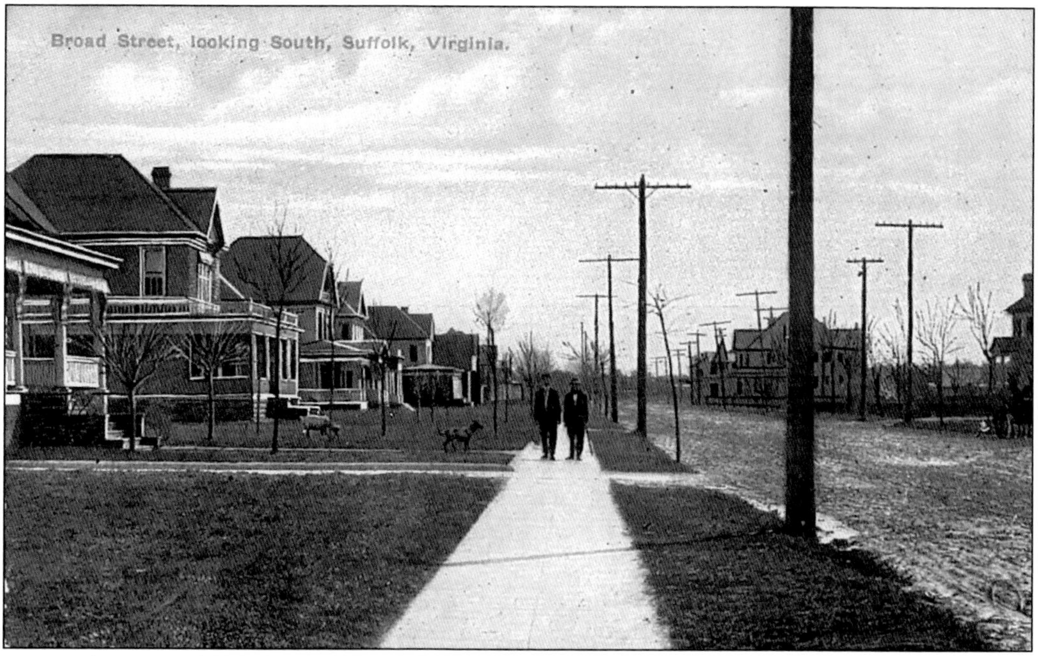

Late in the 1800s the town was growing and prospering. A street car ran in Suffolk for a few years and transported people as far as Broad Street on West Washington. It was a long walk downtown. By the time this *c.* 1909 shot was taken, the east side of South Broad Street was well developed but houses on the West side were few.

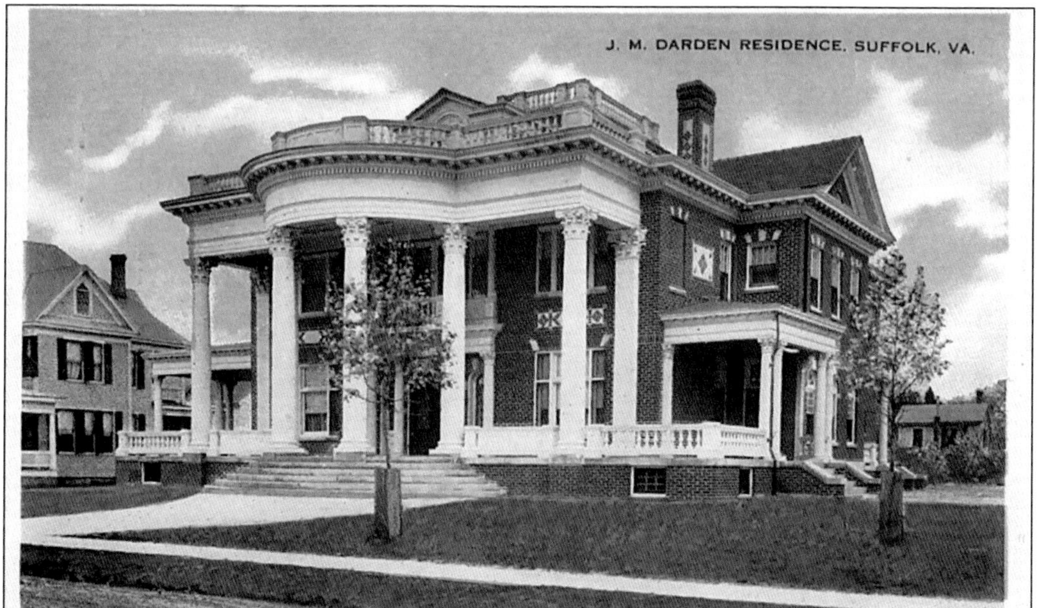

Probably the very finest house on a street of fine homes, J.M. Darden's Broad Street house, with a grand staircase and Tiffany windows, was built to reflect his prosperity. His garden, like those of his most prosperous friends, was later designed by Charles Gillette, who planned the gardens at the Governors Mansion and other fine Virginia homes.

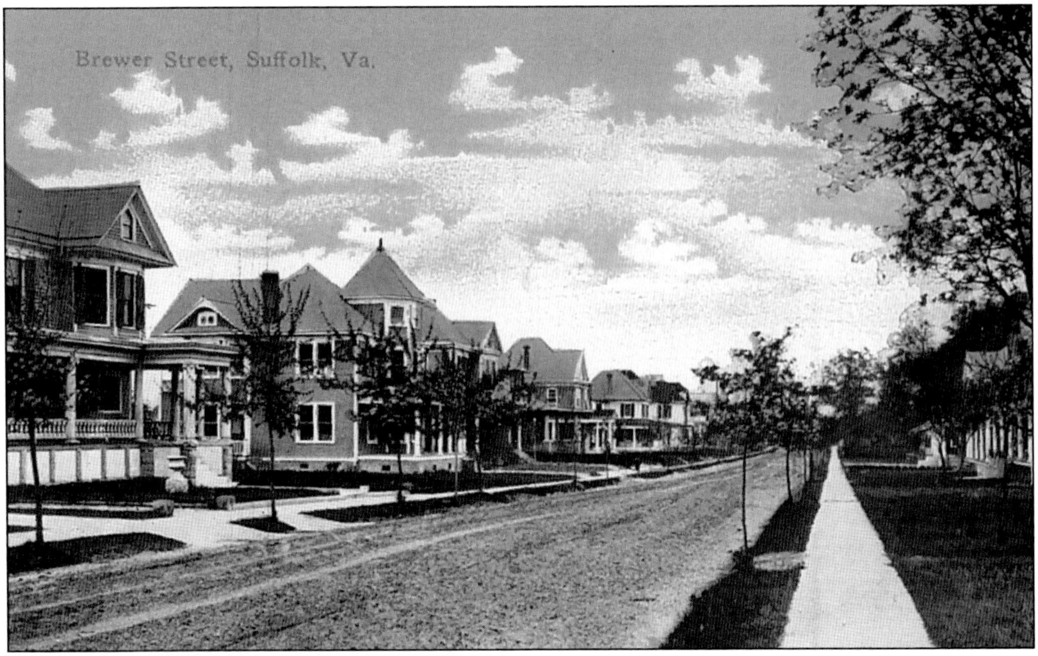

In the late 1800s, R.L. Brewer Sr. began selling lots on his farm at the edge of town. Brewer Avenue was the major street created on Brewer's farm. It runs from West Washington Street to the Seaboard Railroad. The styles range from Queen Anne to Colonial Revival. Two of the most charming bungalows in the city are on this street. The Nimmo house is at the far left.

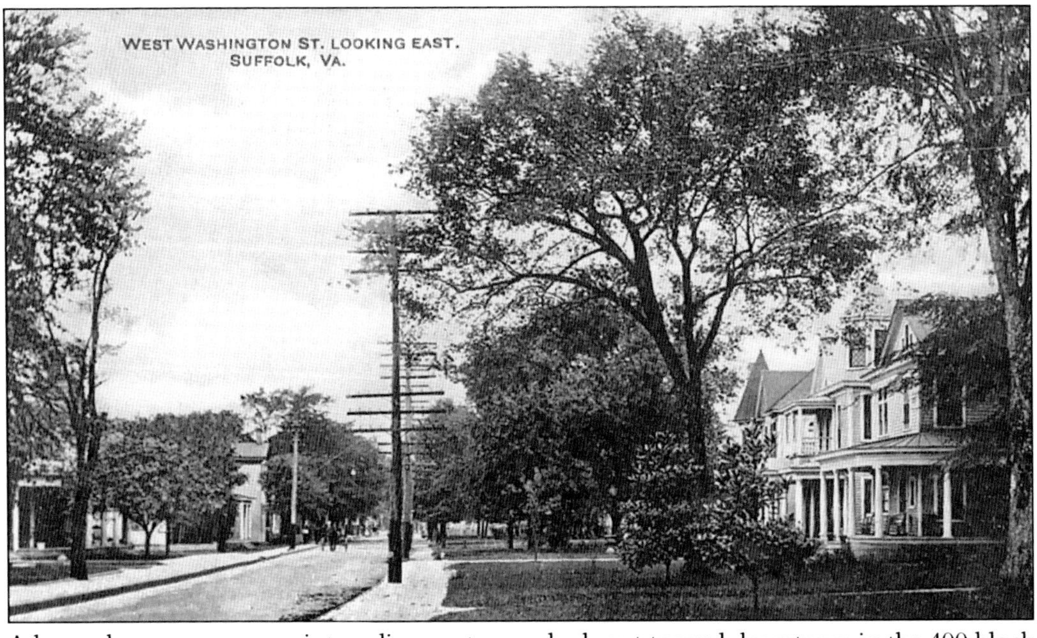

A horse-drawn conveyance is traveling west as we look east toward downtown in the 400 block of West Washington Street. Col. J.E. West's home is just out of the picture on the right. On the left only a porch is visible to mark the home of Col. R.L. Brewer Jr., who served as speaker of the House of Delegates in the 1920s while Colonel West was lieutenant governor.

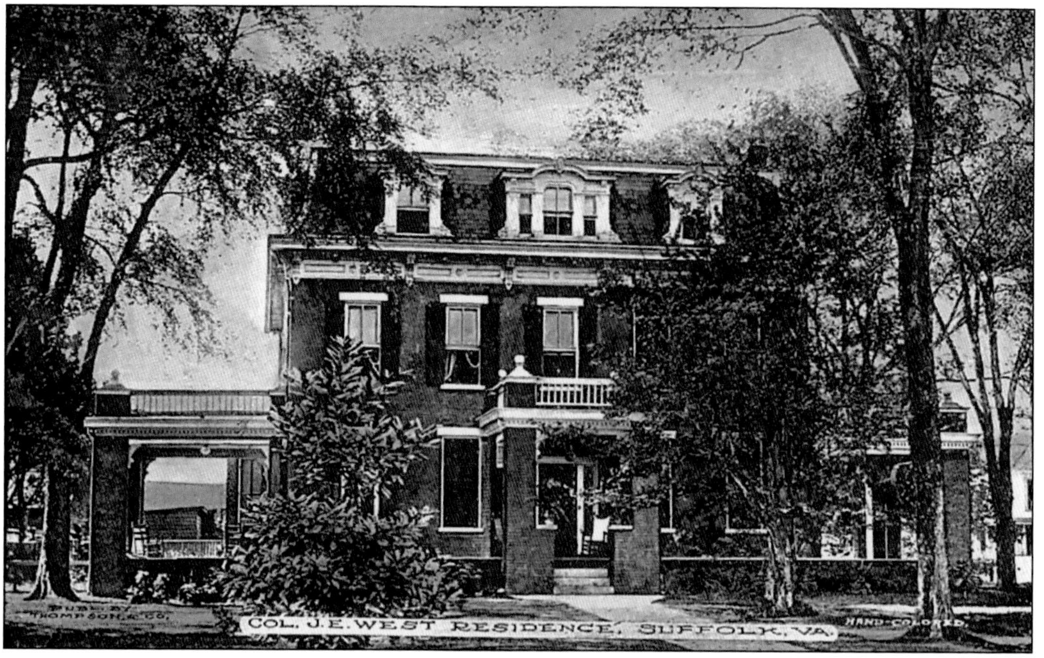

This house was built on West Washington Street around 1885 by Dr. F.W. Skiles. Around 1903 the house was purchased by Col. J.E. West and his wife, who added the two side wings. Colonel West served as lieutenant governor of Virginia from 1922 to 1930 under two governors. Colonel West was very active in the church and the community. The West house is blanketed in snow in the picture below. The garden of the West house was designed by Charles Gillette, the premier landscape architect in Virginia in the first half of the 20th century. The house was demolished in the late 1960s. The two magnolia trees still stand at the entrance of the West End Baptist Church parking lot.

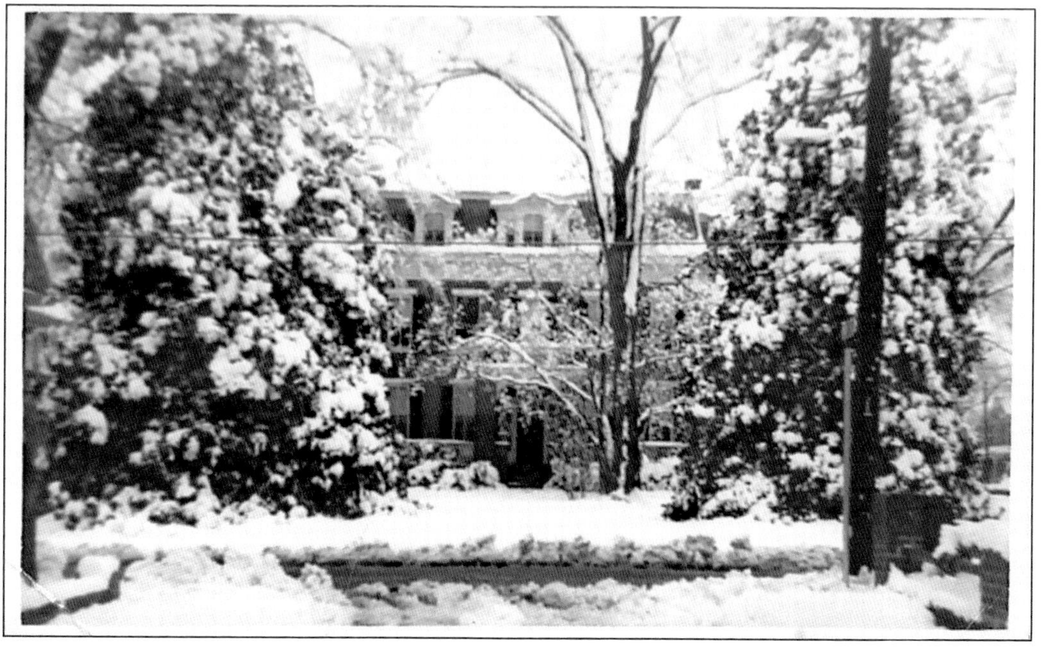

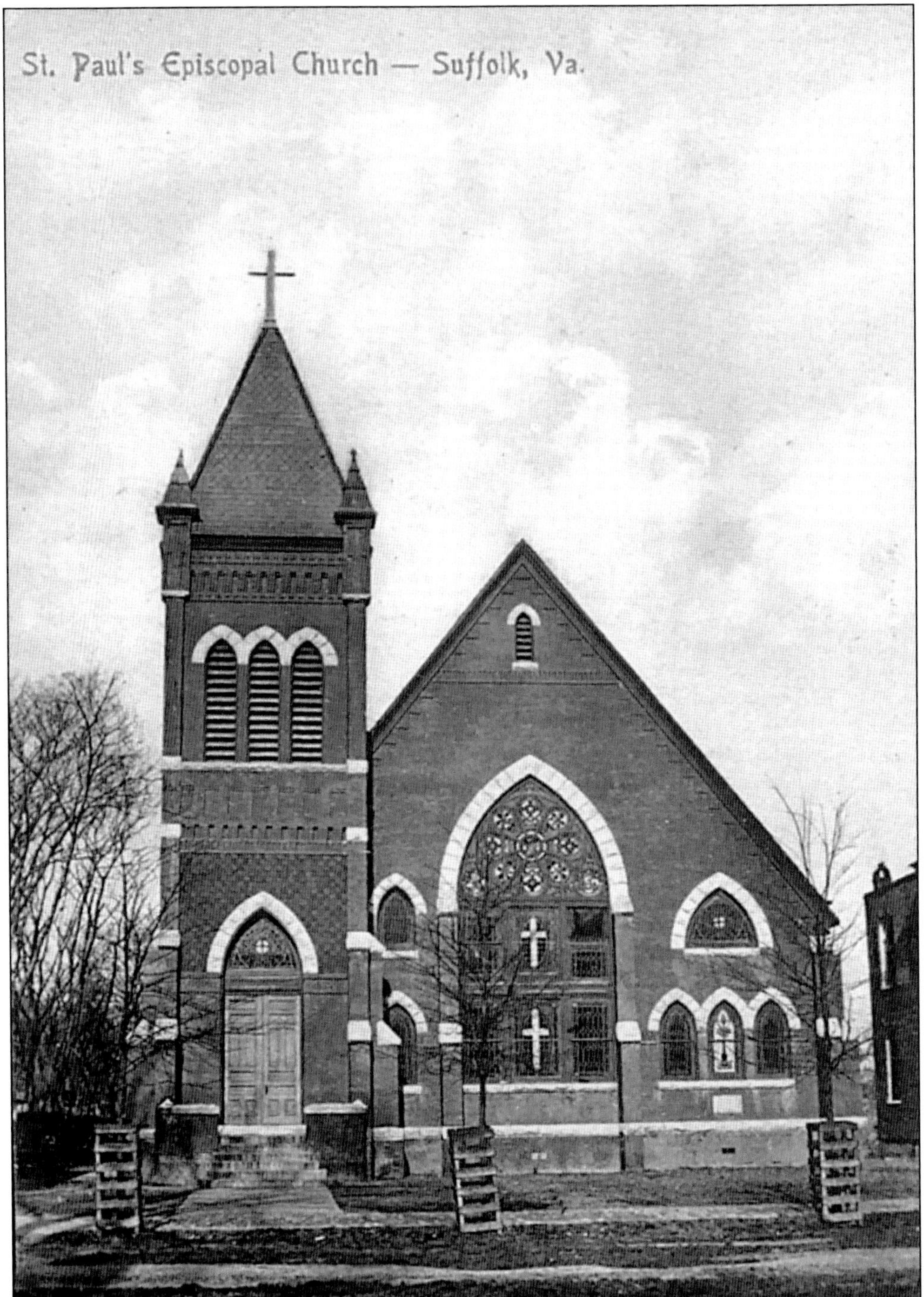

St. Paul's Episcopal Church had its beginning in colonial days as an Anglican Church. First built at Reid's Ferry, the church was moved to town in 1752. After the Revolutionary War the congregants first used the community chapel before they built a church in 1846. This building was completed in 1895 and, with additions, is still in use today.

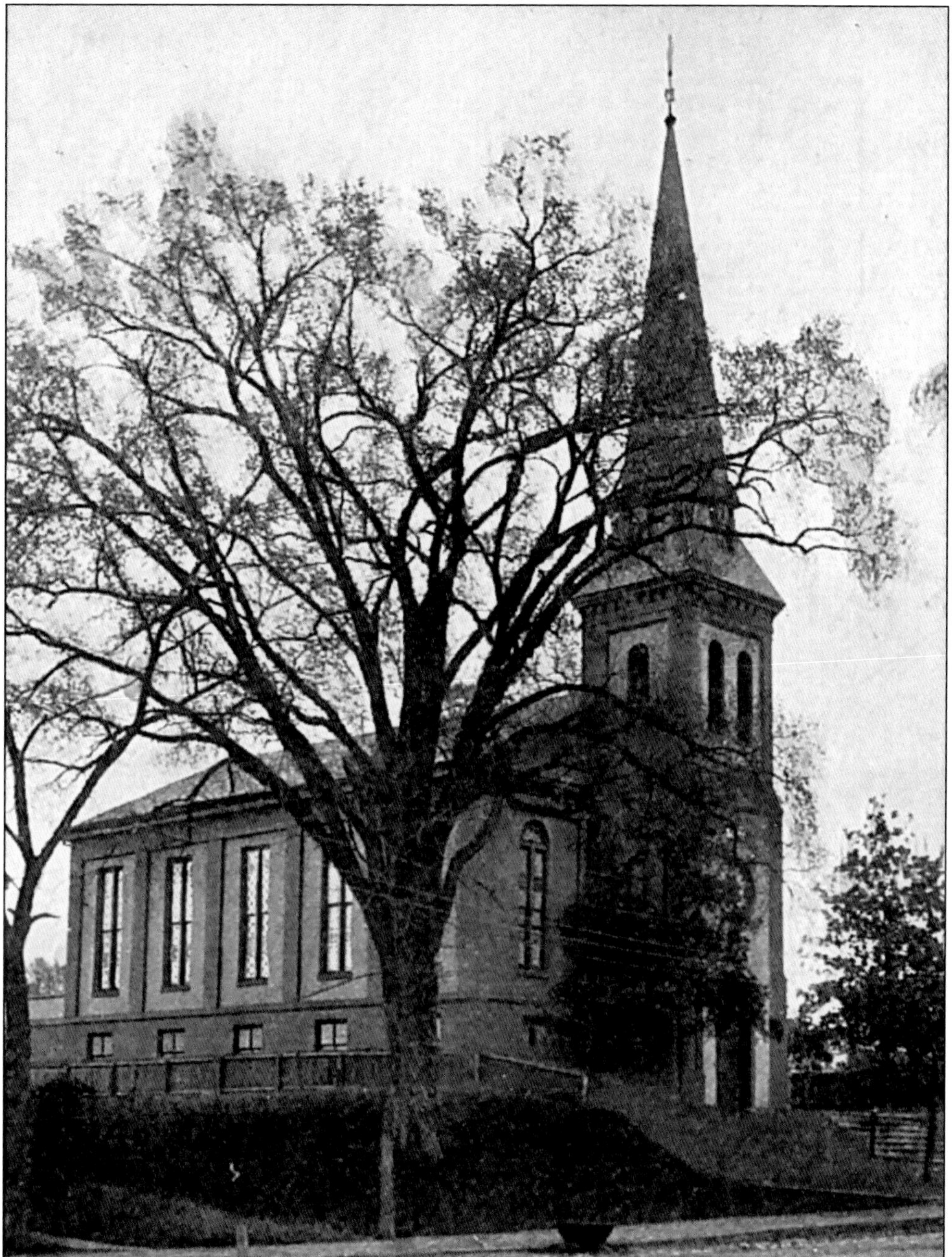

No. 946 M. E. Church South—Built 1860
Main Street—Suffolk, Va.

The Methodist Church was strong in Suffolk soon after the Revolutionary War. The second church built by the Methodists, shown here, was completed in 1861. During the Civil War this church was used as a hospital. In 1916 a new church building was completed. This building still stands and is now Main Street Apartments.

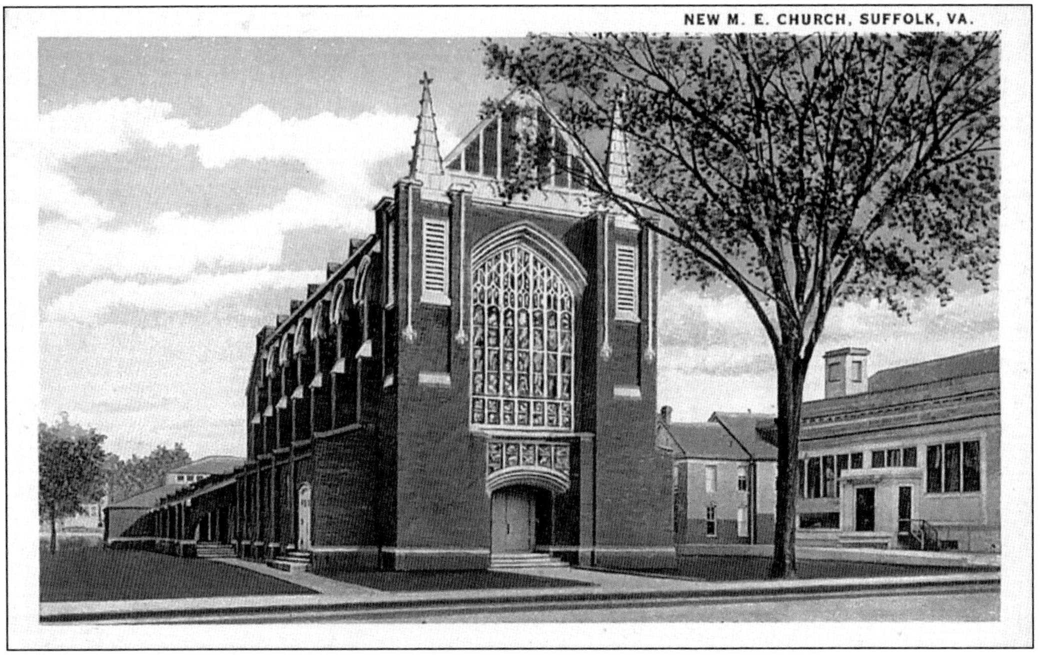

The new Methodist church was built 1914-1916 in the 100 block of North Main Street next to the new post office. The style for the new church was reportedly suggested by the McLemore family who had just taken the Grand Tour. This building, like the three other churches on the block, replaced early residences.

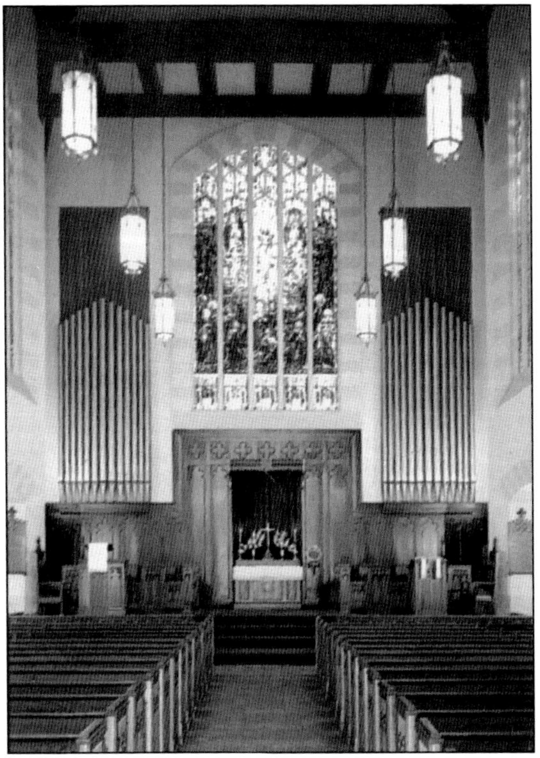

When the Methodist Church was completed in 1916, three of its windows showed scenes from the life of Christ. Over time the other plain stained glass windows were replaced so that each window tells part of the life of Christ. This, the Ascension window, is one of the original windows.

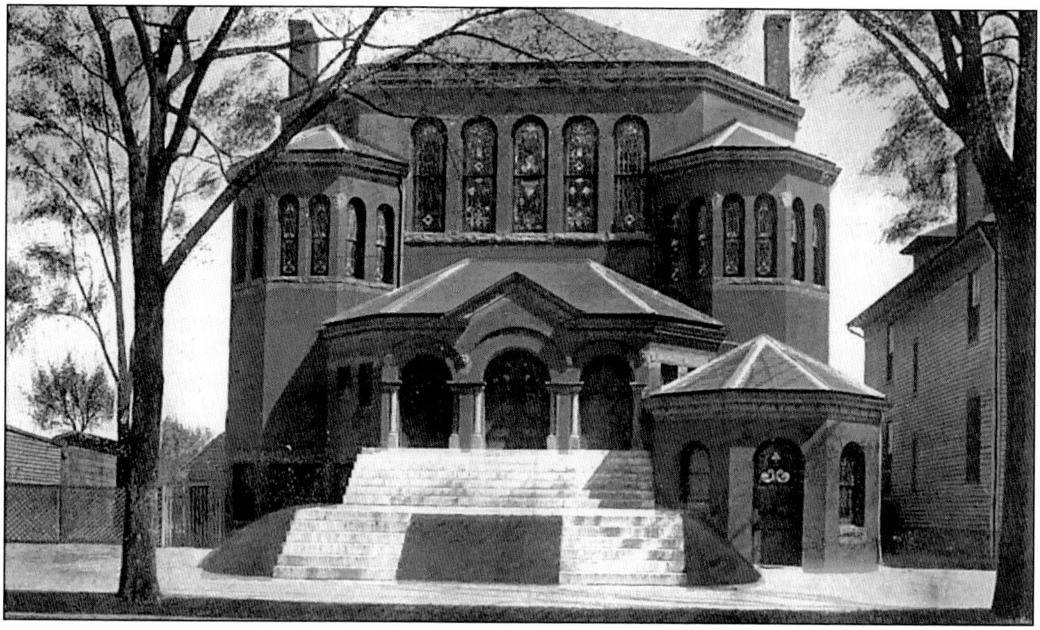

Suffolk Christian Church was started on the eve of the Civil War with its first building constructed in 1860. This church and others of the same denomination were started by the Rev. William B. Wellons, a staunch Confederate who became a Confederate army chaplain. The building shown here was built in the 1890s and replaced the original one. In the 1920s this façade was altered and significant additions were made.

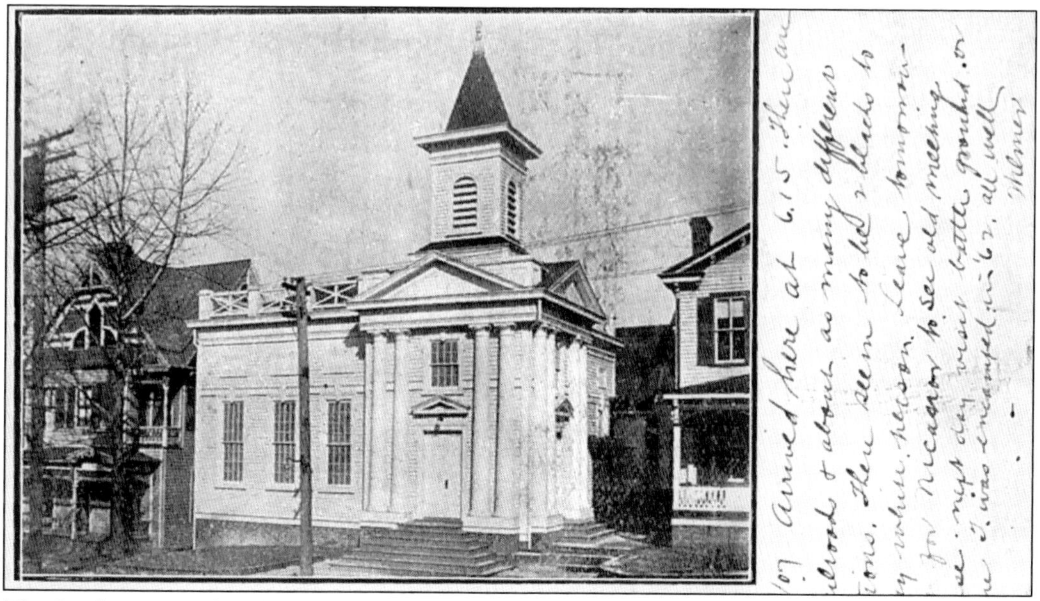

The Presbyterian Church was started in Suffolk in 1876 as new people were lured to town by the booming economy. In 1905 the original church on Bank Street was moved to the rear of the lot and the pictured church was built in front. In the 1920s a new church was built on another site and this one was sold to Agudath Achim Congregation. The synagogue closed in 1995. The card shown here was written by a Civil War veteran in 1907.

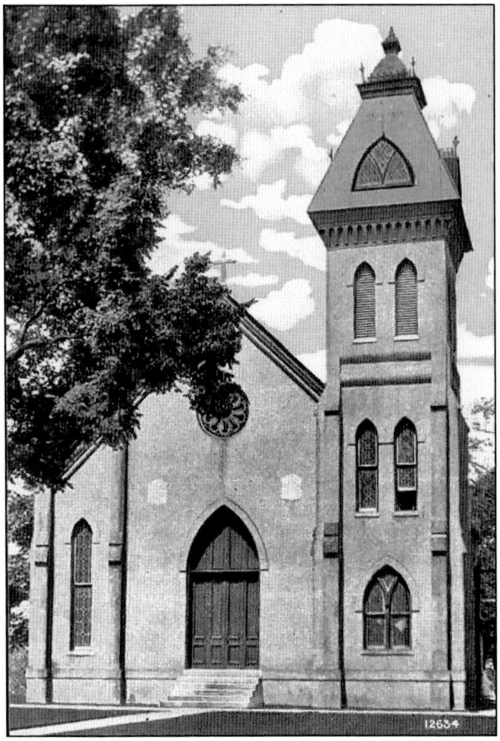

Through the efforts of Elder Robert T. Daniel and several prominent Suffolk citizens, Suffolk Baptist Church was organized in 1827. For several years the church met in the "Old Meeting House" on Cedar Hill. It later moved to Mahan Street and, in 1836, to North Main Street. This building stood on North Main Street from its construction around 1890 until 1911.

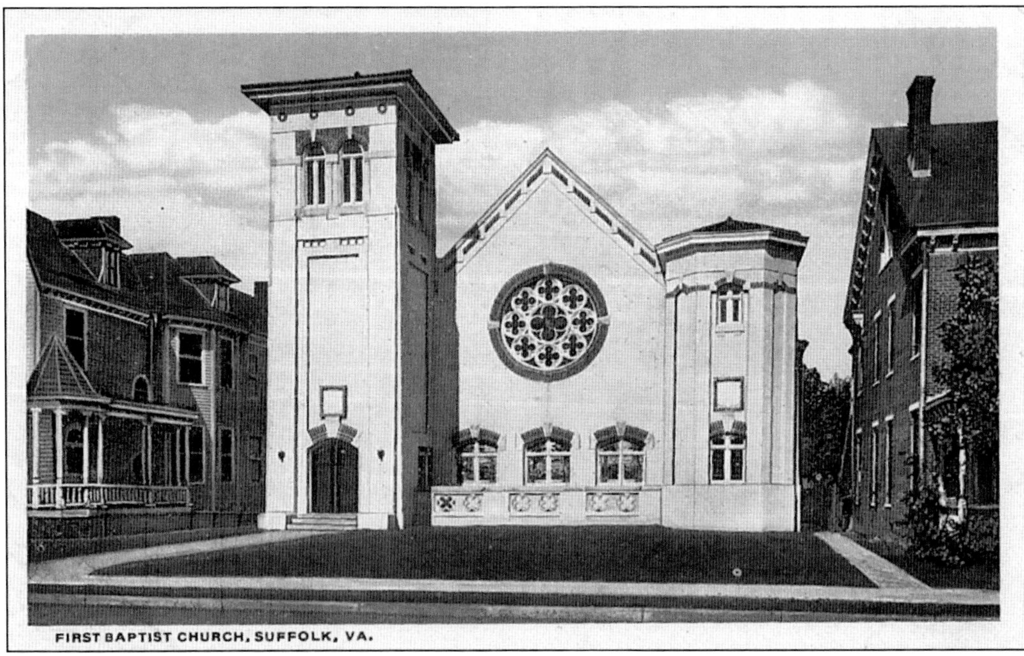

In 1930, Suffolk Baptist Church assumed the new name of First Baptist Church, Suffolk, Virginia. The building shown here was built in 1912 and stood until the mid-1950s. The residence on the right side of the picture was demolished in 1941 to make room for the present Freemason Street.

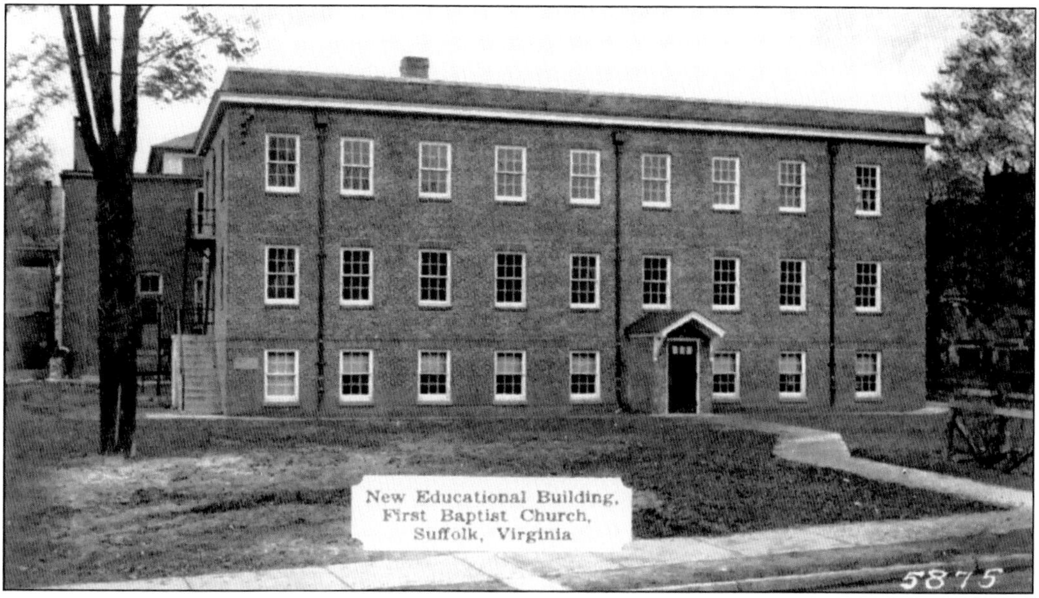

First Baptist Church started work on its new educational building in 1937, and the completed building was dedicated on March 6, 1938. It was named the Goodwin Building for Dr. Harry Jeter Goodwin, pastor of the church. Freemason Street had not yet been built and a parking lot was, at the time, unnecessary. Through the trees on the right we see the tower of Suffolk Christian Church. This view is from North Saratoga Street.

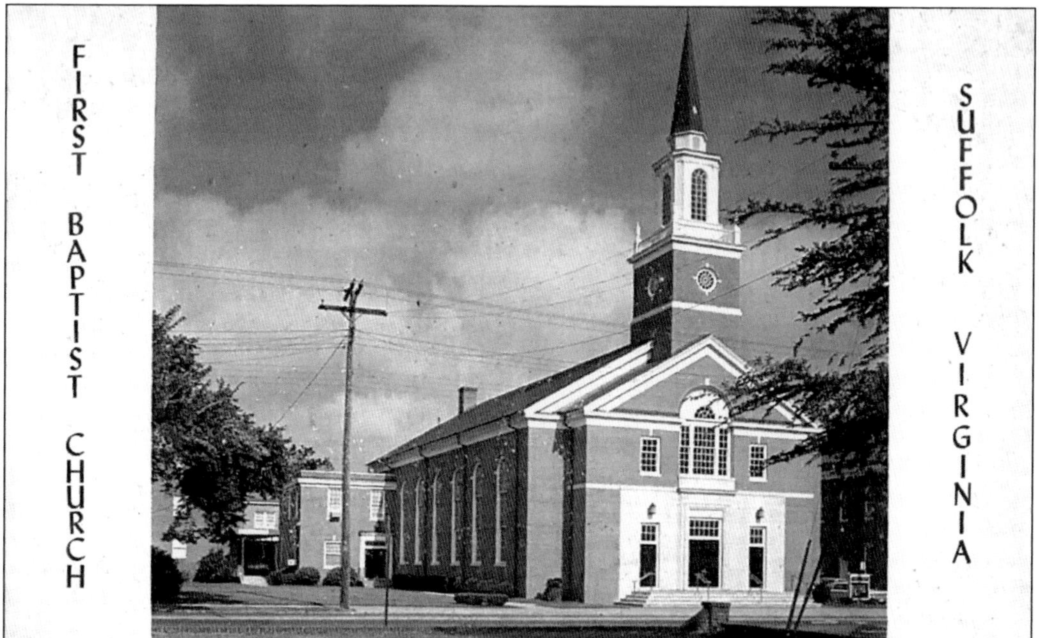

First Baptist Church enjoyed rapid growth in the late 1940s and early 1950s. To meet that need Silas S. Kea and Son was engaged to demolish the old sanctuary and construct a new sanctuary at a cost of $202,126. Construction began in early 1956, and, in May 1957, the new building was dedicated. The church's new pastor, Rev. J.C. Mitchell, led the opening service.

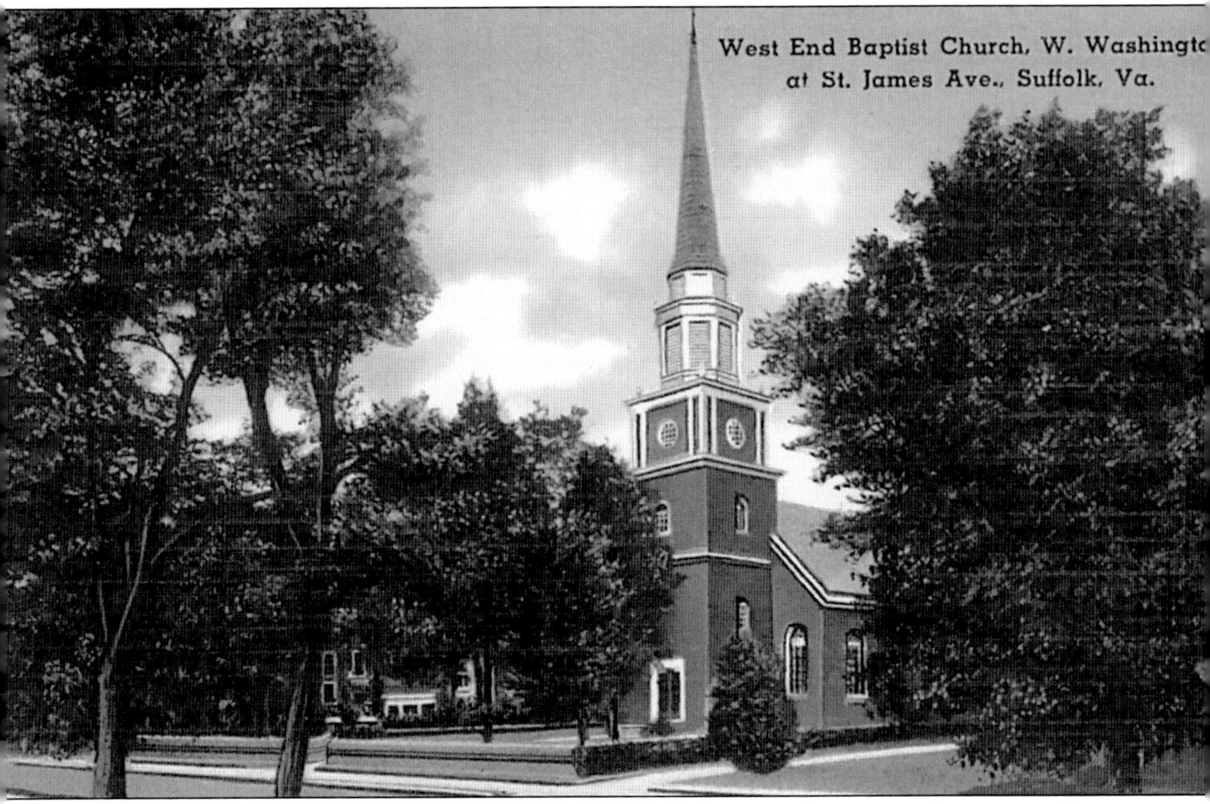

(above and right) West End Baptist Church was built in 1938 at the corner of West Washington Street and St. James Avenue by a group who came out of First Baptist Church on Main Street. Possibly the most handsome example of the work of Suffolk architect Dupree Breeden, the beautiful façade and equally beautiful churchyard remain little changed by the years. Through the trees to the right we see the home of Col. and Mrs. J.E.West. In the inset of the view (left) we see the altar. The window above the altar depicts Jesus the Good Shepherd.

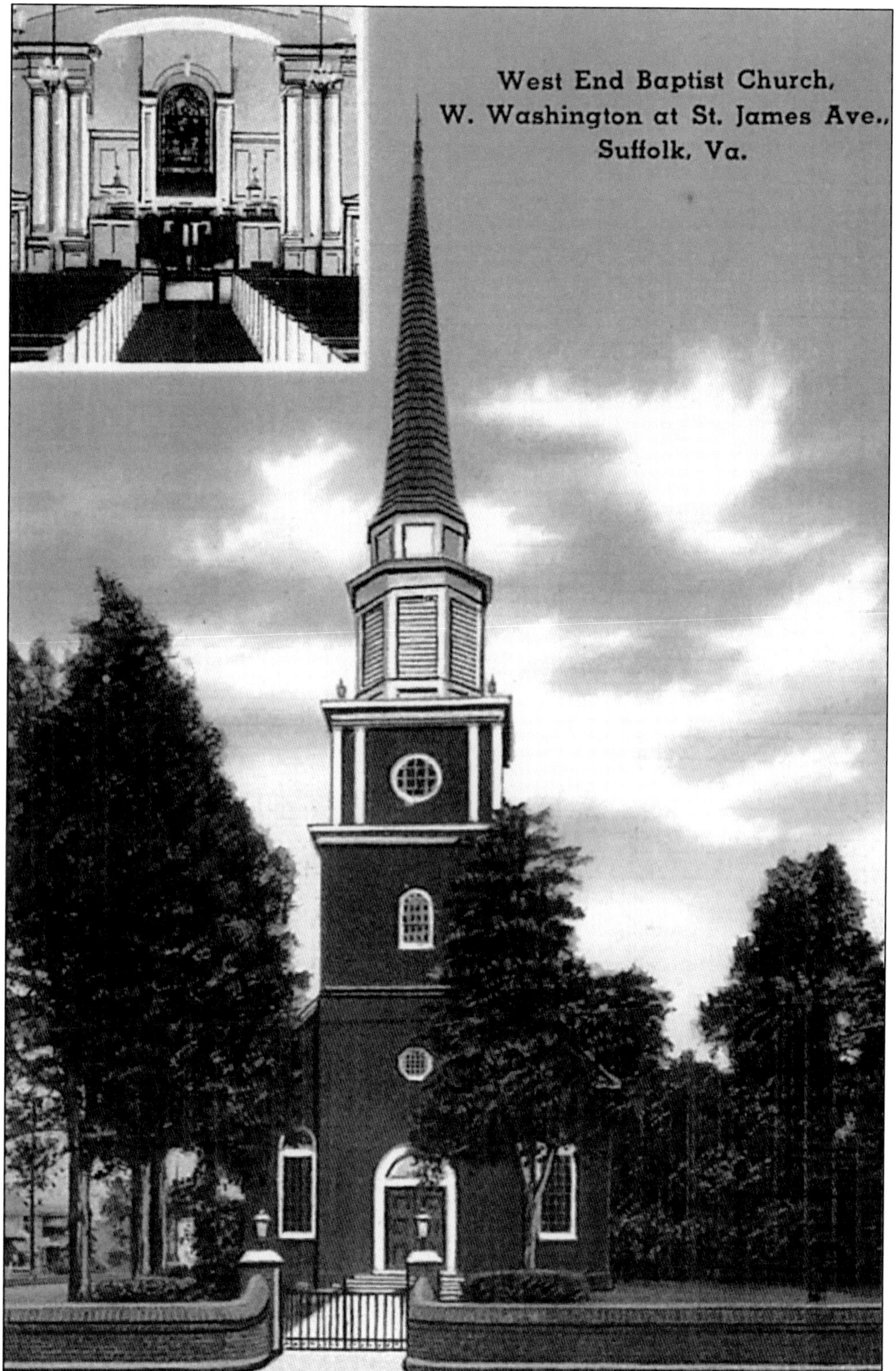
West End Baptist Church,
W. Washington at St. James Ave.,
Suffolk, Va.

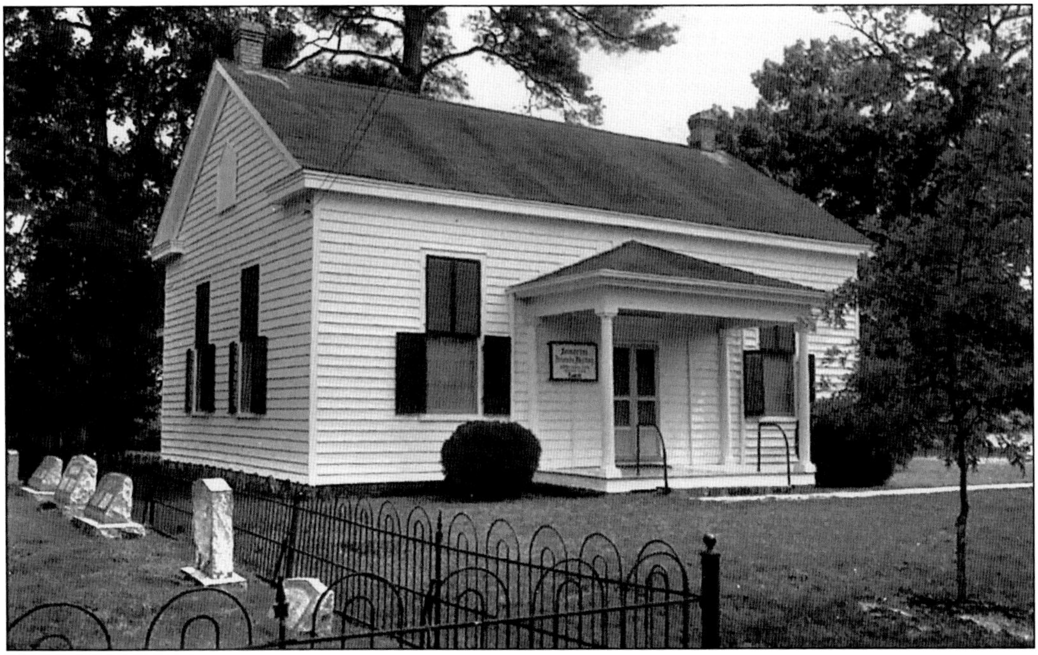

In 1672 George Fox, a Quaker, came through Nansemond County. Though the Quaker religion was frowned upon by the English authorities, Fox found many converts and started several meetings. Somerton Friends Meeting at Box Elder, shown here, is the only one that remains, gathering in a building that was their new church in 1828.

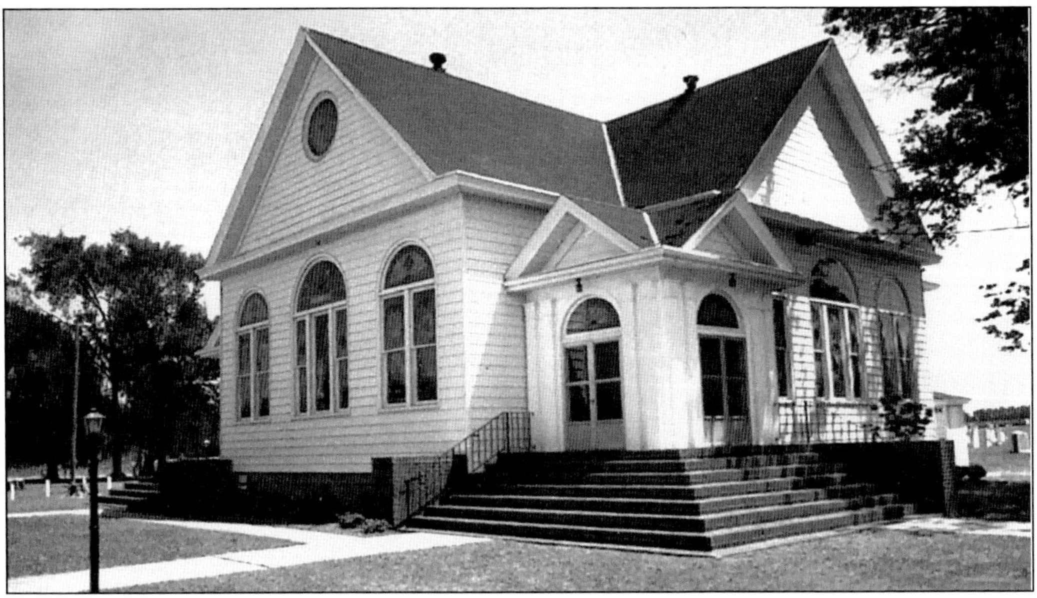

Cypress Chapel was founded in 1746 as an Anglican Glebe Church. After the Revolutionary War the congregation severed its tie with the Anglican Church and became a Methodist Church. In 1794, under the influence of James O'Kelly, it became a Christian Church. The present building was constructed in 1925. A village once grew around the church with a school, a post office, and other commercial buildings. Only the church remains.

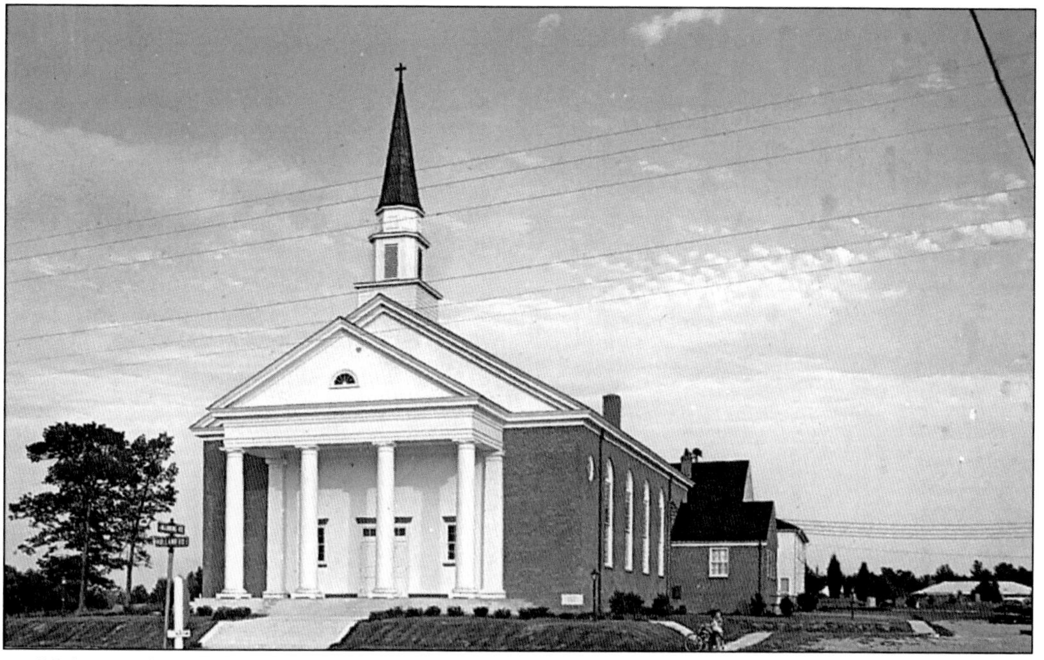

Bethlehem Christian Church was organized in 1847 by Rev. William B. Wellons. The church was built on South Quay (Holland) Road and flourished until 1862 when it was devastated by war. The church was reorganized in 1866. In 1923 a new building was dedicated and in 1961 this new sanctuary was built.

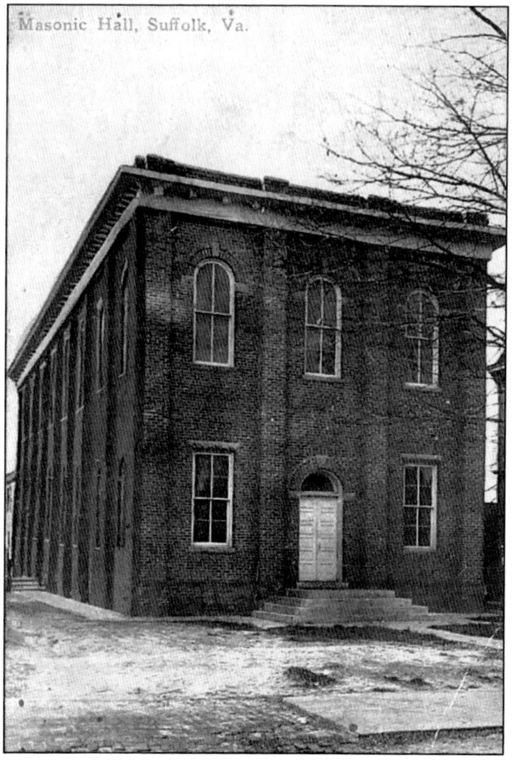

Dating back to the 1790s, the Masonic Order was probably the first of many fraternal orders in Suffolk. This building was constructed on North Main Street around 1910 to replace an earlier one on the same lot. Some Suffolk students went to school here and the Agudath Achim congregation first used this building for worship. It is still being used by the Masons.

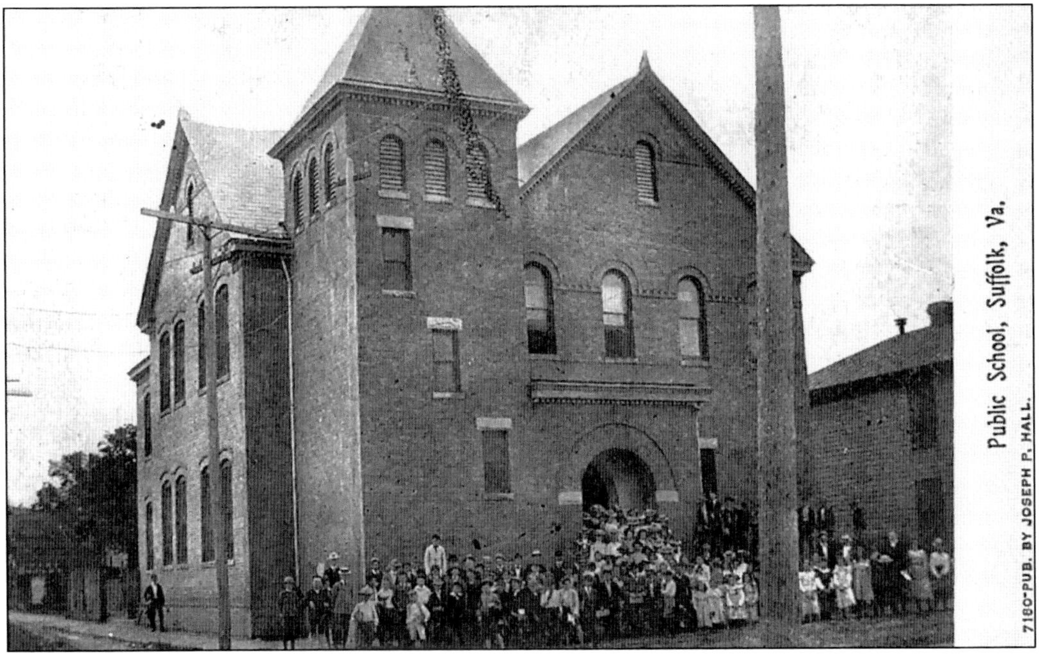

Though Suffolk's public school system was established in 1871, it was not until 1893 that the first school building was constructed. School had previously been held in a variety of other buildings in town. When Thomas Jefferson School opened in 1911, this building became the Municipal Building. It stood on the southeast corner of Market and Saratoga Streets until it was demolished in the 1960s.

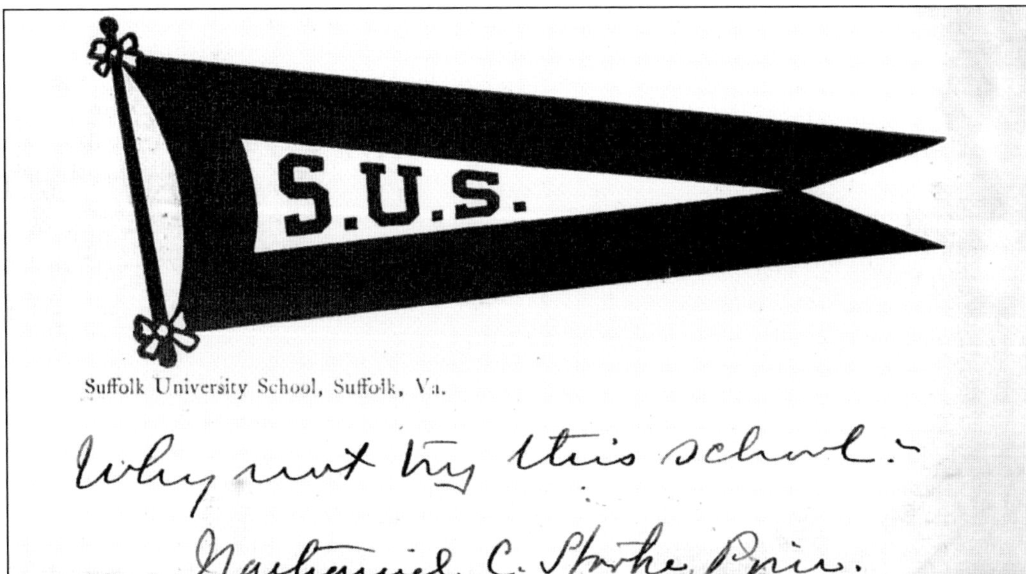

Suffolk University School was one of the lesser-known private schools in Suffolk in the late 1800s and early 1900s. Professor Nathaniel C. Starke operated the school, which is believed to have been held at the Masonic Hall after 1910. Apparently, only boys studied under "Old Man Starke" (as one former student called him).

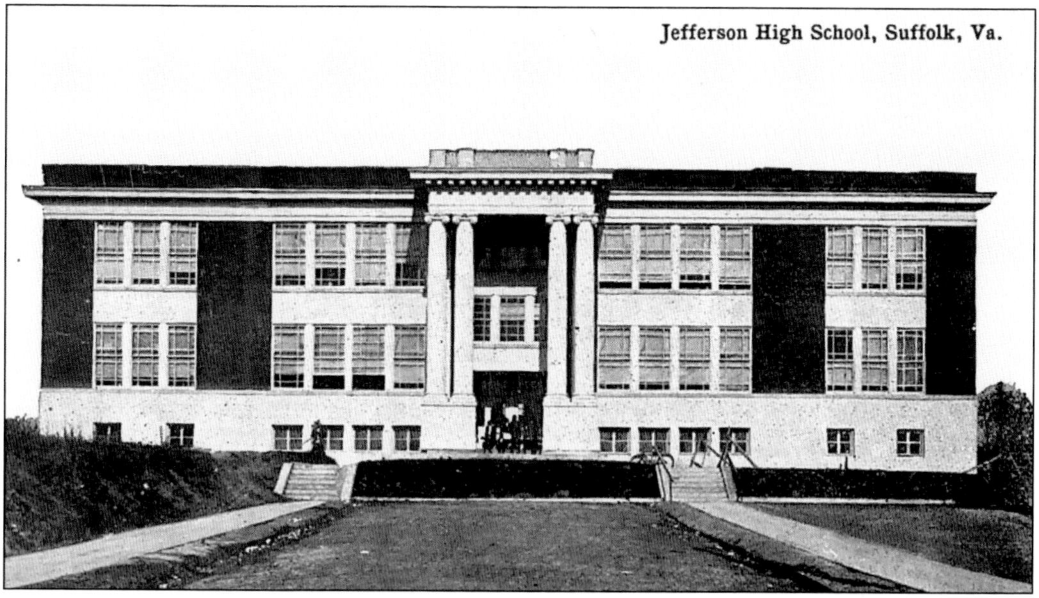

Thomas Jefferson School or Jefferson High School was a handsome, impressive structure built in 1911 at the north end of the newly-opened Clay Street. It was the city's only white high school until 1922 when the new Suffolk High School was completed, built in the thicket on the right of the picture. Jefferson was used as an educational facility of one kind or another until 2002.

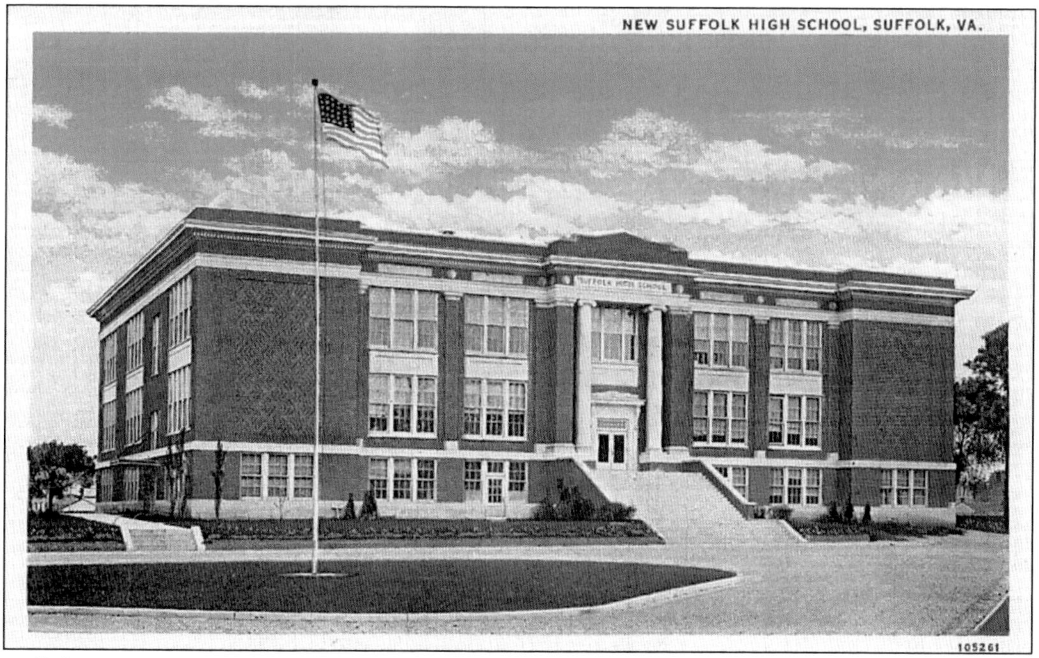

Suffolk High School opened in 1922, and with some additions in the 1950s, it served students in the City of Suffolk, as well as county students who paid tuition until 1990. The school and the community were closely linked. The yearbook was called the *Peanut* and the school newspaper was the *Peanut Picker.* Plans are now being finalized for the creation of a cultural arts center in the old school building.

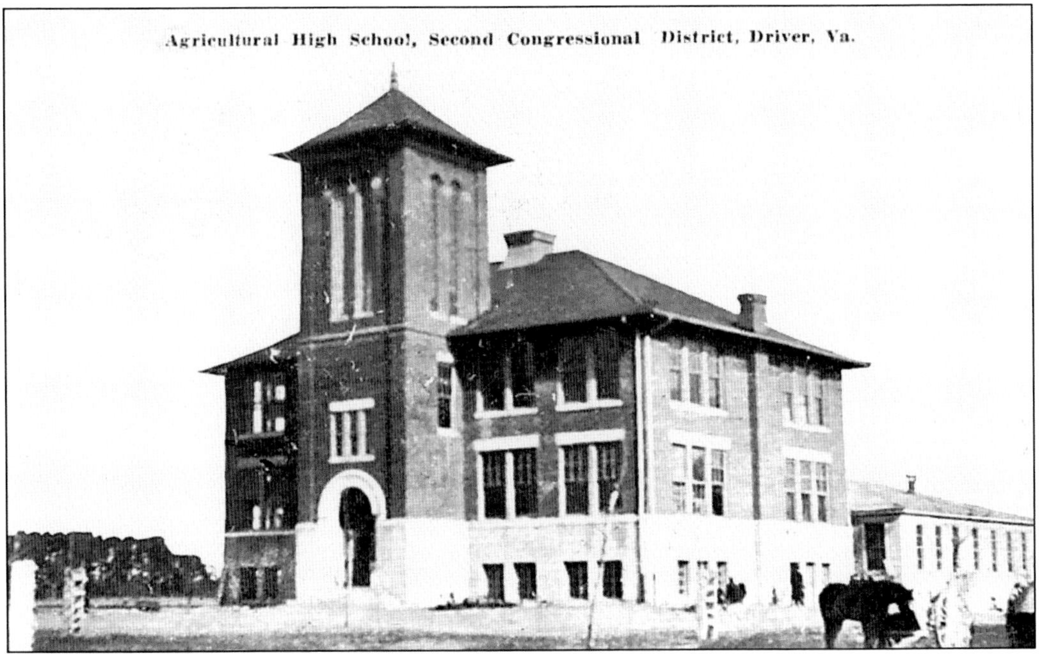

The school in Driver had a special distinction. Built around the turn of the century, the Second Congressional District Agricultural High School had dormitories for students who came from surrounding areas to study here. The school was eventually named the DeJarnette School for J.B.L. DeJarnette, superintendent of public instruction in Driver.

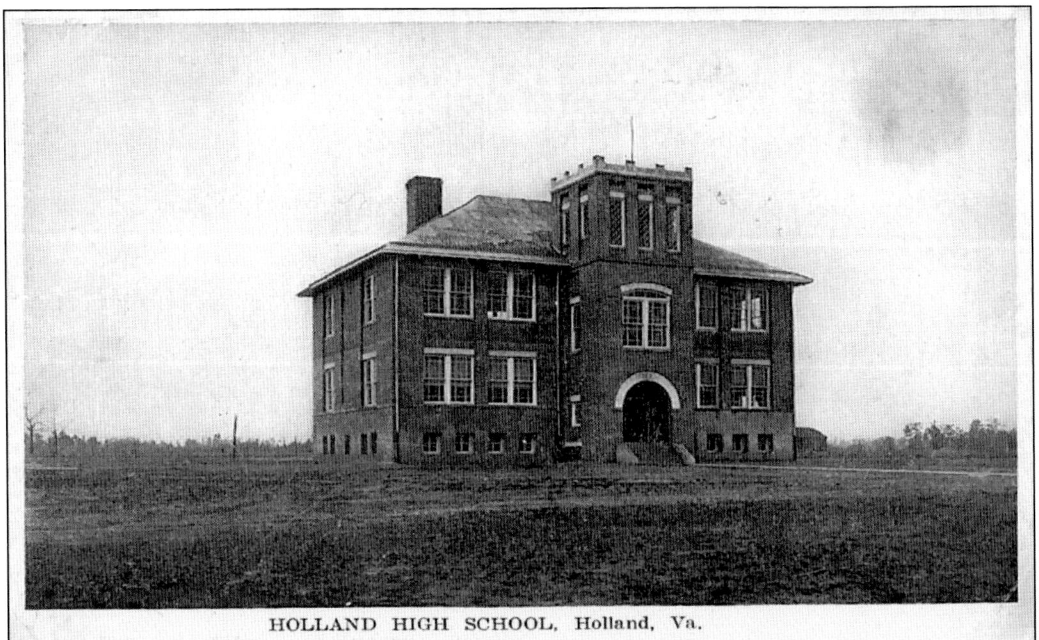

This structure was the third building erected for use as a public school in Holland. In 1924 it became an elementary school when a new high school was built on an adjoining lot. This building had been abandoned for several years when it was destroyed by fire in 1992.

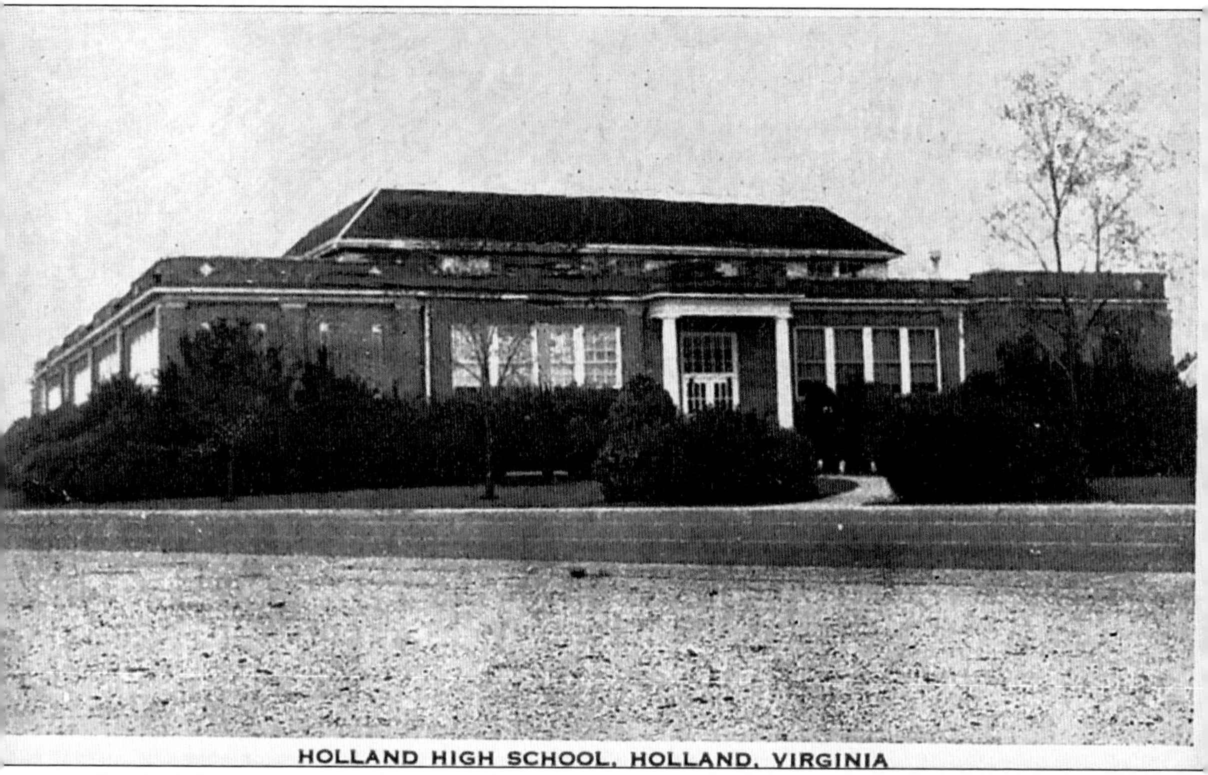

Holland High School was built in 1924 for white students in grades eight through eleven. Holland was the largest town in Nansemond County and its school was considered one of the finest in the area. Holland High School closed in the 1960s. The building was used as an elementary school for a while before it was destroyed by fire in 1991.

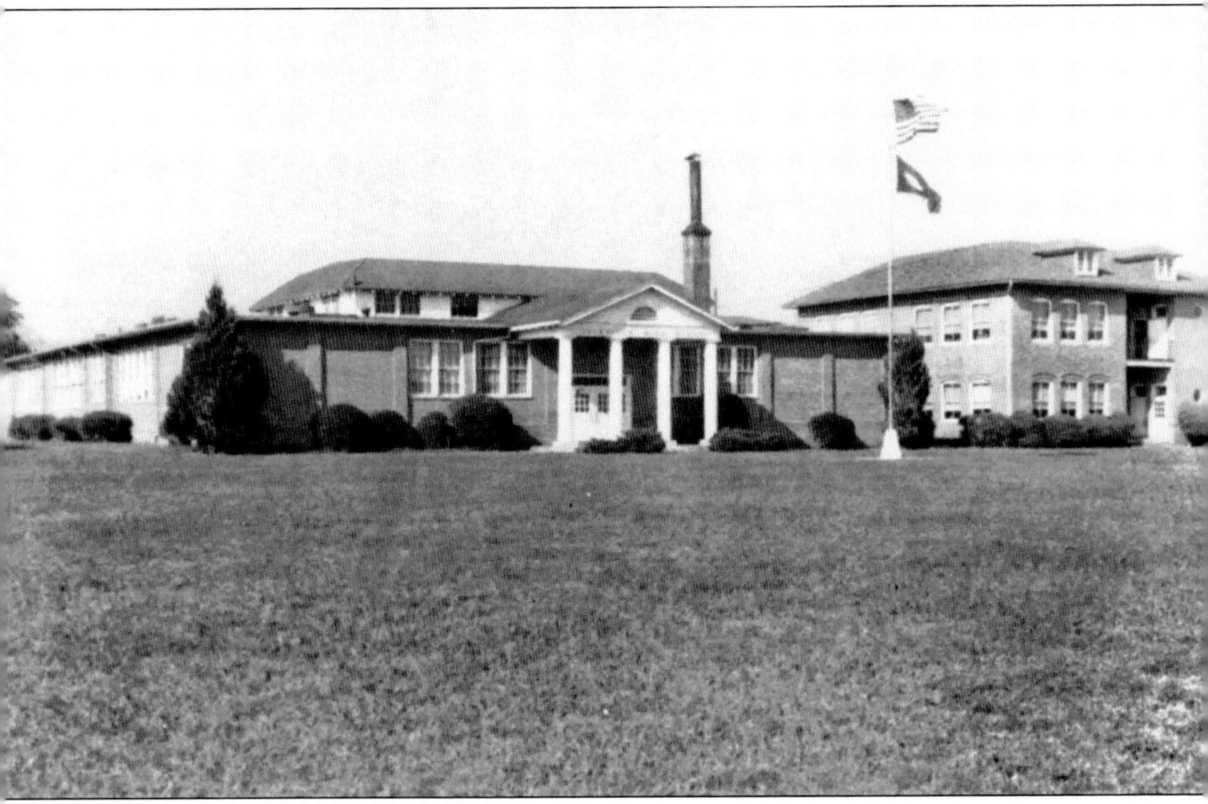

Chuckatuck High School was completed in 1924 as a district high school serving the Crittenden, Driver, and Kings Fork areas of Nansemond County. The two-story building, constructed *c.* 1890, served all Chuckatuck students and became the grammar school in 1924. Chuckatuck High School was replaced by John Yeates High School in 1965. The Chuckatuck High School complex served as Chuckatuck Middle School from 1965 until 1977. It now houses a building supply company.

Two

Landmarks and Institutions

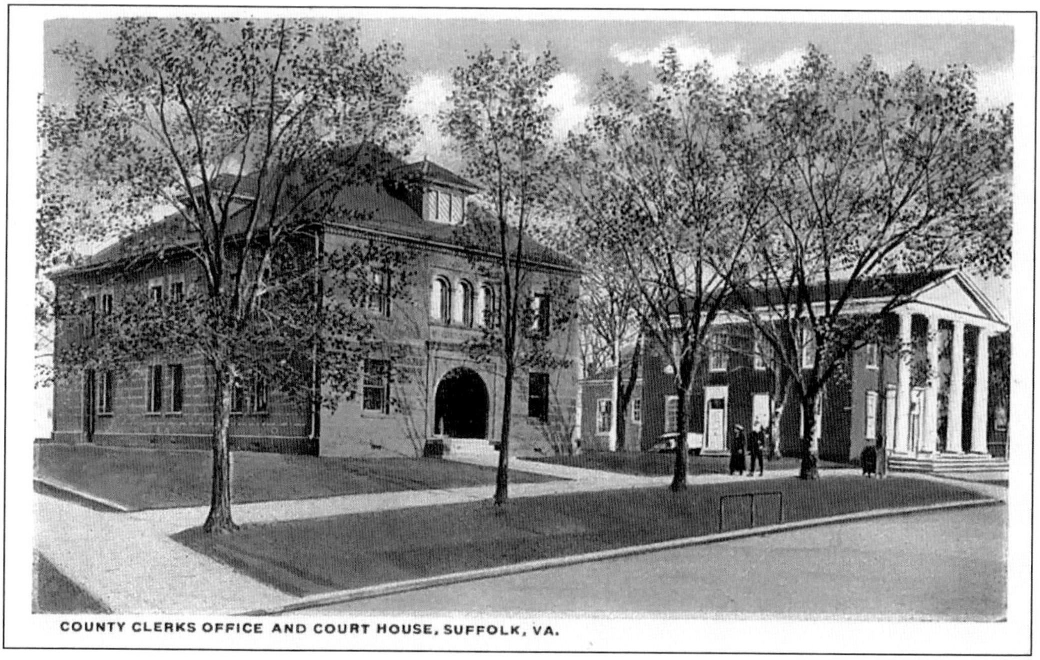

When the original courthouse was built on the hill overlooking the river, it was the absolute center of town. Through the years, business activity moved away from this corner. The river hill still seems like the perfect place for what was once the Nansemond County Courthouse, which now houses city offices. Note the hitching post in front of the clerk's office.

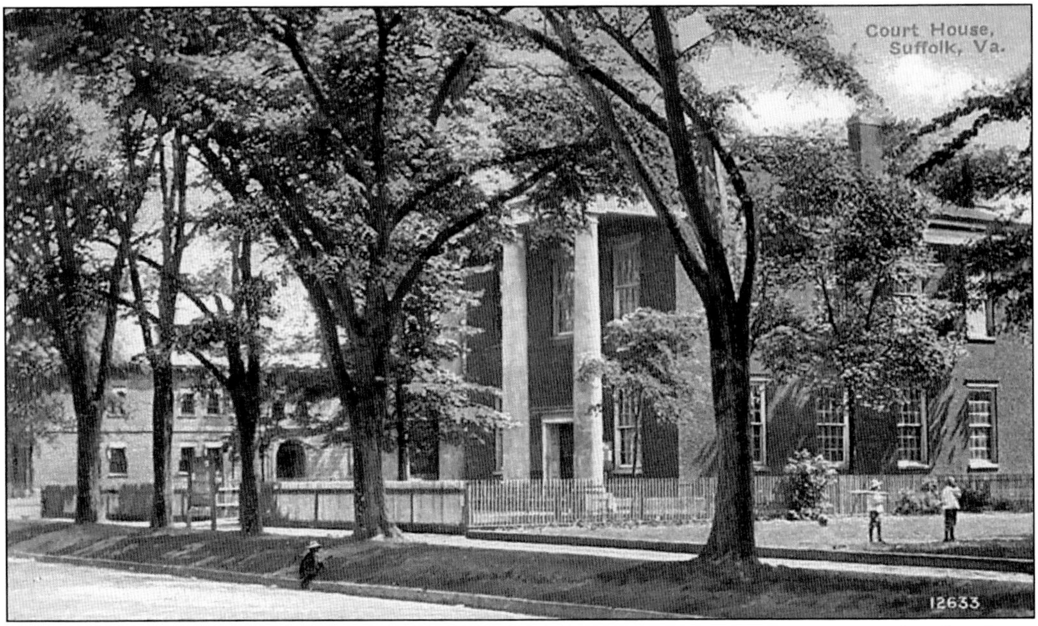

The Greek-Revival style Nansemond County Courthouse was rebuilt on this site after the Great Fire of 1837 destroyed the previous one. Necessary announcements were posted out front. Perhaps the fence was to keep small boys at a distance. The 1894 clerk's office is to the left.

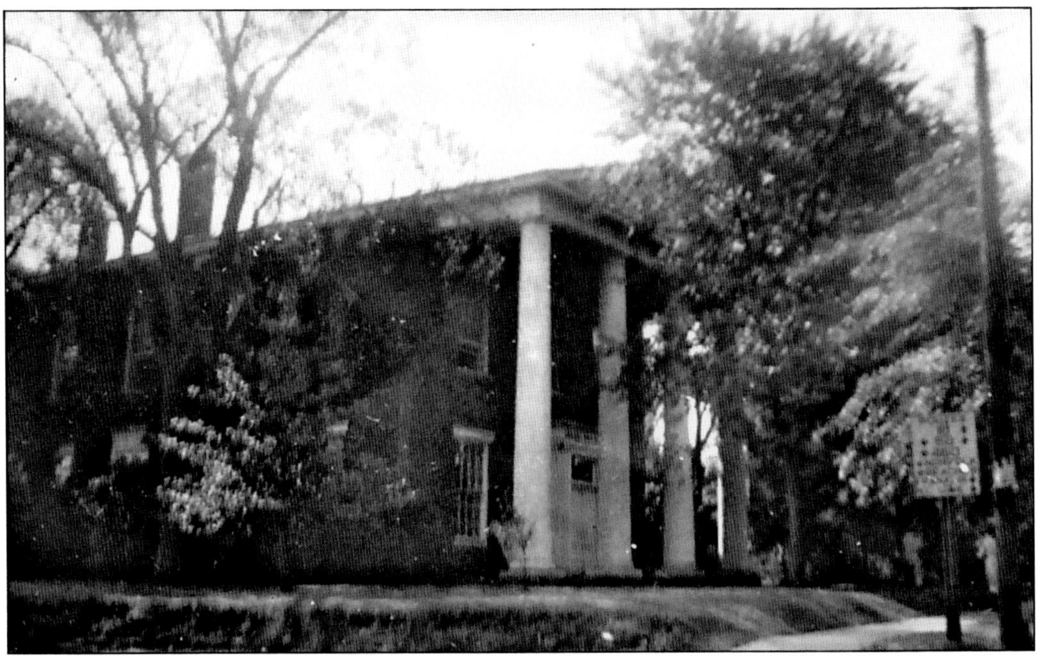

The courthouse faces Main Street but this hazy view is taken from Milner Street (first called First Cross Street and now known as Constance Road.) The highway markers were much more discreet. This was one of the first impressions of Suffolk one would receive when entering the city from the north.

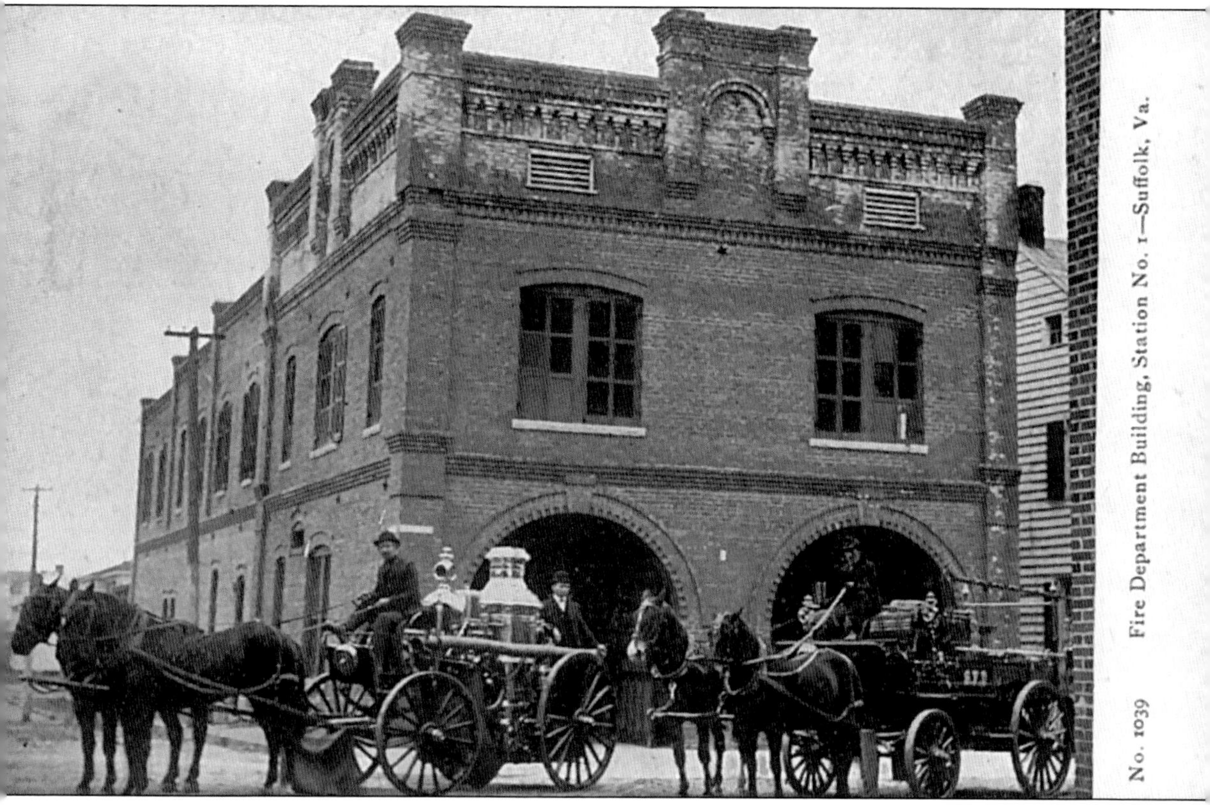

Fire Station # 1 was built in 1888 on the corner of Saratoga and Market Streets by and for the Phoenix Fire Company. No doubt the big downtown fires in 1885 and 1888 had shown the need for organization and equipment. The Phoenix Fire Company had a band that often played at the Joyner Park Bandstand and other pleasant spots.

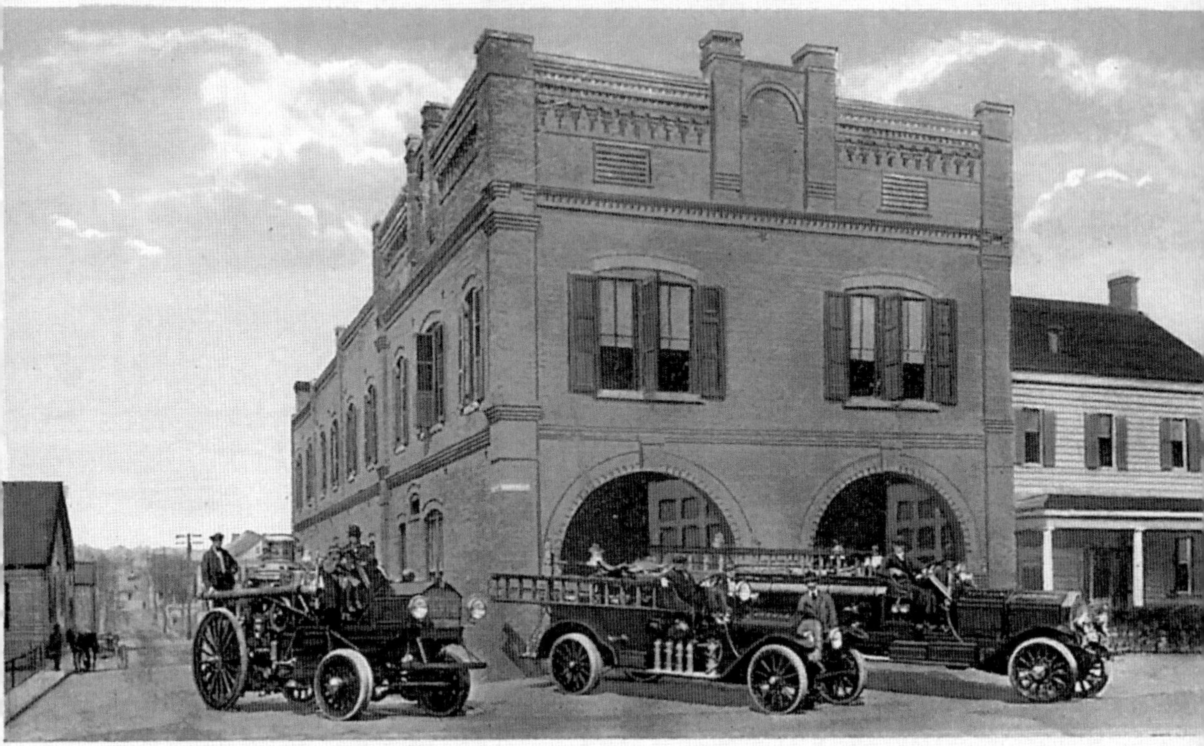

SUFFOLK FIRE DEPARTMENT, SUFFOLK, VA.

Early in the 20th century, the fire department had acquired motorized vehicles—the first in 1914. By the time this picture was taken, horses had been retired. Across the street from this building stood the Pythian Castle, a meeting place for several fraternal orders. The Pythian Castle was lost at an unknown date. The fire house was demolished in 1963. An insurance agency now occupies the site.

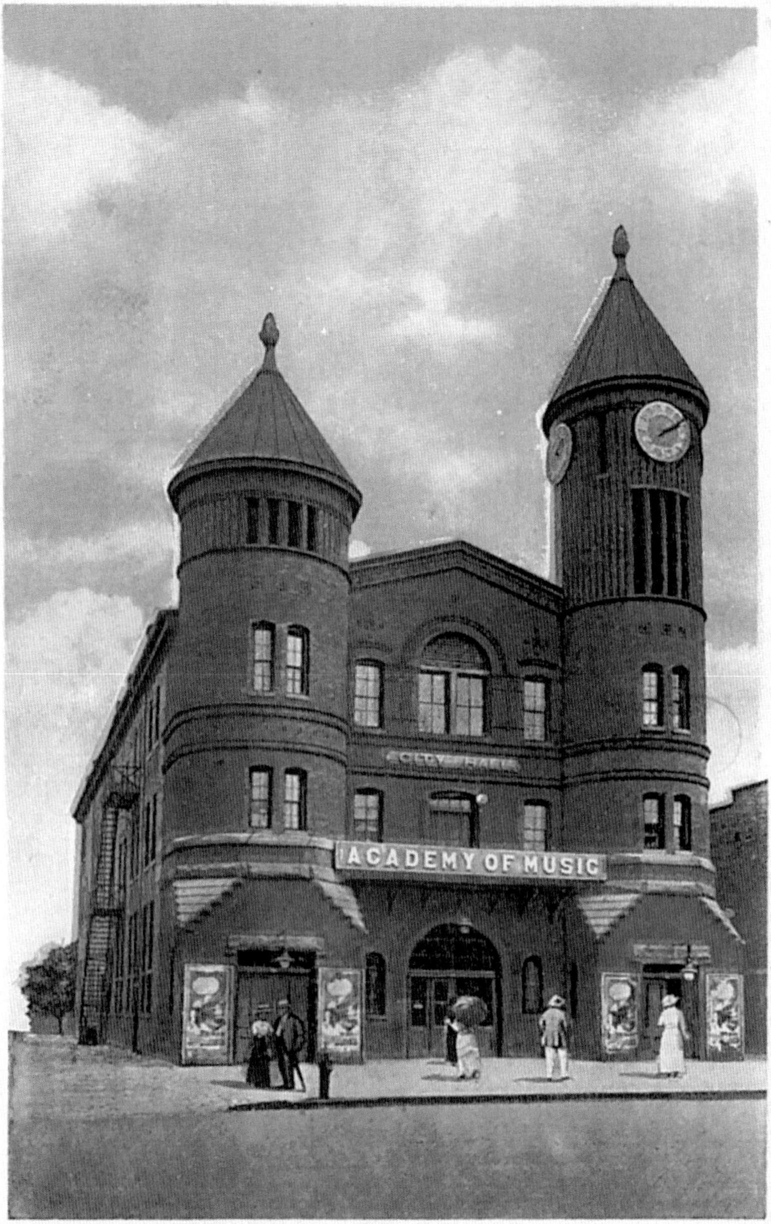

CITY HALL, SUFFOLK, VA.

A clear favorite lost landmark for people from Suffolk and old Nansemond County is the City Hall/City Market. It was built on the east side of Main Street in 1890 and 1891. Before the days of motion pictures, the Academy of Music was the place for entertainment. There were vaudeville shows, music recitals, lectures, and plays. The police department was here as well. The market, designed by George C. Moser of Norfolk, was the spot for dances, basketball games, roller skating, graduation exercises, and even Sunday school classes. The latter occurred when both the Christians and the Episcopalians were building new churches. Merchants sold live chickens and fresh produce here. For Memorial Day, country ladies would bring flowers to sell. The building was demolished in 1962.

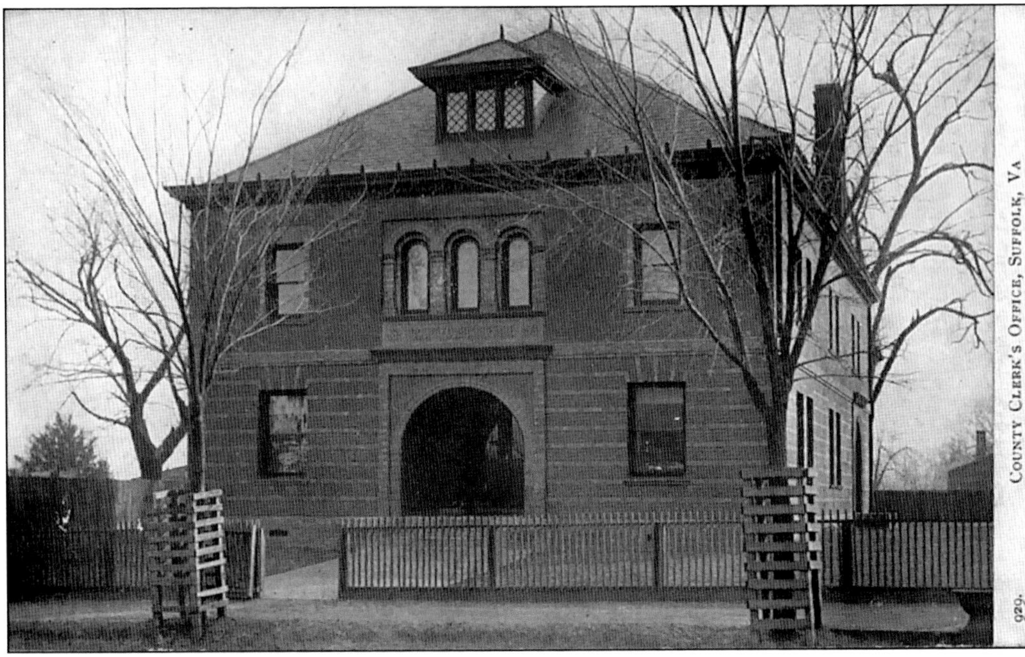

This clerk's office was built in 1894. The previous office was damaged by fire in 1866 and patched up to "make do" until the county could afford a new one. Every effort was made to construct as sturdy and fireproof a building as possible. It was demolished with some considerable effort in the 1980s because of a highway widening project.

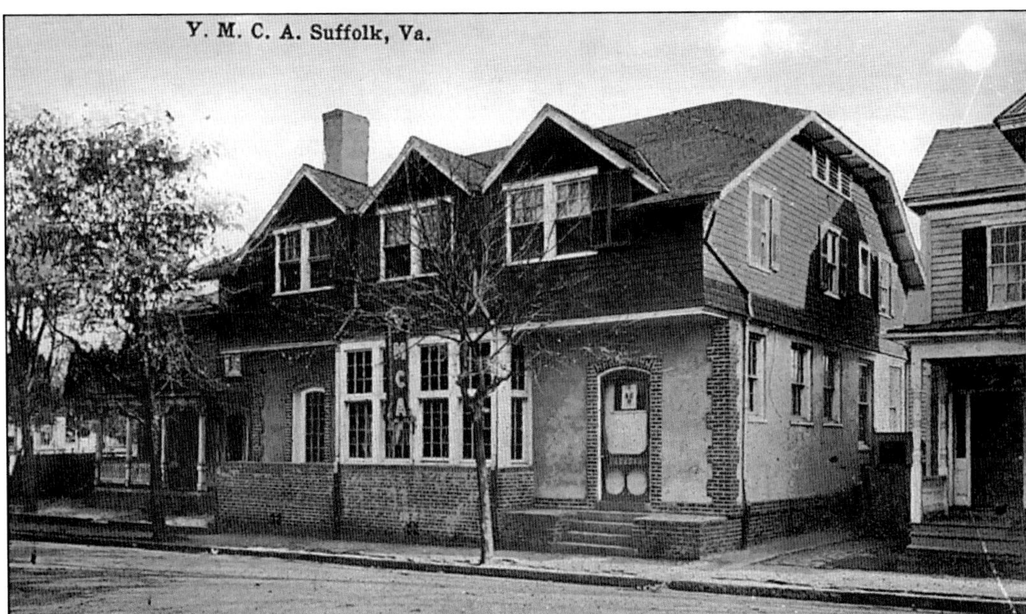

This building once stood in the 100 block of North Saratoga Street early in the century. It was originally built to house the Young Men's Christian Association, but there was insufficient support for the organization. It was eventually used by the chamber of commerce and then the Boy Scouts before it was demolished several years ago.

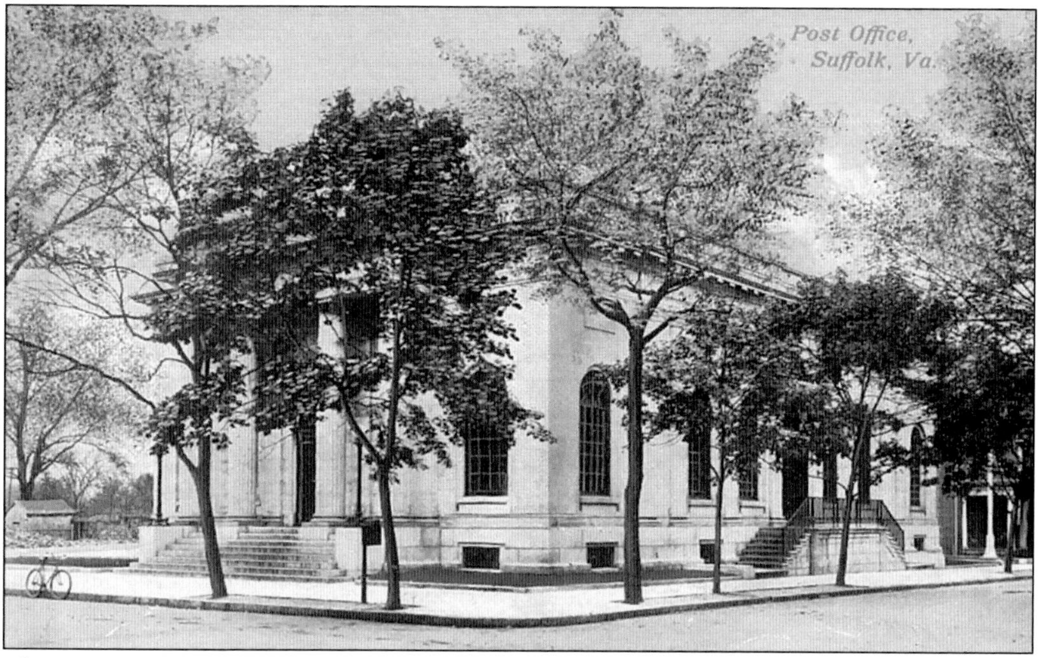

This picture of the handsome 1913 post office building must have been taken around 1914 as work was beginning on the new Methodist Church building visible on the left. The ever-present bicycle is at the curb. This post office closed in the 1980s and is now a law office.

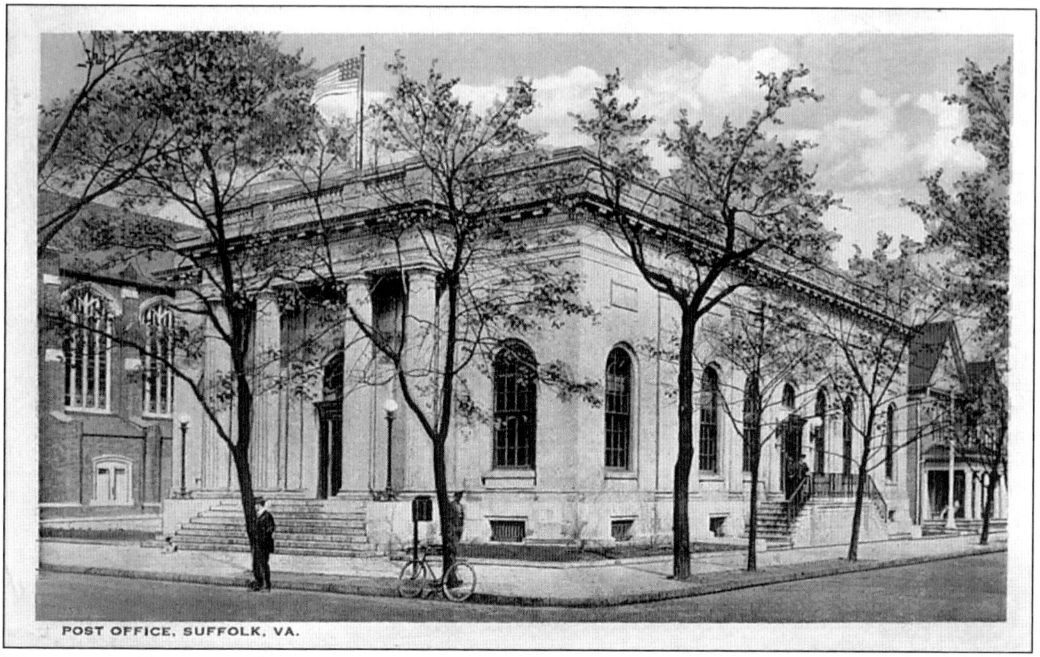

The steps of the post office were a popular perch for idlers The world as Suffolk knew it passed by this spot. Men from the Methodist Church (seen to the left) and the Christian Church (a few doors north of the Methodist Church) posed for a group picture here shortly after the post office opened. This splendid public building was a great source of community pride.

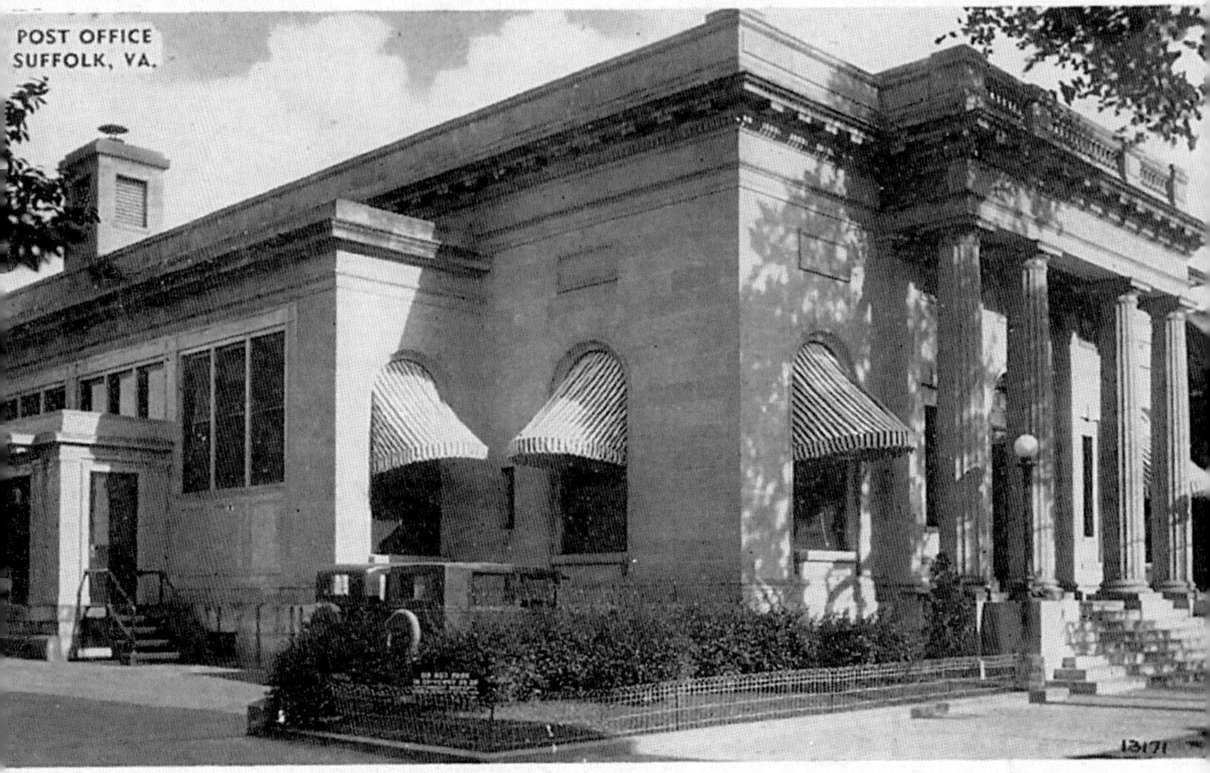

In its early years, the post office relied on awnings and shade trees to keep it cool during the summer. In the mid-20th century there were two mail deliveries per day and the building offered a shower room so that the mailmen could cool off and start fresh. There was also a "cat walk" inside for use by the postmaster or postal inspector to insure that mail was being handled properly.

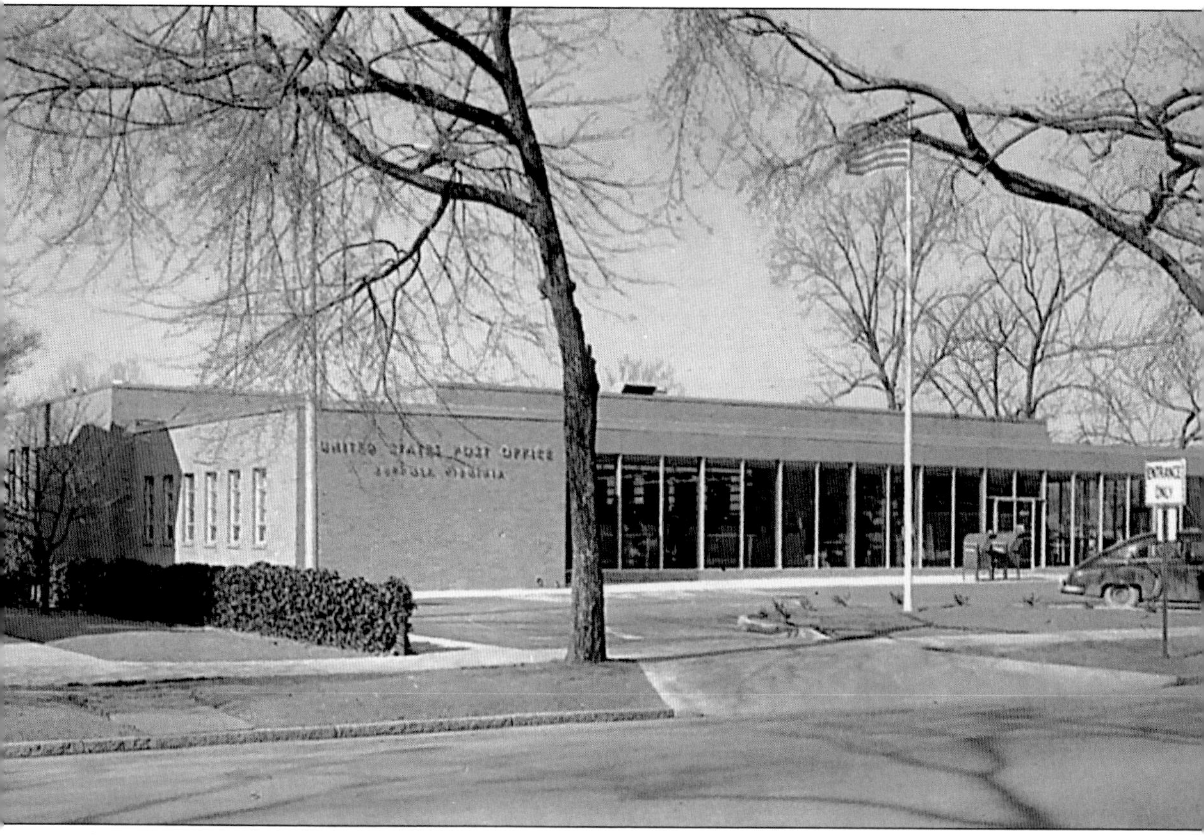

Like many other buildings of its style and age, the 1960s post office at the corner of North Main Street and Western Avenue replaced an older home that once stood on the spot. It became the only downtown post office in 1987 when the older one on the corner of Main and Bank Streets closed.

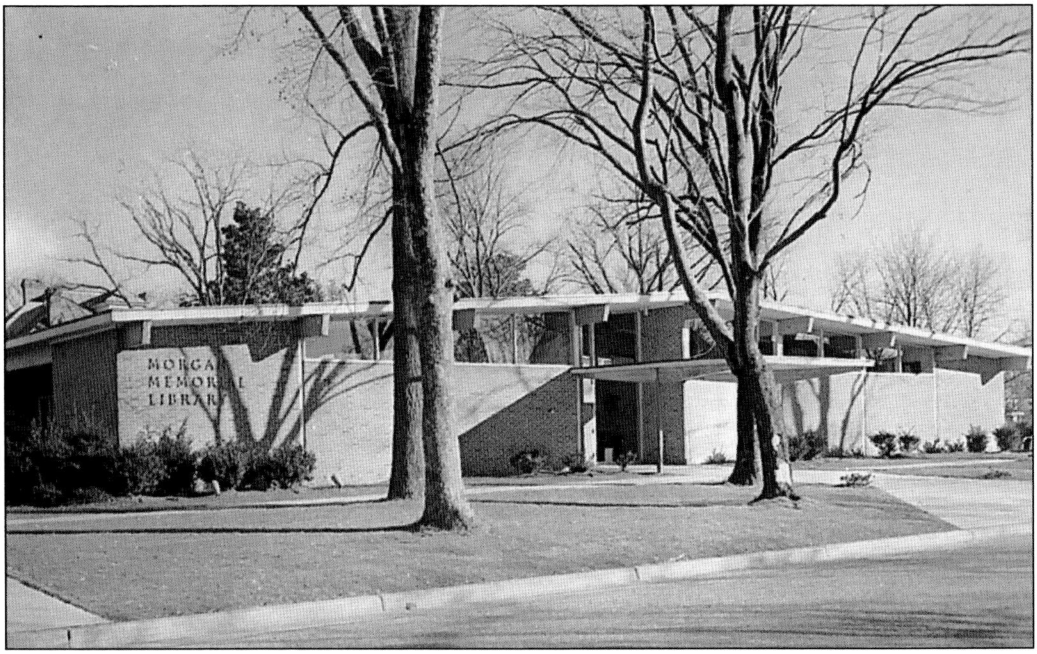

Morgan Memorial Library was built on Bosley Avenue in 1957 with money left for that purpose by Lizzie Morgan as a memorial to her parents. Before the construction of this library, the Woman's Club had operated a library from their headquarters at the corner of Bank and Pinner Streets. Morgan Library moved to larger quarters in 1986 and this building eventually became the Suffolk Museum.

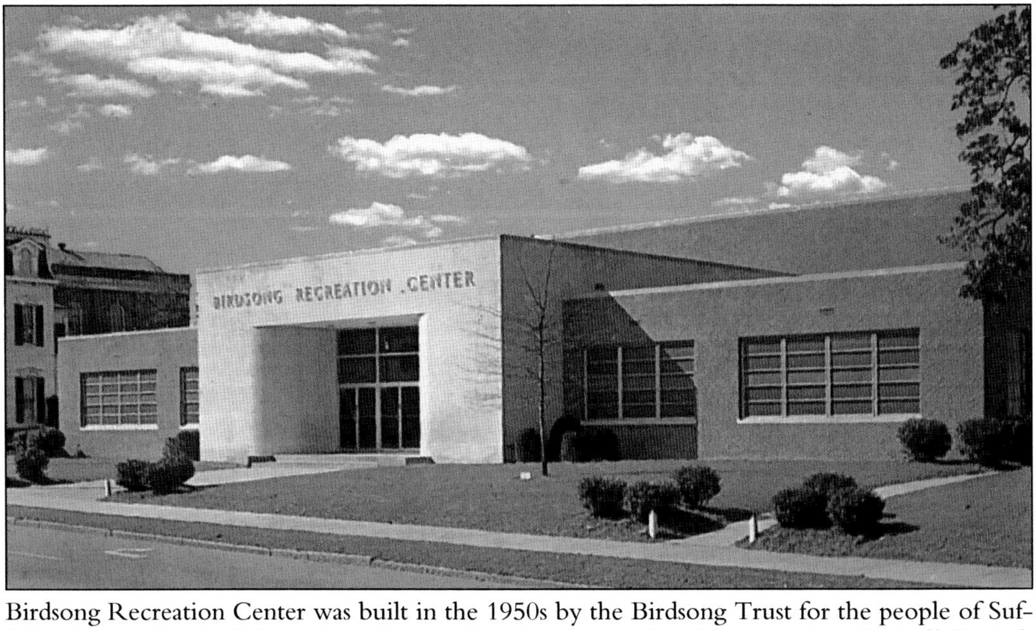

Birdsong Recreation Center was built in the 1950s by the Birdsong Trust for the people of Suffolk. Designed by Suffolk architect Dupree Breeden, it served as the gymnasium for Suffolk High School from the time the center was built until Suffolk High School closed in 1990. It is now used by the City Department of Parks and Recreation.

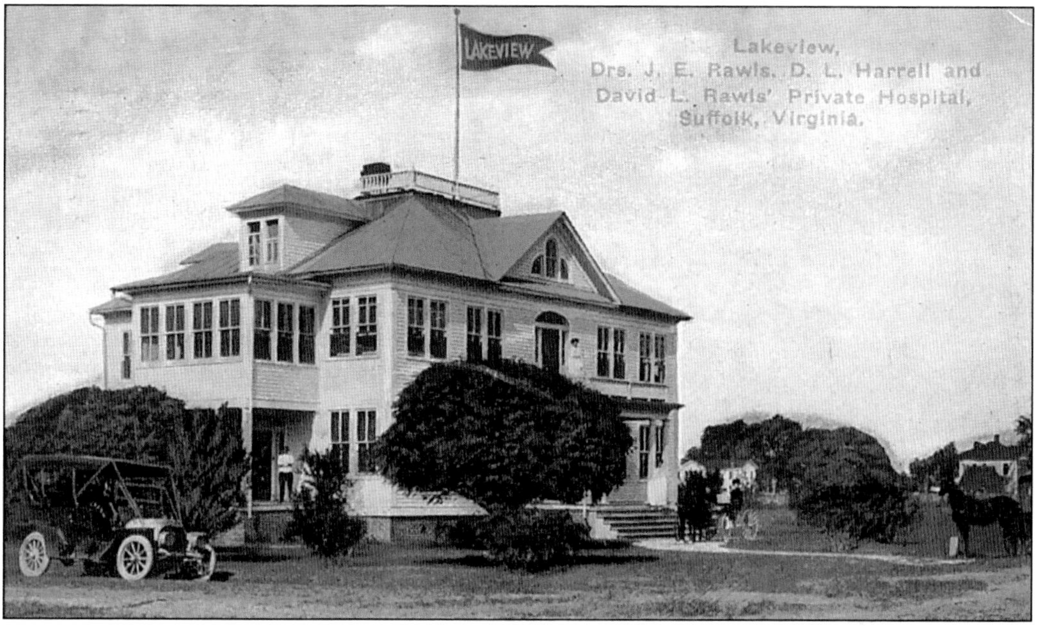

Lakeview, Suffolk's first hospital, was built in 1906 at the west edge of town on two lots at the corner of Smith Street and Bosley Avenue. It was so far from downtown that one account of its history referred to Lakeview as "the hospital in the field." It was organized and built by Dr. J.E. Rawls and Dr. E.R. Hart.

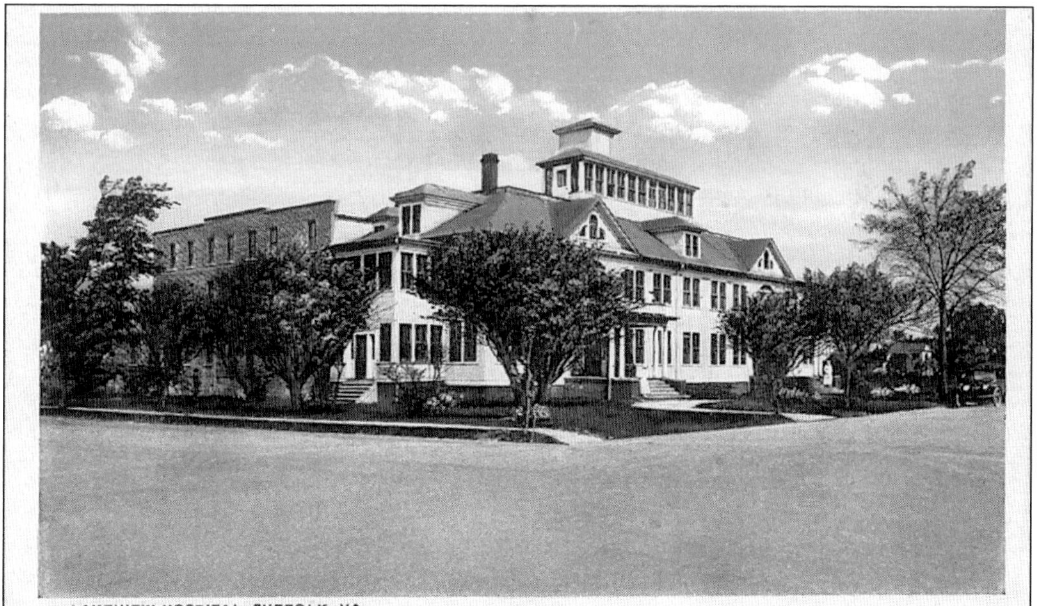

Over the next few decades, the hospital grew to cover most of the block. The staff grew as well. Lakeview Hospital closed in 1951 when Obici Hospital opened. The old Lakeview building was used as doctor's offices for a few years until Lakeview Clinic was built on part of the hospital property. The old hospital was demolished. The former clinic now houses other offices and Lakeview Clinic has moved to a new site.

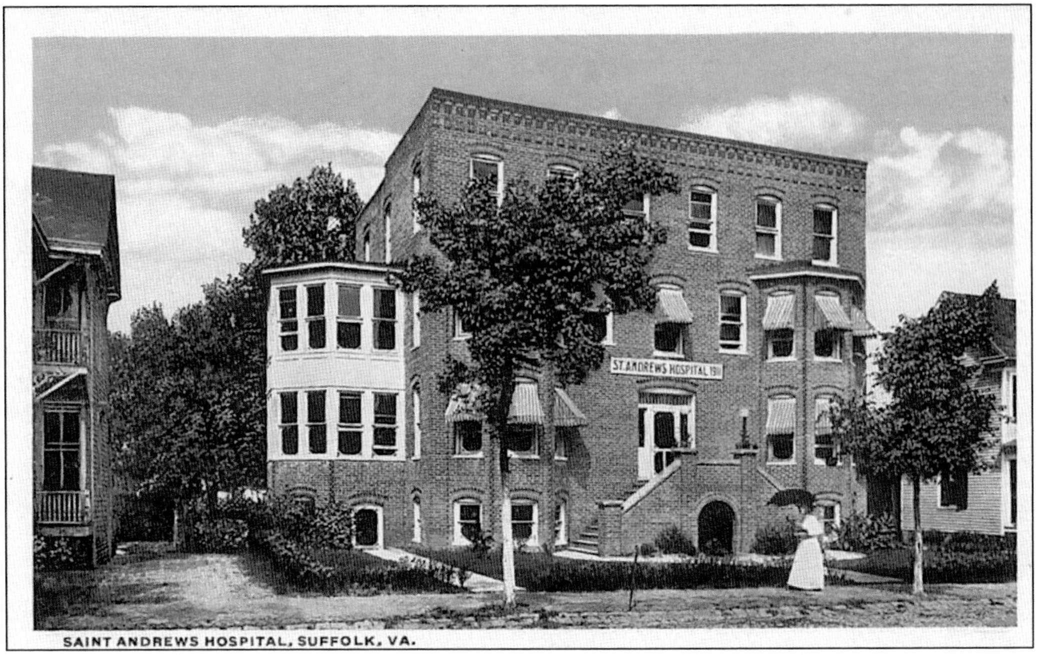

St. Andrews Hospital was built on Clay Street in 1911 by Dr. Frank J. Morrison and Dr. E.R. Hart (who had sold his share in Lakeview.) In 1917 it was reorganized as the Virginia Hospital. It always operated as a small, private downtown hospital, and it closed when Obici opened in 1951. The building was demolished in the 1960s.

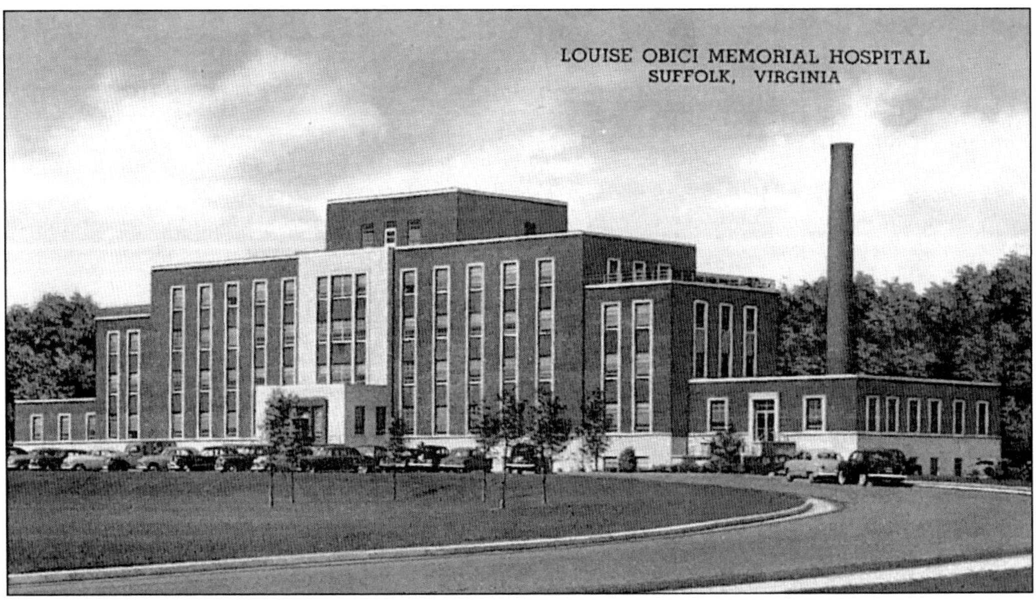

Louise Obici Memorial Hospital opened in 1951 on Route 460 just north of the old City of Suffolk. The hospital and its adjacent nursing school were constructed with funds left for that purpose by Amedeo Obici, founder of Planters Peanuts, as a memorial to his wife. The hospital was at this site until April 2002 when a new Louise Obici Memorial Hospital opened nearby on Route 10.

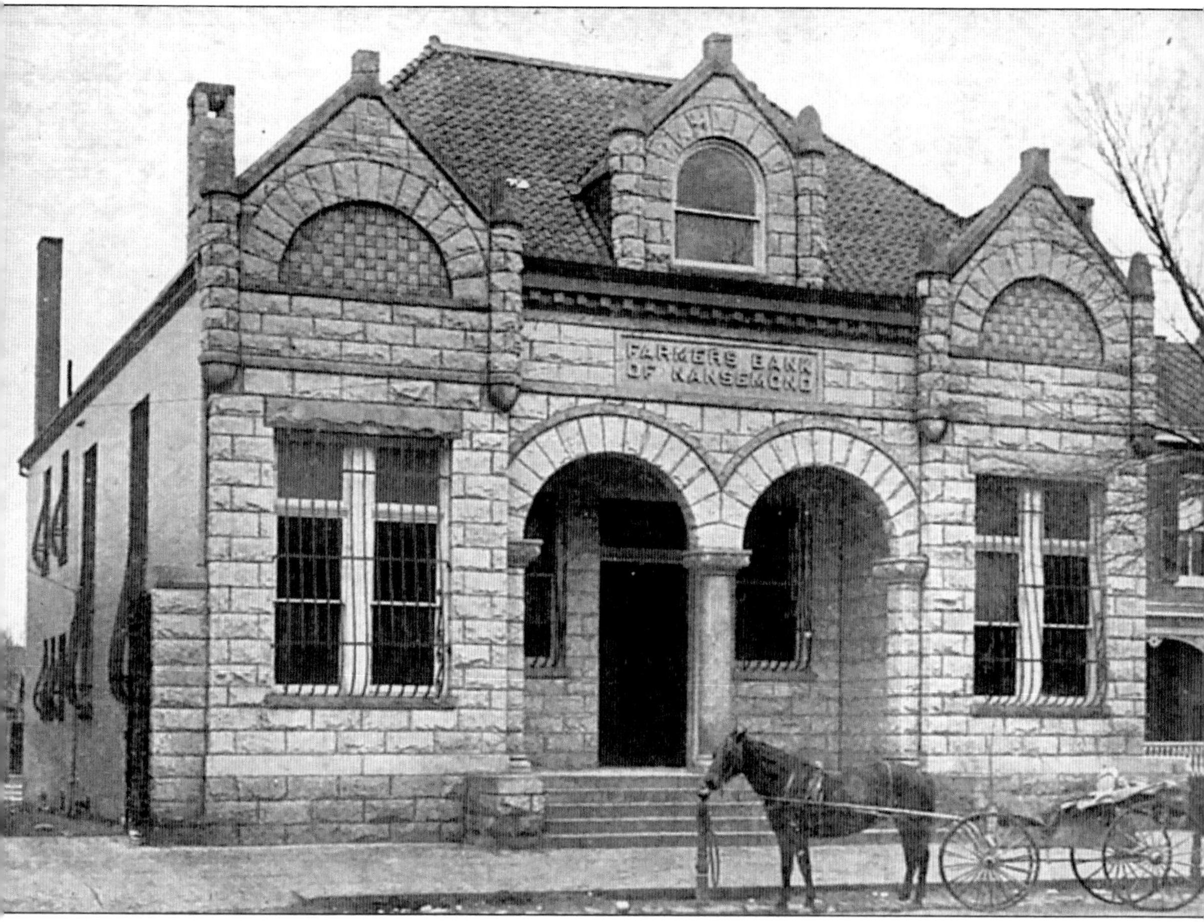

Farmers Bank of Nansemond was not the first bank in Suffolk, but it was the first successful one. Originally in another building, it was organized by Col. John R. Copeland in 1869. When the building shown here opened in 1899, it was called "one of the handsomest of its kind in the state." It was altered in 1922 and demolished in the 1960s when a more modern building was constructed.

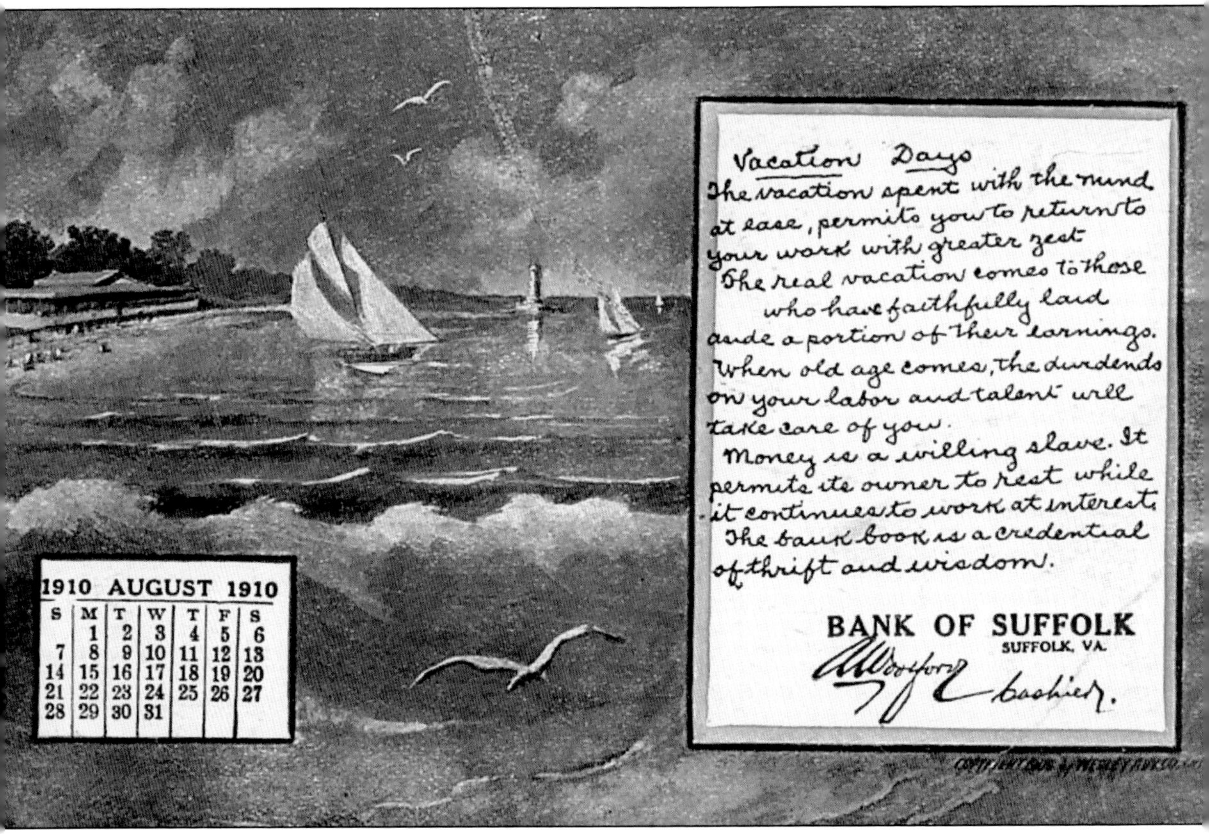

Organized in 1899 as the Bank of Suffolk, the institution advertised on this card was soon known as the National Bank of Suffolk. A. Woolford was the cashier in 1910. The bank was started by James L. McLemore along with A. Woolford, Thomas Birdsong, R. Howard, R.A. Pretlow, J.A. Pretlow, C.A. Shoop, and N.R. Withers.

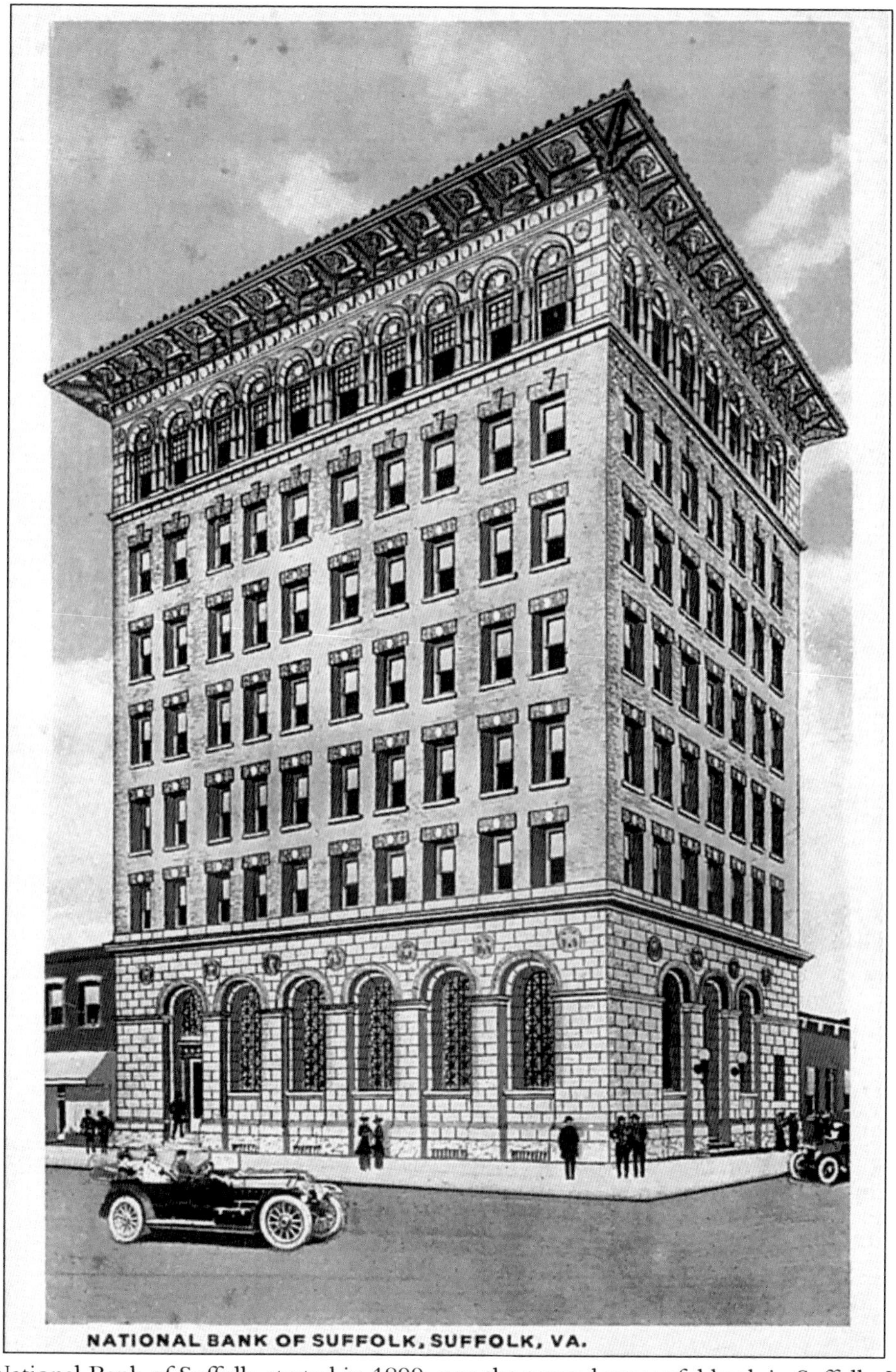

The National Bank of Suffolk, started in 1899, was the second successful bank in Suffolk. It first used an existing building on Main Street at the Square. That building was demolished to make way for this one in 1916. No longer used by the bank, this handsome building is still in use as an office building. On the south wall a bronze tablet was displayed for many years listing the local men who died in World War I. It is now posted in Cedar Hill Cemetary.

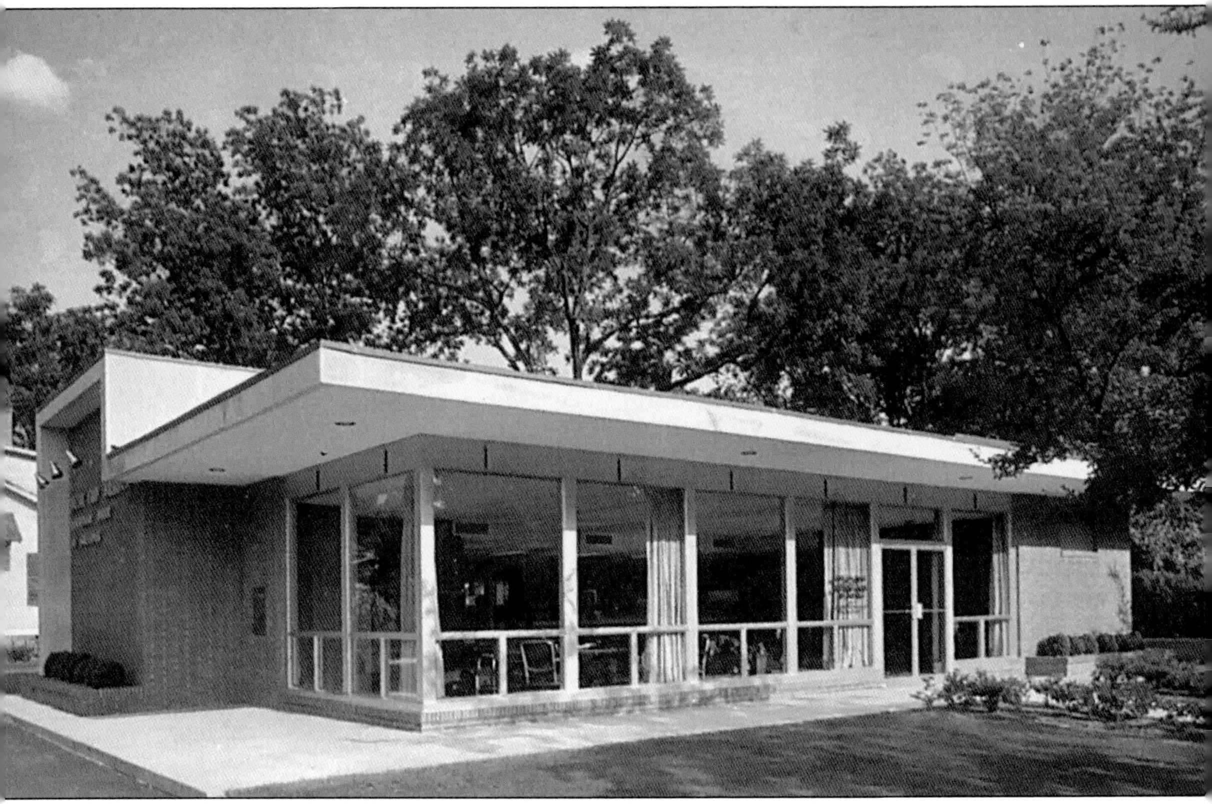

This branch of the National Bank of Suffolk was built at the corner of Bosley Avenue and West Washington Street in the late 1950s. It was the first branch office built by a Suffolk bank and had the first drive-through window in Suffolk. It now houses the newly-opened Suffolk First Bank.

Three

Downtown

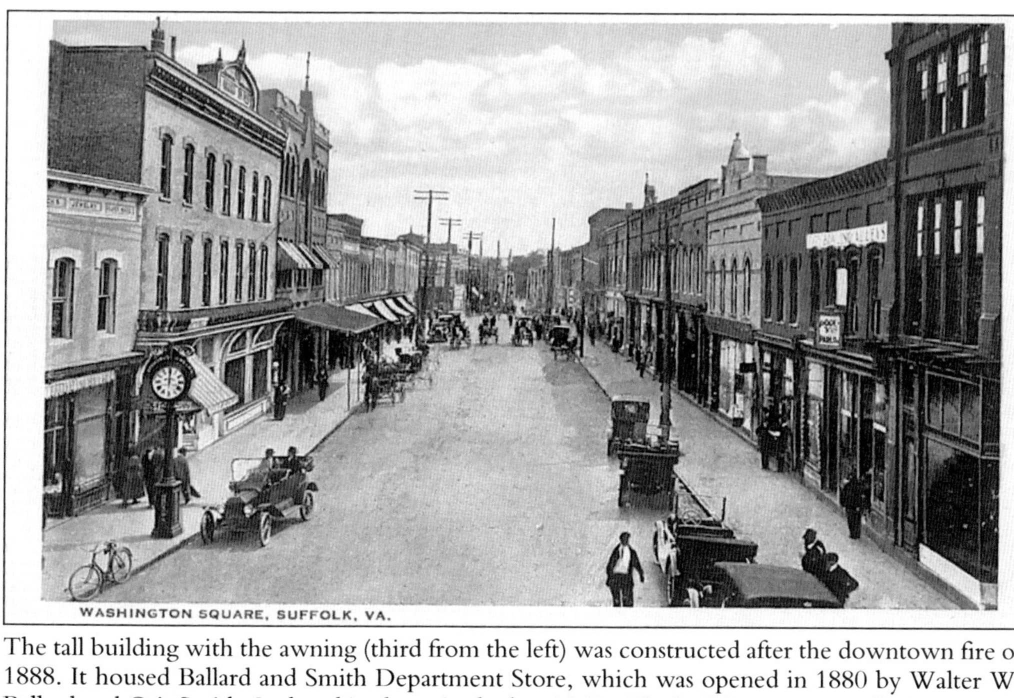

The tall building with the awning (third from the left) was constructed after the downtown fire of 1888. It housed Ballard and Smith Department Store, which was opened in 1880 by Walter W. Ballard and Otis Smith. It closed its doors in the late 1960s. The building was partially demolished and the remaining section was covered with new materials in the 1970s.

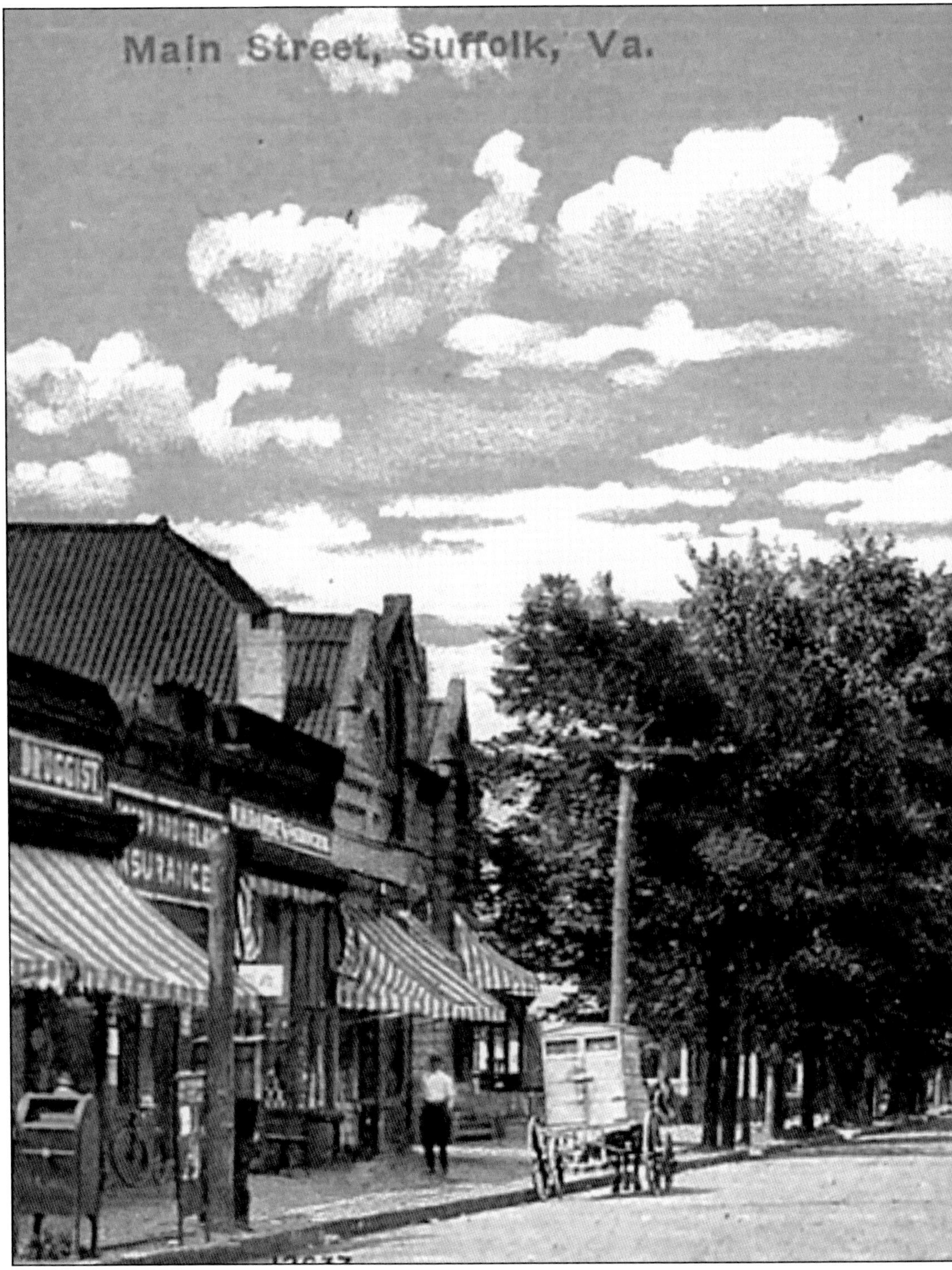

The Main Street business district has little business on a hot summer day. The City Hall/City Market towers over the other buildings, dominating the block. Out of sight here are the horse troughs that were up and down the street. The bicycle might have belonged to a delivery boy.

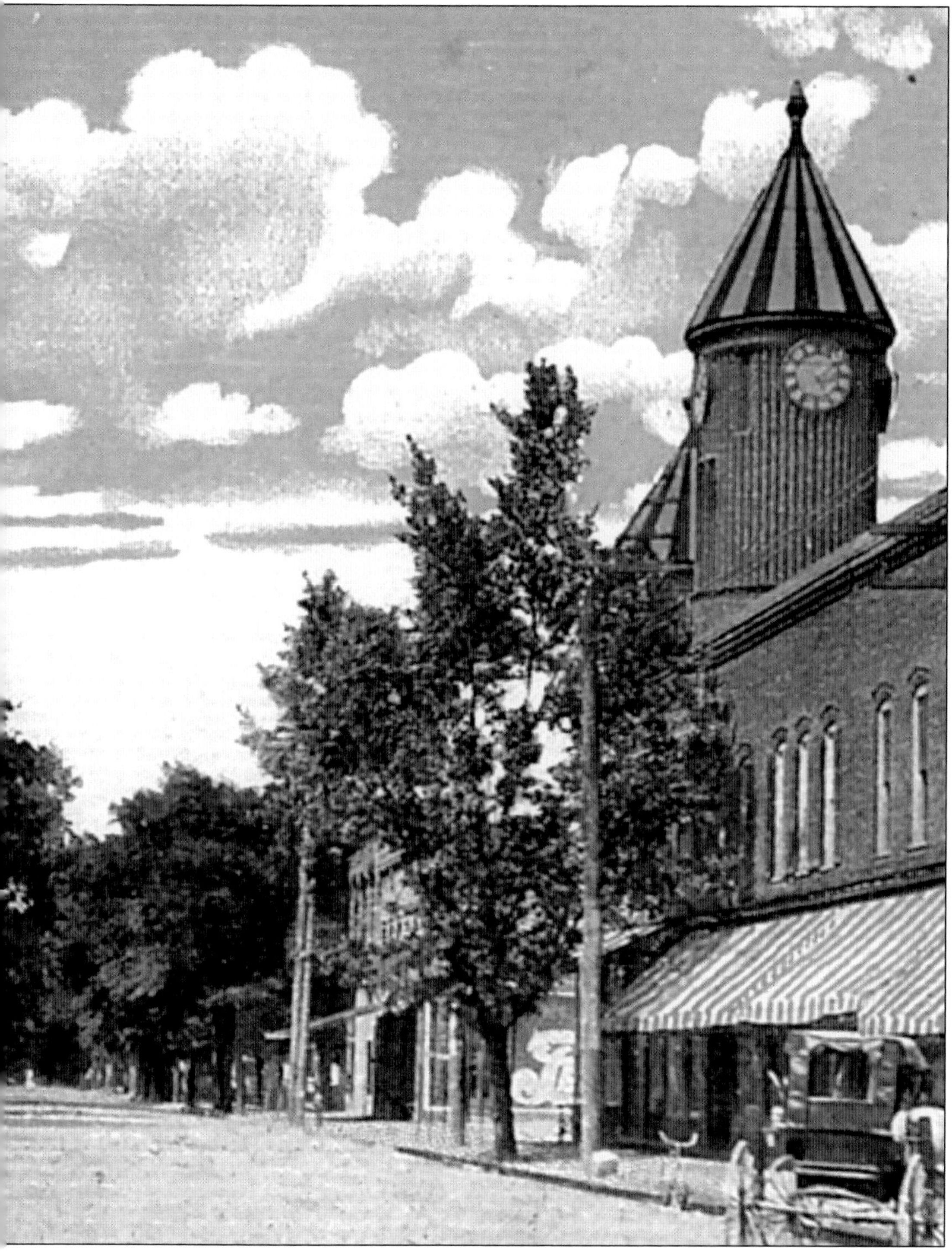

This is just a few doors from the intersection of Washington and Main Streets, an important east-west junction. Peace reigns here, of course, partly because of the heat but largely because the railroads—not highways—are carrying the traffic east, west, north, and south through Suffolk.

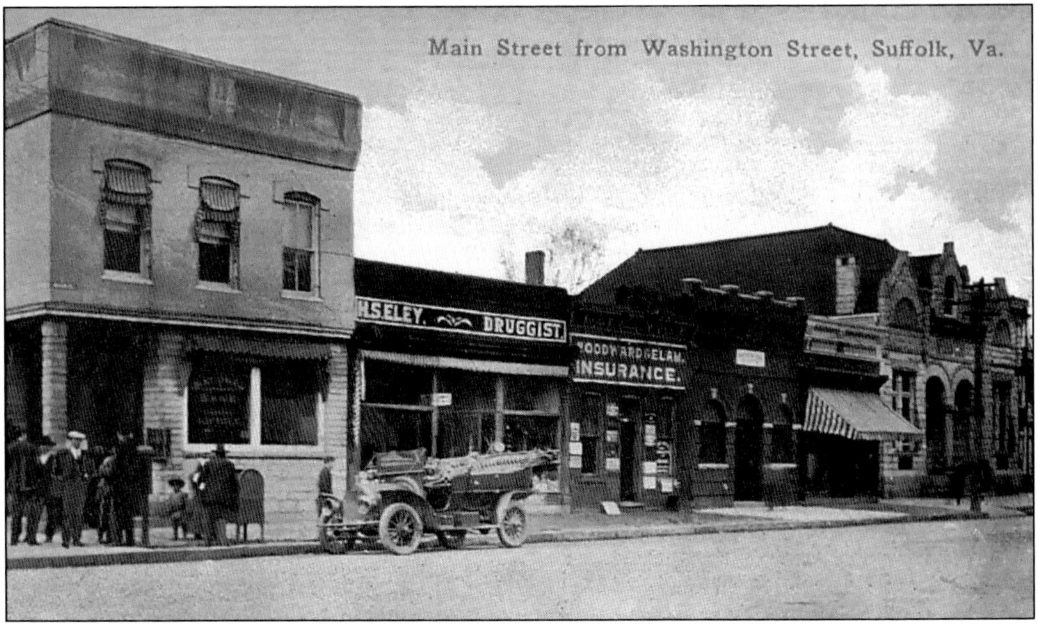

At the corner of Washington and Main *c.* 1915, a group of men gather outside the National Bank building. Next door is Henry S. Eley's Drug Store. Beyond that are Woodward and Elam Insurance, an unidentified business, West and Withers Insurance, and Farmer's Bank, which was built in 1899 and used until 1922.

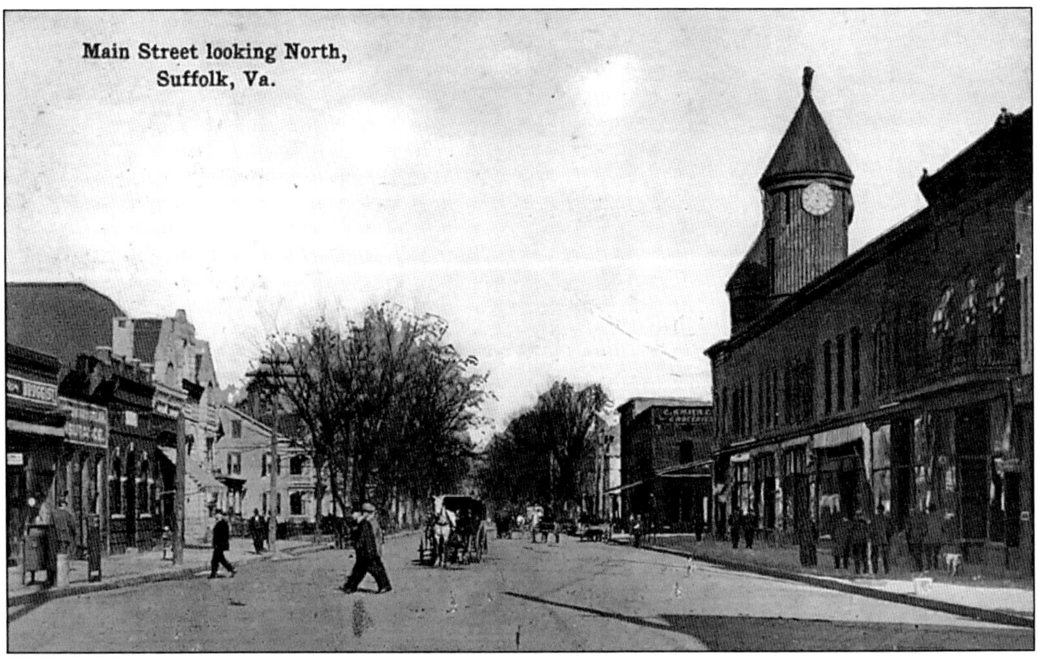

Cool weather finds awnings closed or removed and customers out and about. The City Hall/City Market dominates the scene. Its clock marked the passage of time in Suffolk. The clock tower held a bell for tolling the hour. Similar to Washington Square, these buildings replaced those destroyed by the 1888 fire.

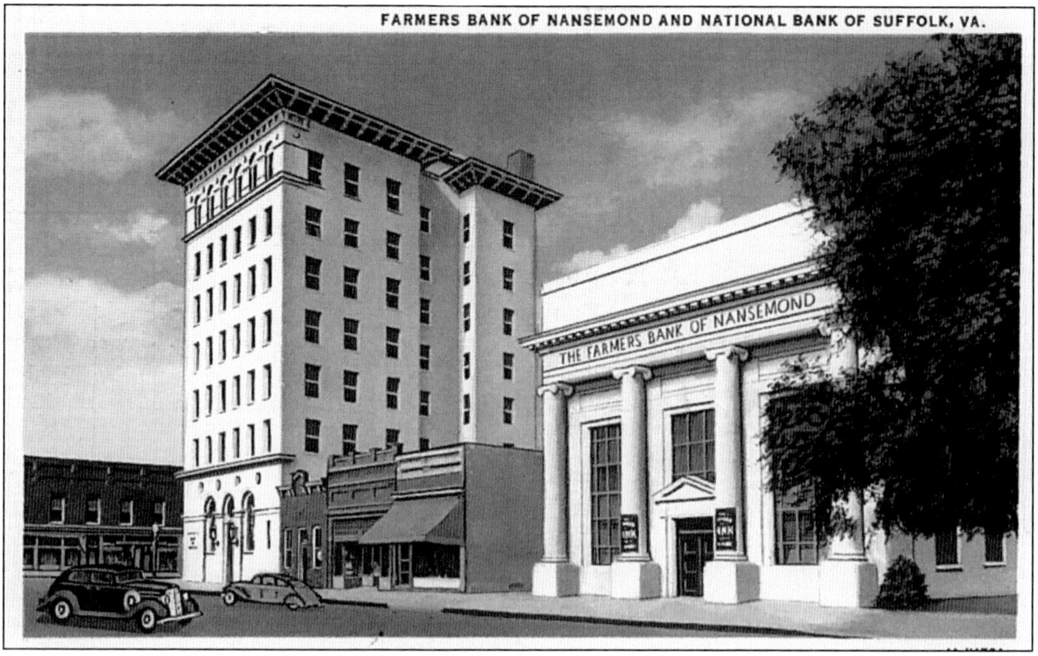

By the mid 1920s both the National Bank and the Farmers Bank had constructed new buildings. The high-rise National Bank still stands, but the Farmer's Bank building, shown here, was demolished in 1966 in favor of a more modern building.

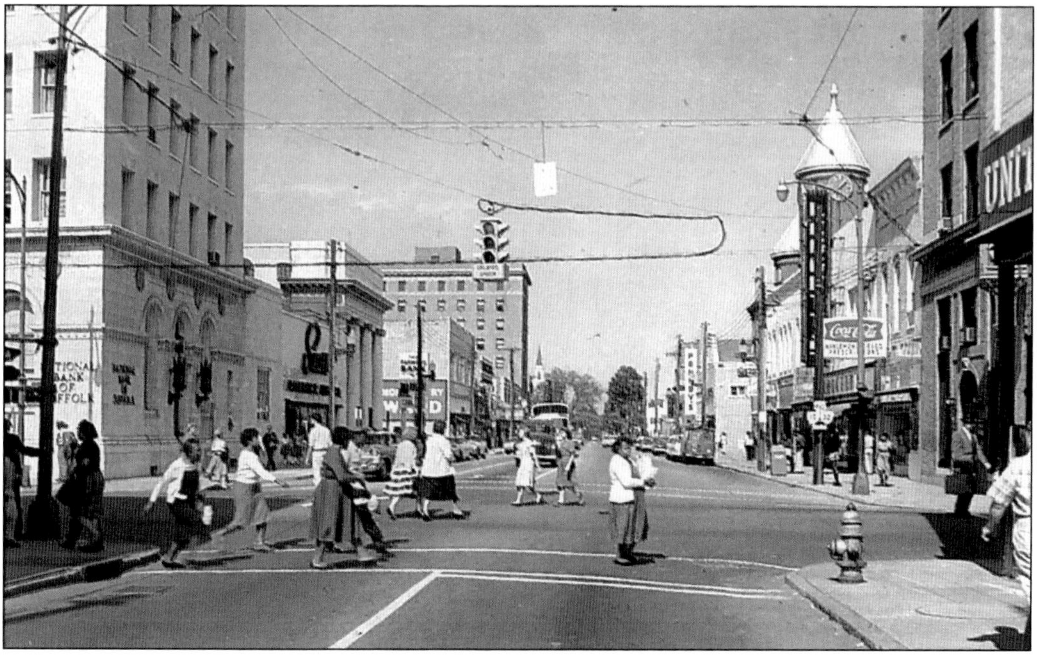

Seen from South Main at the Square (about 40 years after the view shown on page 56), North Main Street offered Sears and Montgomery Ward on one side of the street with Leggett Department Store and J.C. Penney on the other side. A corner of the United Dollar Store is just visible on the right. The towers of City Market would soon be gone from the landscape.

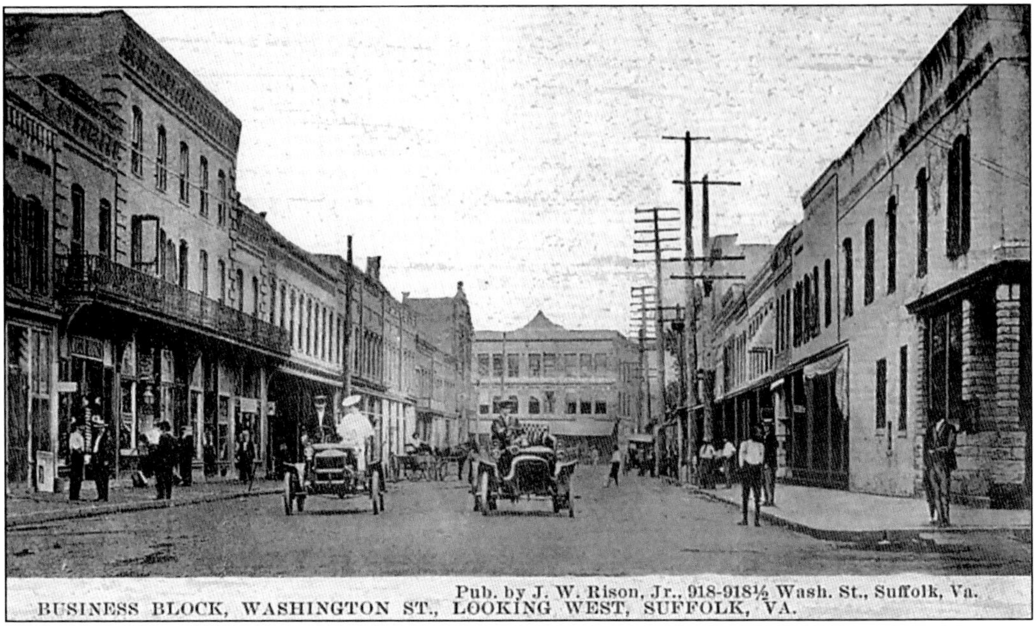

The main business block of Washington Street took the name Washington Square. This area suffered terrible fires in 1885 and 1888, so most of the buildings shown were built after that time. Some of Suffolk's oldest and finest businesses were on that block as was the office that produced this postcard.

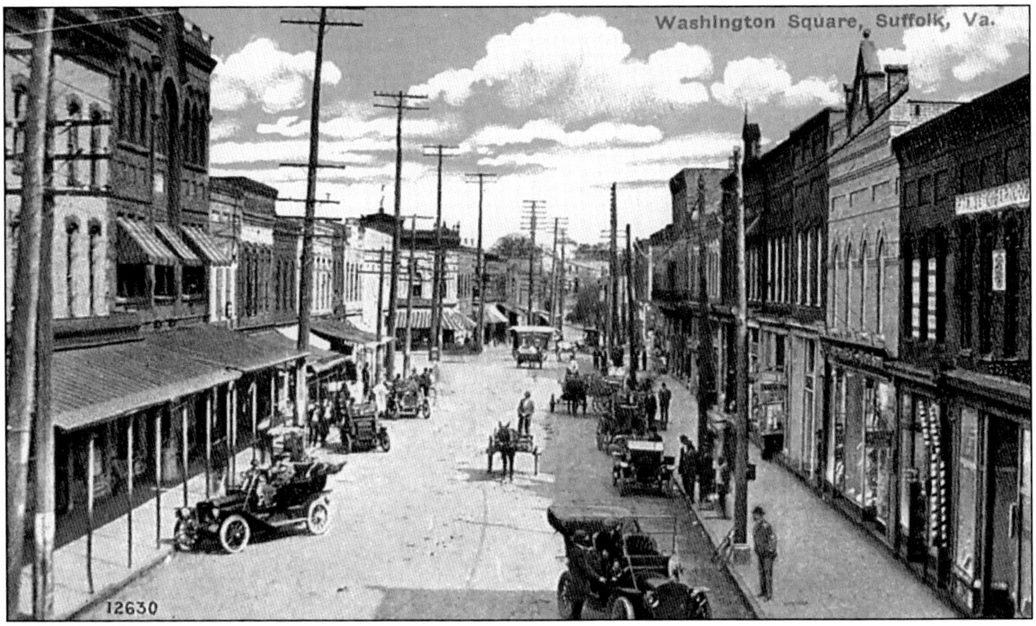

Business seems brisk enough on this pleasant day downtown. Marmaduke Jones's striped summer awning can be seen down on the corner of Washington and Main where M. Jones and Son offered fine men's clothing. Pedestrians still outnumbered motorists (or equestrians) so there was no plan for parking. The good old mule and cart are still doing work despite a growing interest in the automobile.

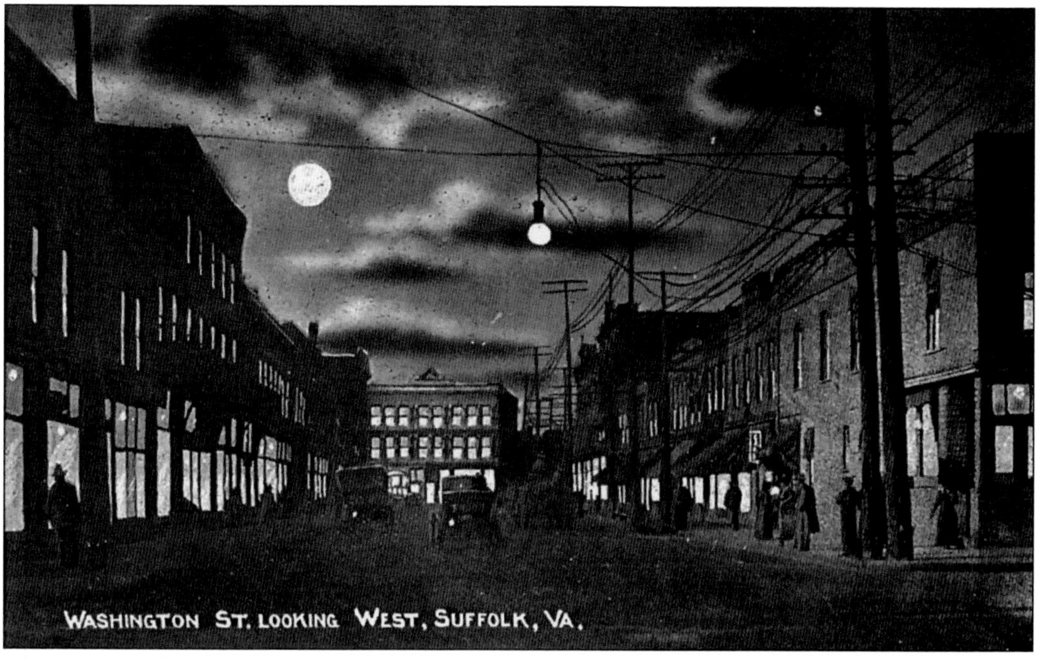

The Law Building can be seen at the end of the block. Though it appears that businesses found it advantageous to be open at night, men were abroad and few proper city matrons were out and about at night. One farm cart seems to be making its way home.

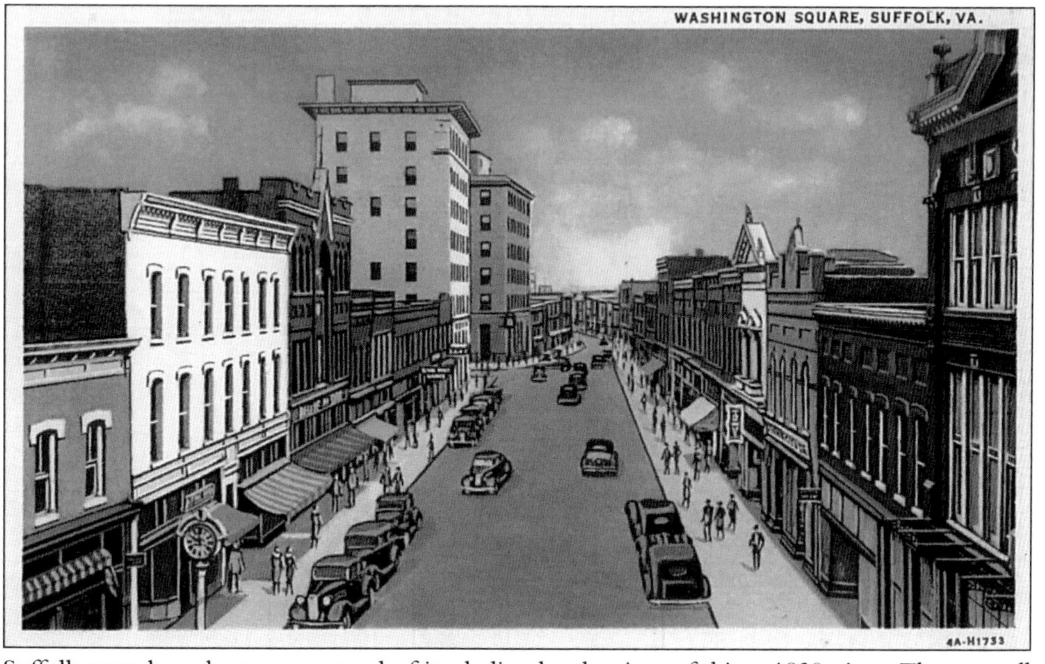

Suffolk must have been very proud of its skyline by the time of this *c.* 1930 view. The two tall banks—National Bank of Suffolk and the American Bank—faced each other across Main Street. Happily both buildings still stand.

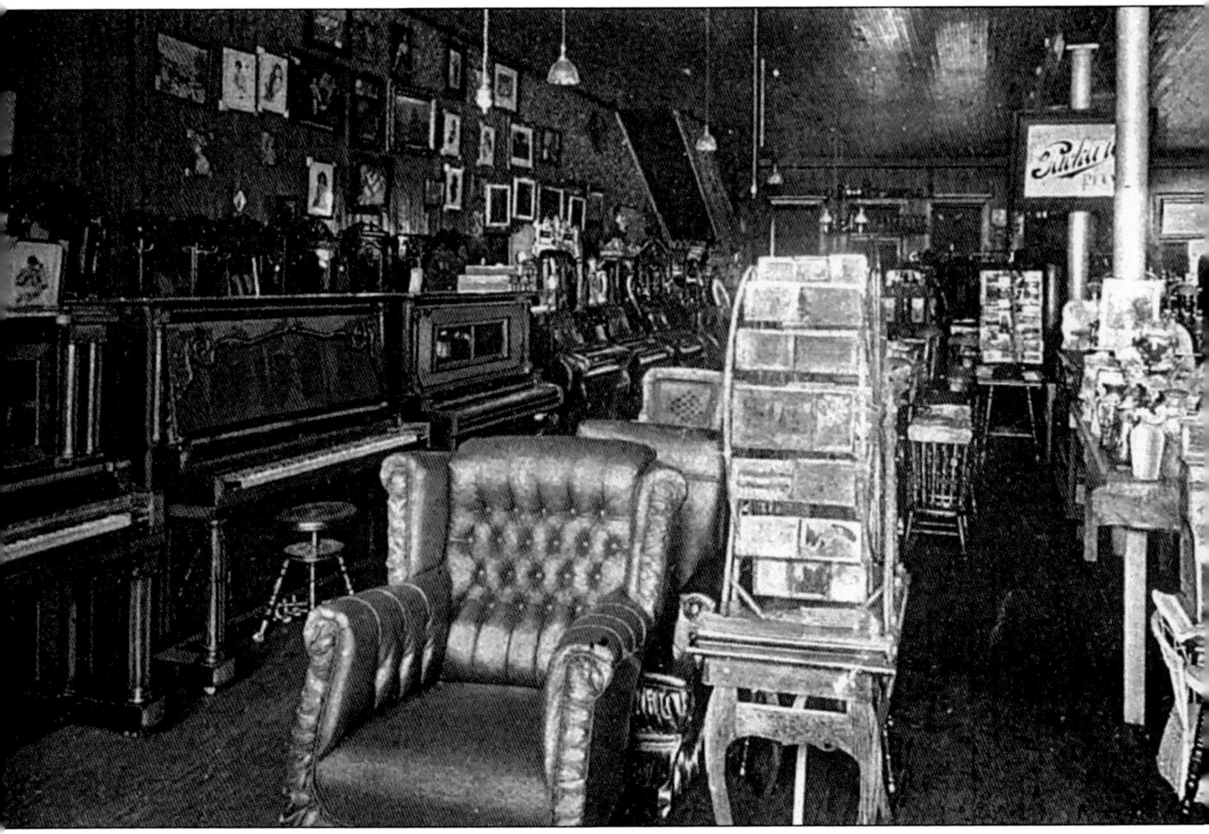

This *c.* 1915 double-sized advertising card for Thompson & Company gives a good view of the way middle-class families furnished their homes early in the century. Thompson & Company was established in 1903 with R.O. Chandler as an associate. He soon bought Mr. Thompson's interest and became the sole proprietor. Chandler, a native of Danville, offered furniture, stoves and mat-

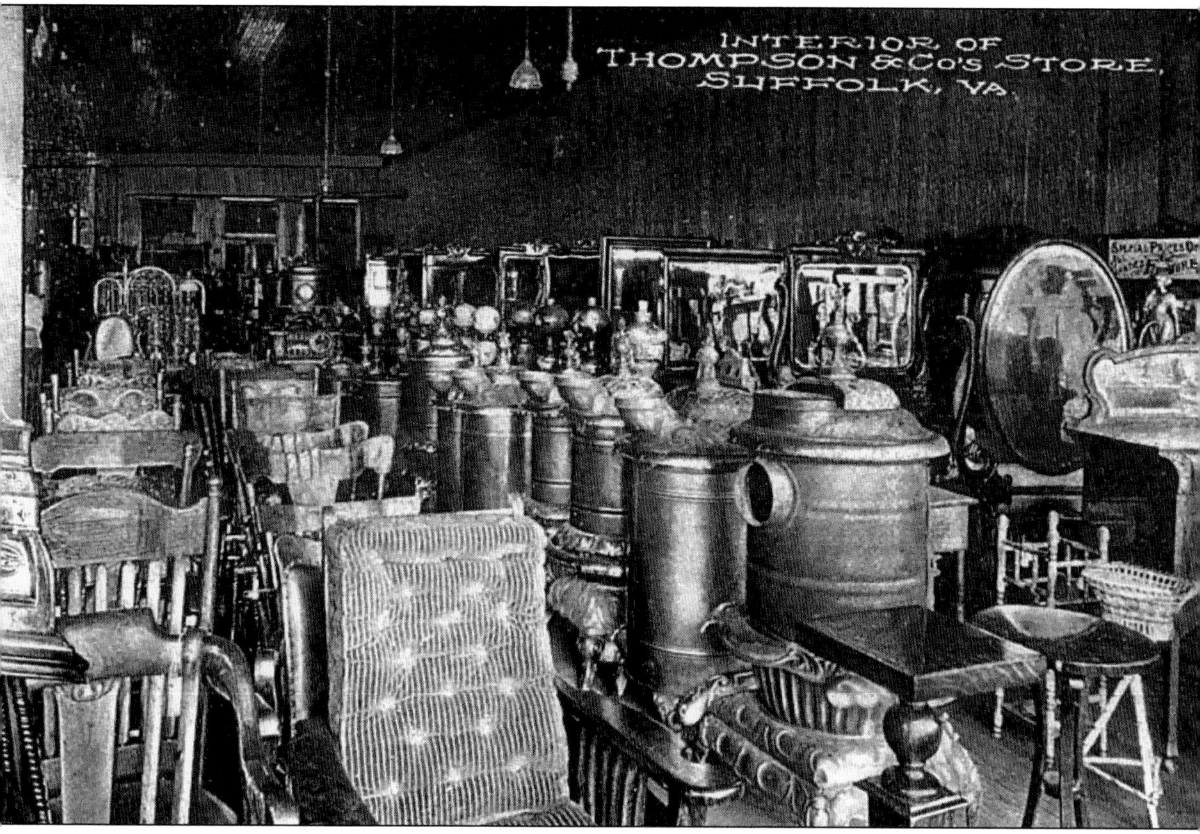

ting, pianos, organs, Victor goods, and general house furnishings. Thompson & Company was in the 100 block of North Main Street in a large two-story building. An ad from the period promises "goods sold on the most convenient terms." Mr. Chandler also owned Chandler's Dairy.

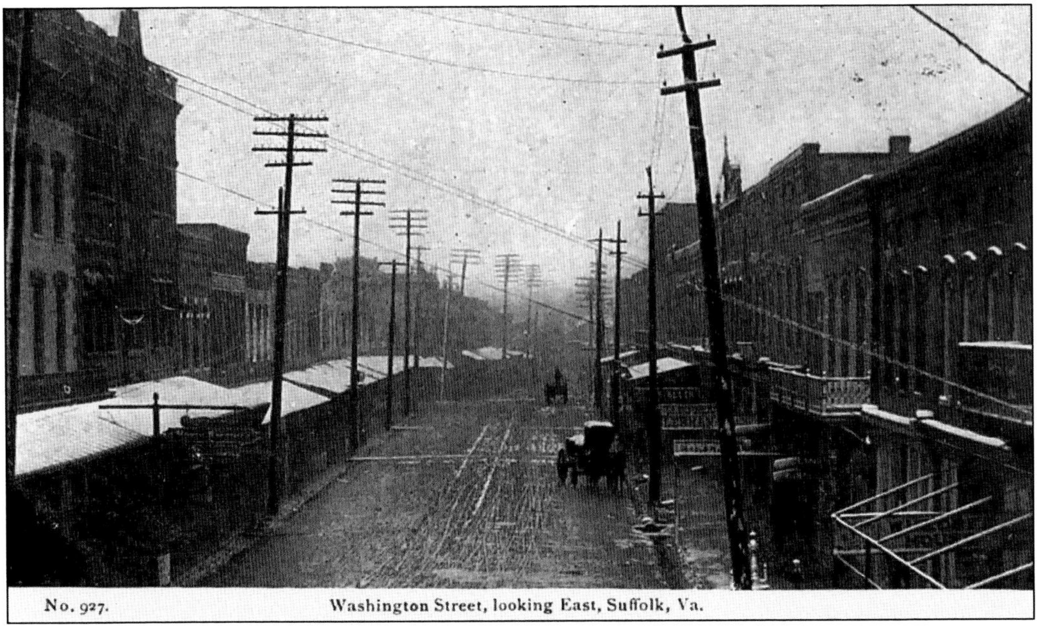

The south facing stores provided their own shade in summer and shelter from the elements anytime with the metal canopies shown here. Across Main Street on East Washington "the bottom" or low point near present Commerce Street was a murky mess in weather like this. Back on the Square, Nathan Lehman's mercantile establishment is advertised in one of the few legible signs.

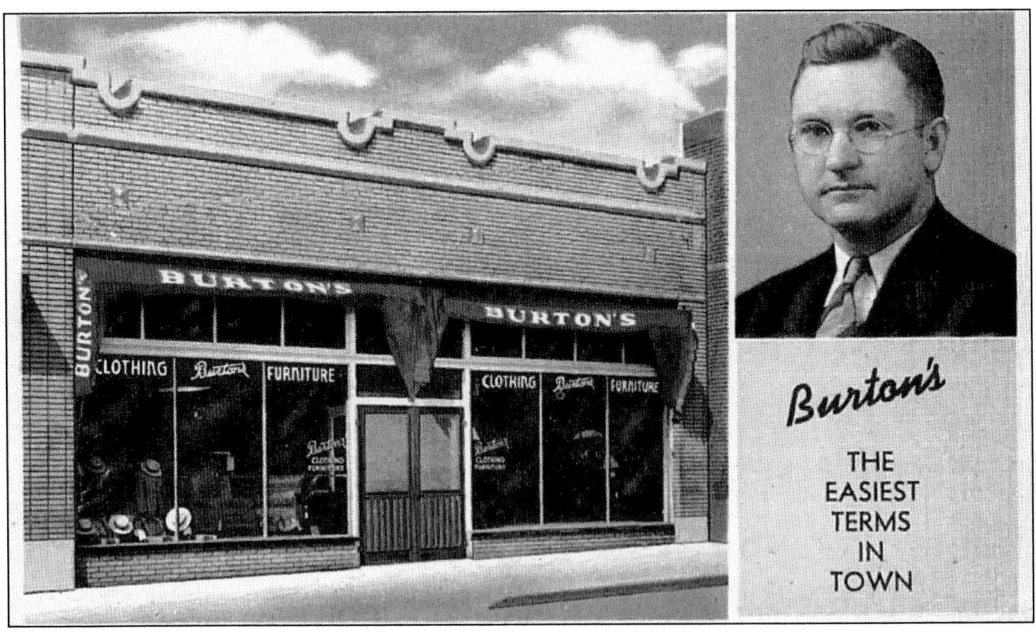

L.S. Burton came to Suffolk in the early 1930s to work at Suffolk Overall Factory in a managerial capacity. In 1937 he opened his own retail establishment and, in 1940, moved to this modern building on East Washington Street. He specialized in clothing for the whole family and home furnishings. Holland Produce now occupies this building.

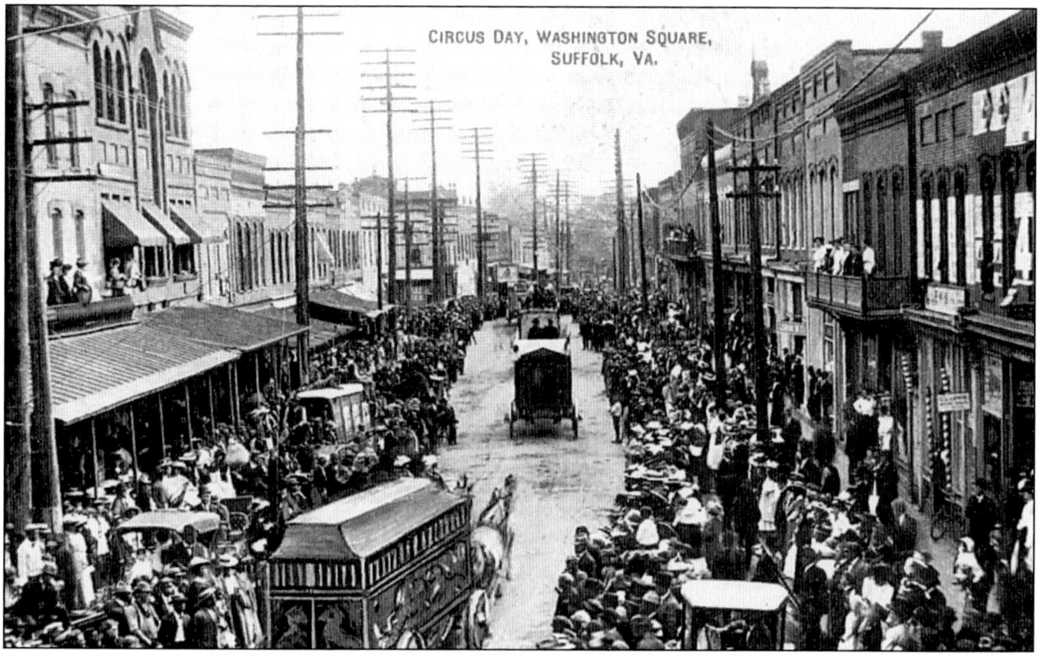

Circuses provided excitement a-plenty in those pre-television days. Numerous small circuses traveled about the countryside in horse-drawn carts that were gaily decorated as rolling advertisements. The crowd makes good use of the beautiful balconies that once graced Washington Square buildings. In spite of what the caption on the card below says, this is not just a busy day. In this view, the circus crowd disperses.

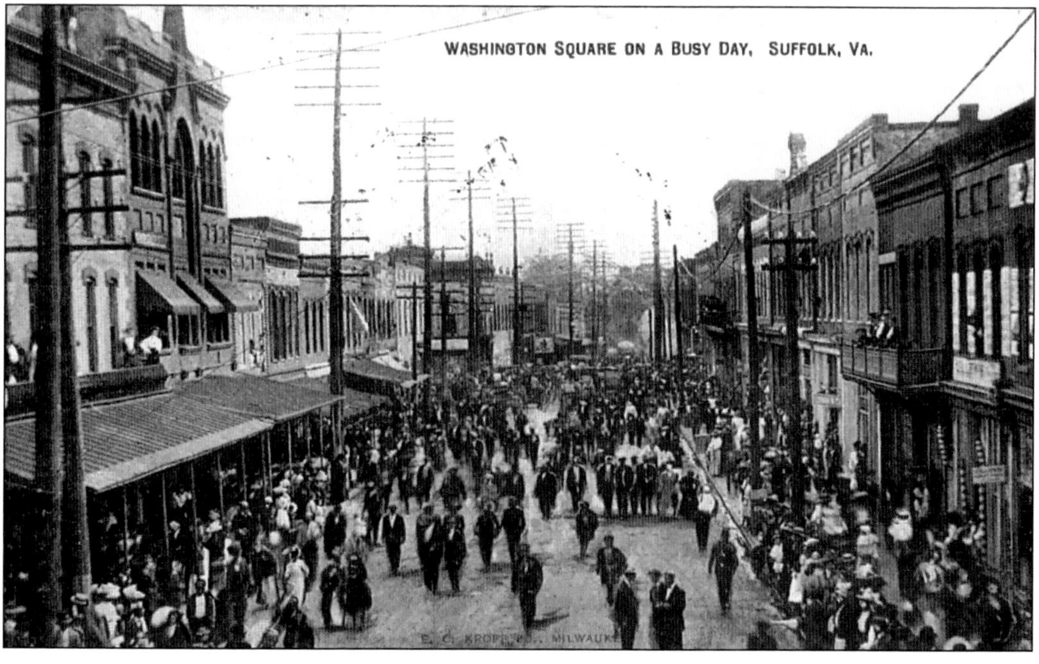

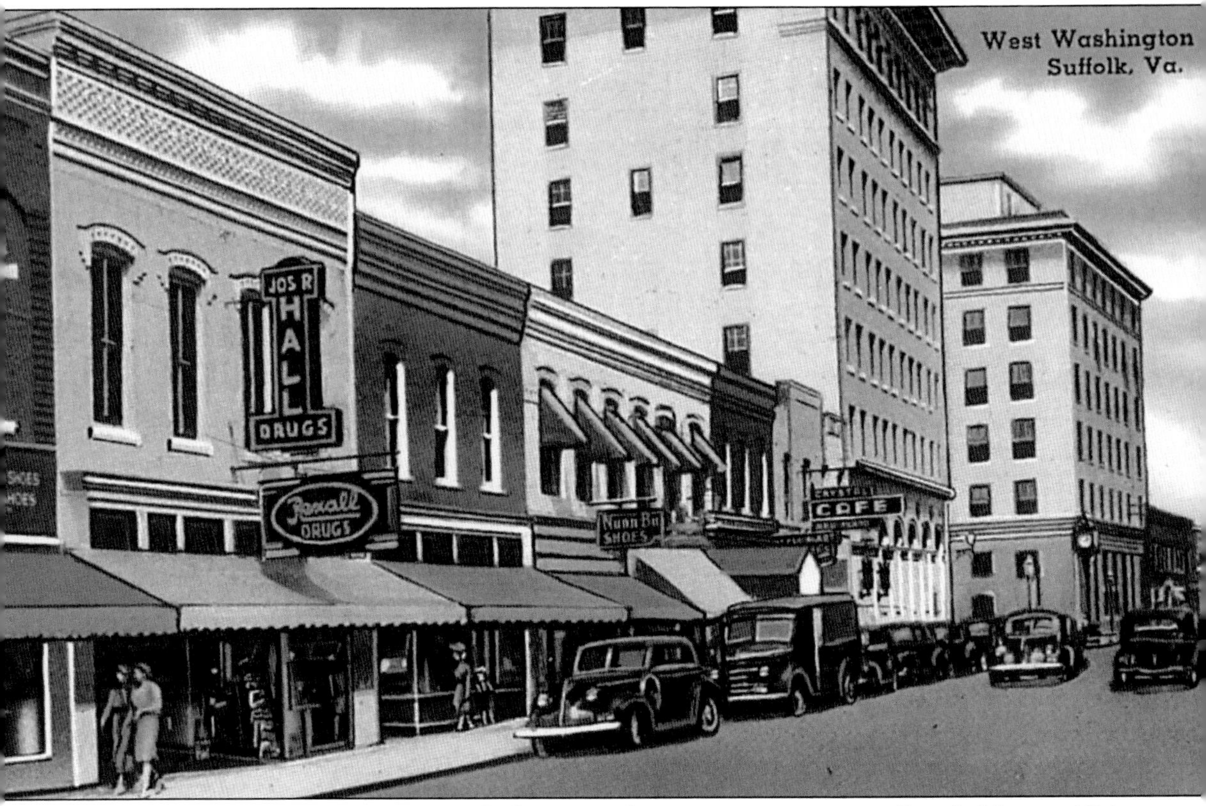

From the 1880s all the way through the 1960s there were numerous quality clothing establishments on the Square. There are two stores in this view offering shoes for sale. Near the National Bank on the corner (and the American Bank across the street) is the Crystal Café. Operated by the Thanos family, it was a popular gathering spot for businessmen until it closed in 1988. Though the building still stands, at this writing it is unused. Joseph P. Hall Drugstore was then, and remains, a fixture on the block. In this view we are reminded of the day when people dressed in hats and gloves to go downtown.

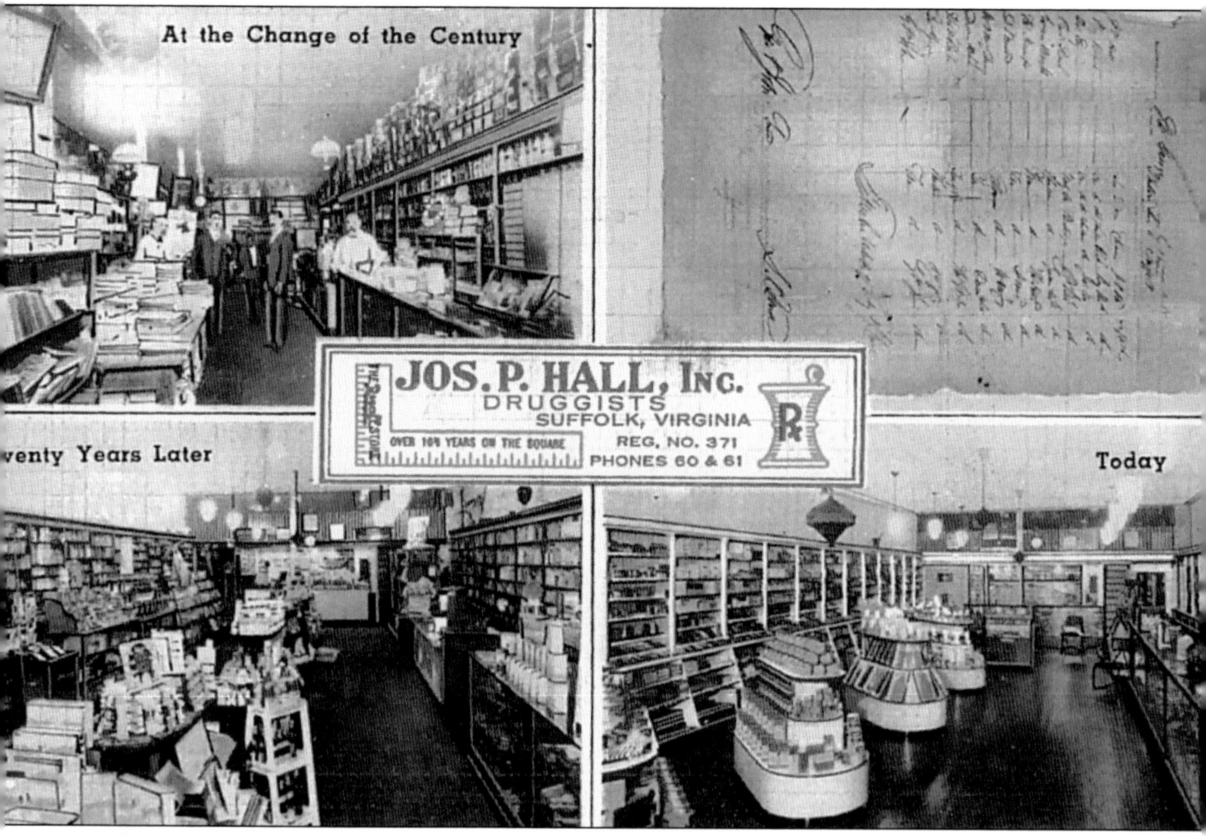

Joseph P. Hall opened his drugstore on the Square in 1837. Over the years it has had different owners and been in a couple of different locations. Today it is back on the Square—across the street from the location shown on the opposite page—still operating under the name of Joseph P. Hall. The *c.* 1940 postal advertisement above marked one of the milestones in its history. Around the turn of the century (and before and after that) school textbooks were sold at Joseph P. Hall, as were other school supplies. Hall Avenue along the Norfolk and Western Railroad is named for Joseph P. Hall, who lived in a house that faced the railroad.

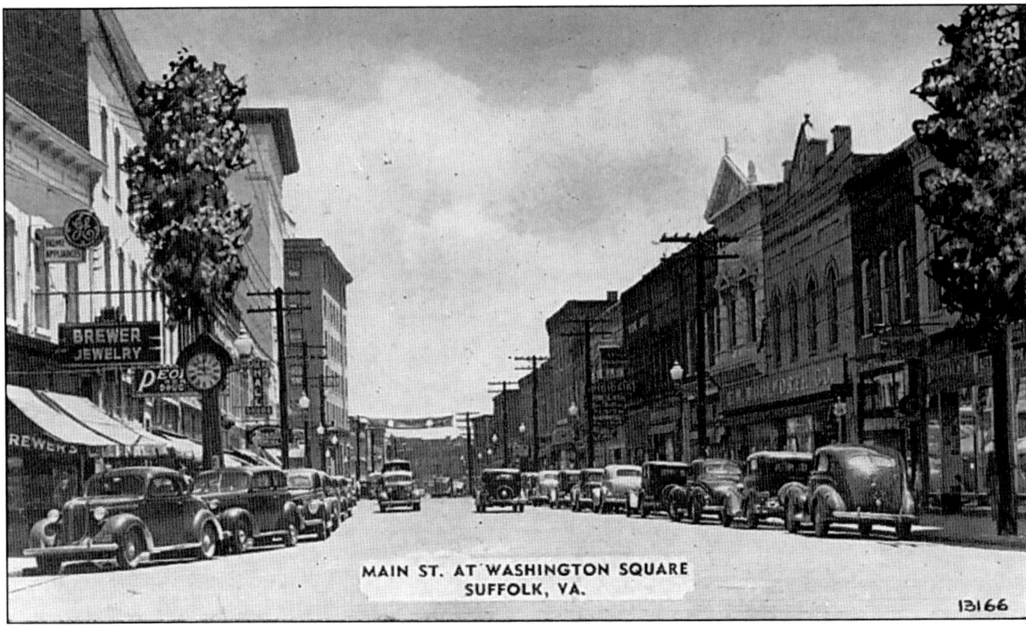

R.L. Brewer Sr. bought his jewelry business in 1875 from Thomas Hannaford. Brewer later passed it to his son who sold it to Floyd Turner in 1924. In 1976 it passed to Floyd Turner's son, Johnson Turner. It was sold again in the 1980s. Brewer Jewelry remained at this spot (at left in picture) with the same name until around 1990. This view is of the Square from Saratoga Street, not Main Street from the Square.

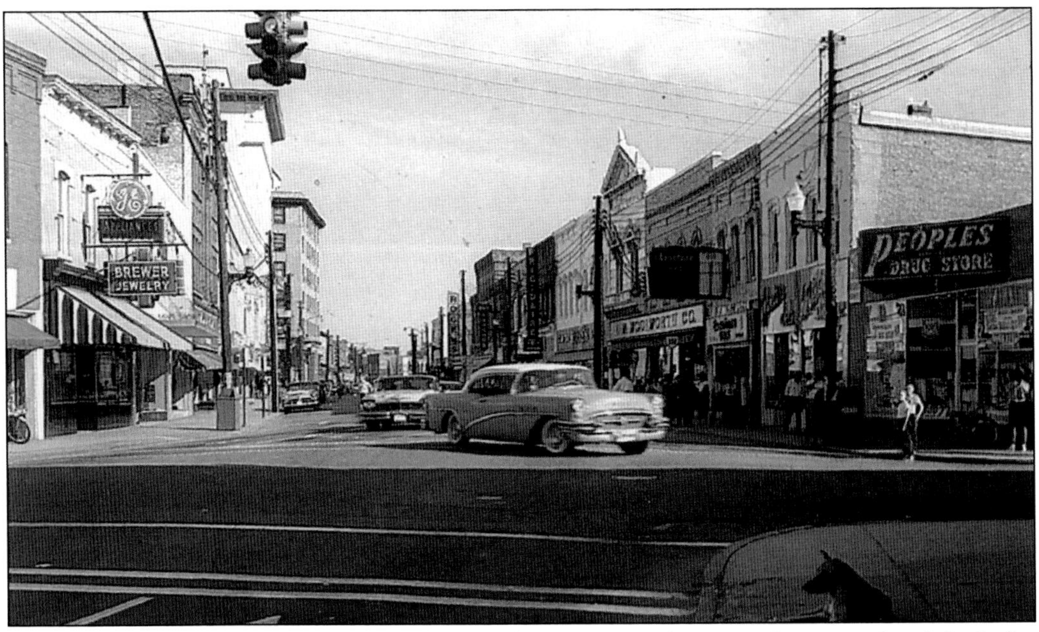

Baby Boomers will recall Washington Square this way. Peoples Drug Store on the right had a lunch counter for shoppers and downtown workers. Beside it the Little Shoppe and Junior Deb dressed children and young ladies, and down the street, F.W. Woolworth offered all kinds of treats as well as Christmas jobs for teenagers.

Four

Agriculture and Industry

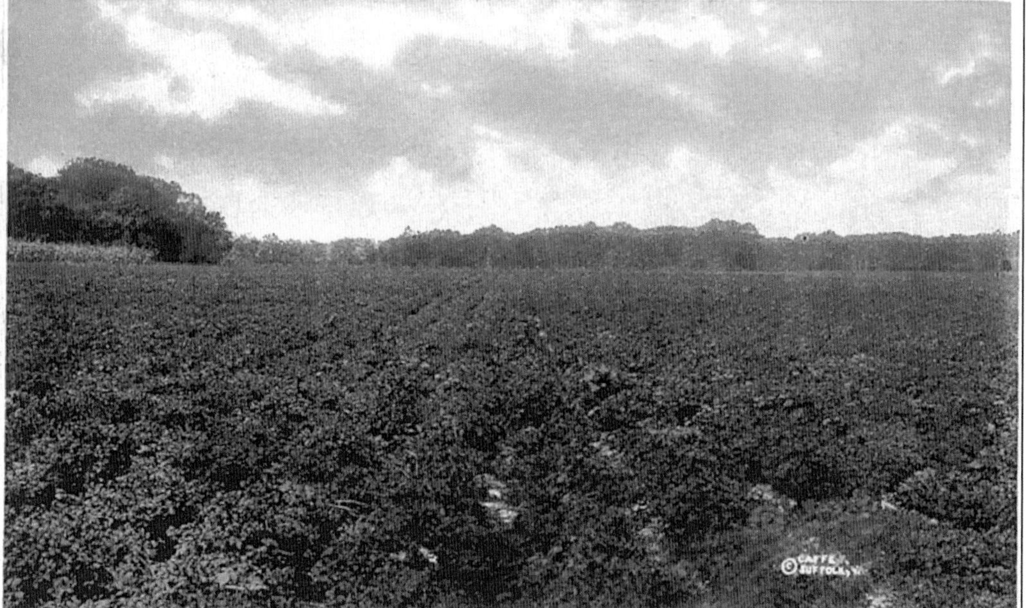

A GROWING FIELD OF PEANUTS, NANSEMOND CO., SUFFOLK, VA.

Few people, other than those who grow them, realize that peanuts are not really nuts but rather legumes. They grow underground, attached to the root of the *Arachis hypogaea* plant and thrive in the light sandy Nansemond County soil. The harvesting process requires that they be carefully dug from the ground so that their delicate stems do not break loose from the vines. The plants shown in this picture appear ready to be harvested.

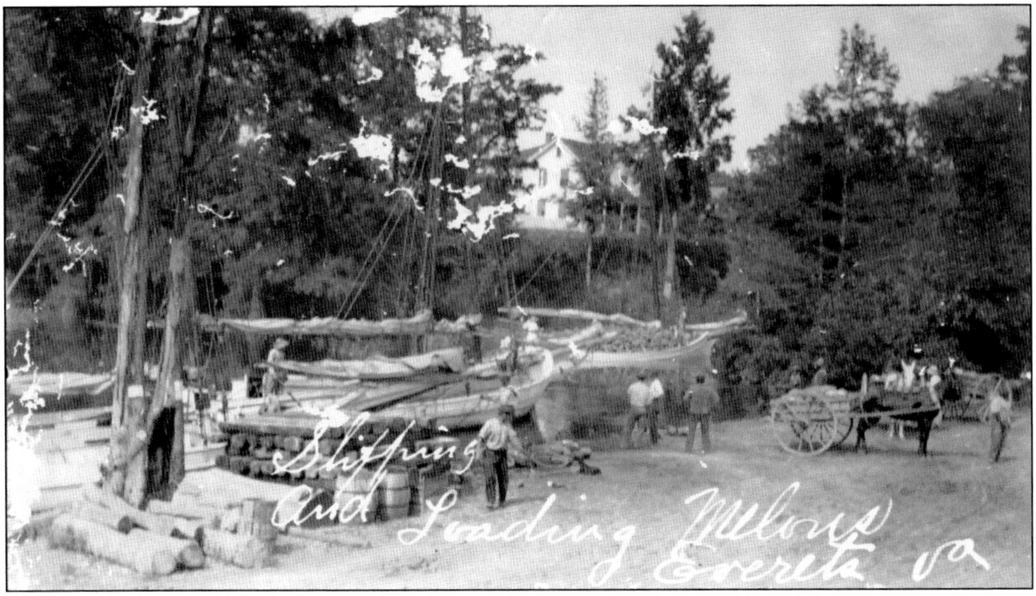

Everets is a small community once located on Everets Creek, the northwestern branch of the Nansemond River. Schooners visited the active port weekly, bringing supplies for two general stores, mail for the post office, and items such as fertilizer for the surrounding agricultural community. Local farmers and merchants shipped out many products including watermelons, barreled potatoes, cotton, peanuts, corn, boxes, barrels, and lumber. The home of William G. Saunders Sr. is shown in the background above. The *Ocean Star* was owned and captained by John Martin of Elipse. In 1962 Everets Creek was dammed to create the Western Branch Reservoir, an approximately 1,500-acre lake that supplies drinking water to the city of Norfolk.

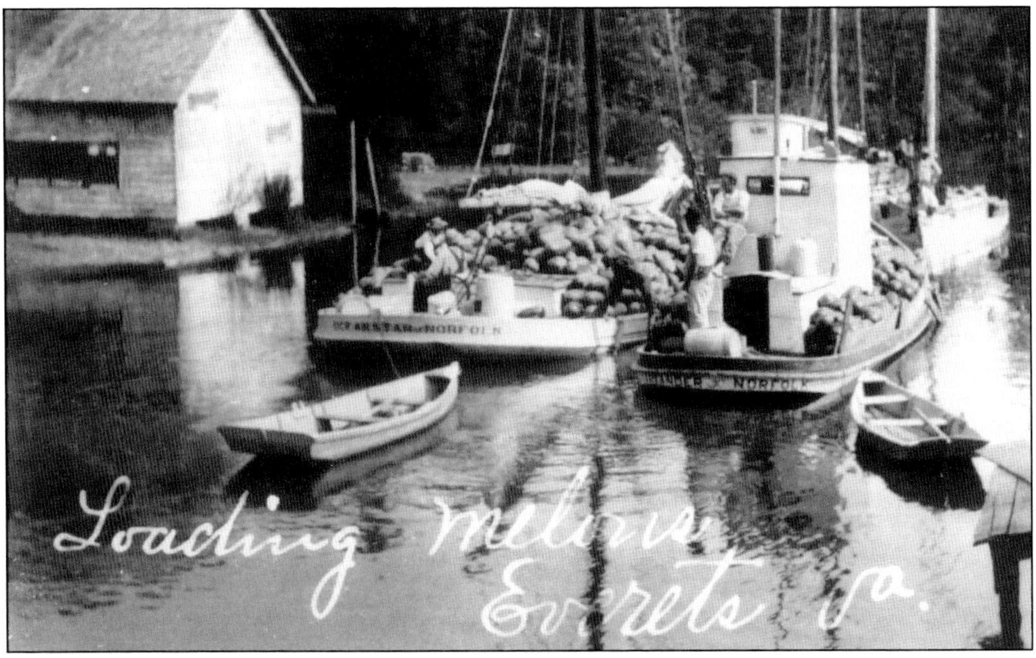

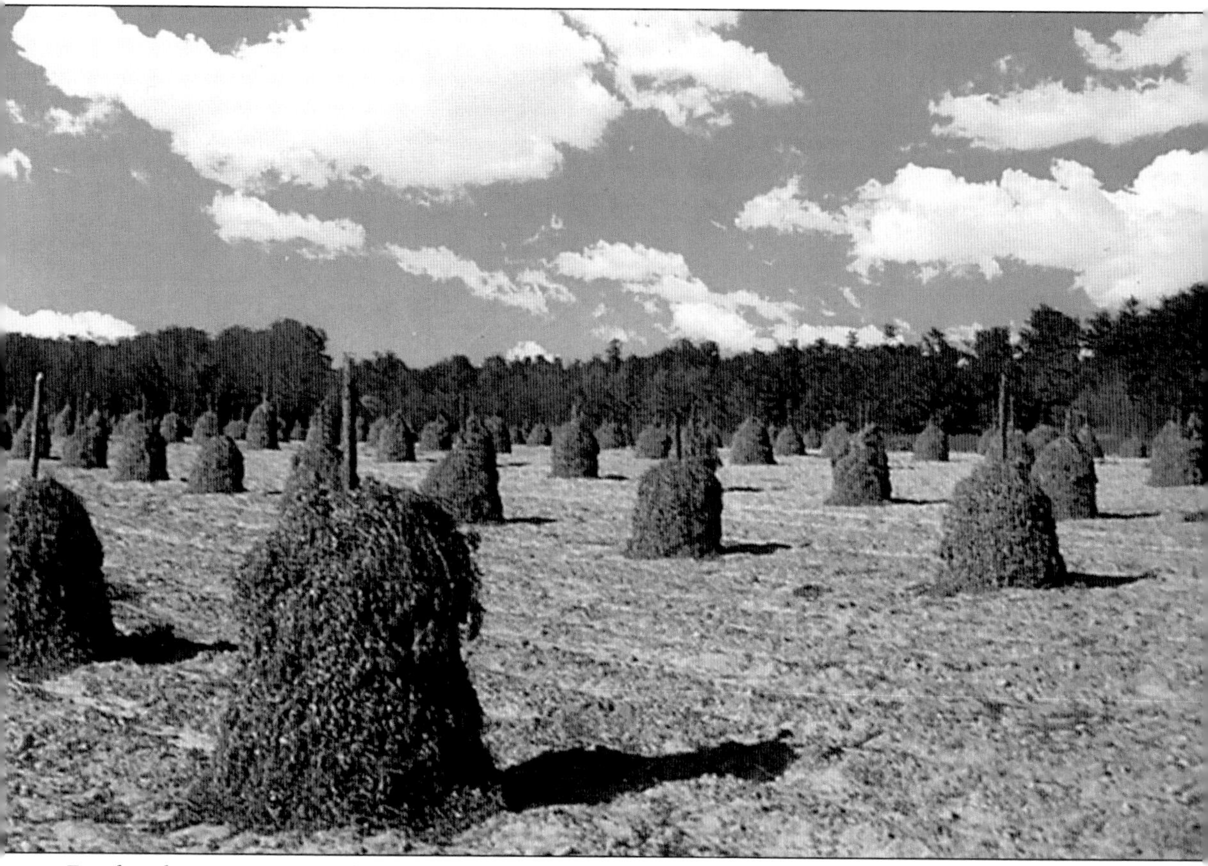

For decades, peanuts were harvested by stacking the dug peanut vines, with peanuts still attached, onto pointed poles as shown here. The peanuts were allowed to dry naturally for a period of a few weeks until they were ready for "picking," either by hand or by machine. The stacking technique lasted until the 1960s and is remembered nostalgically by many Suffolk residents.

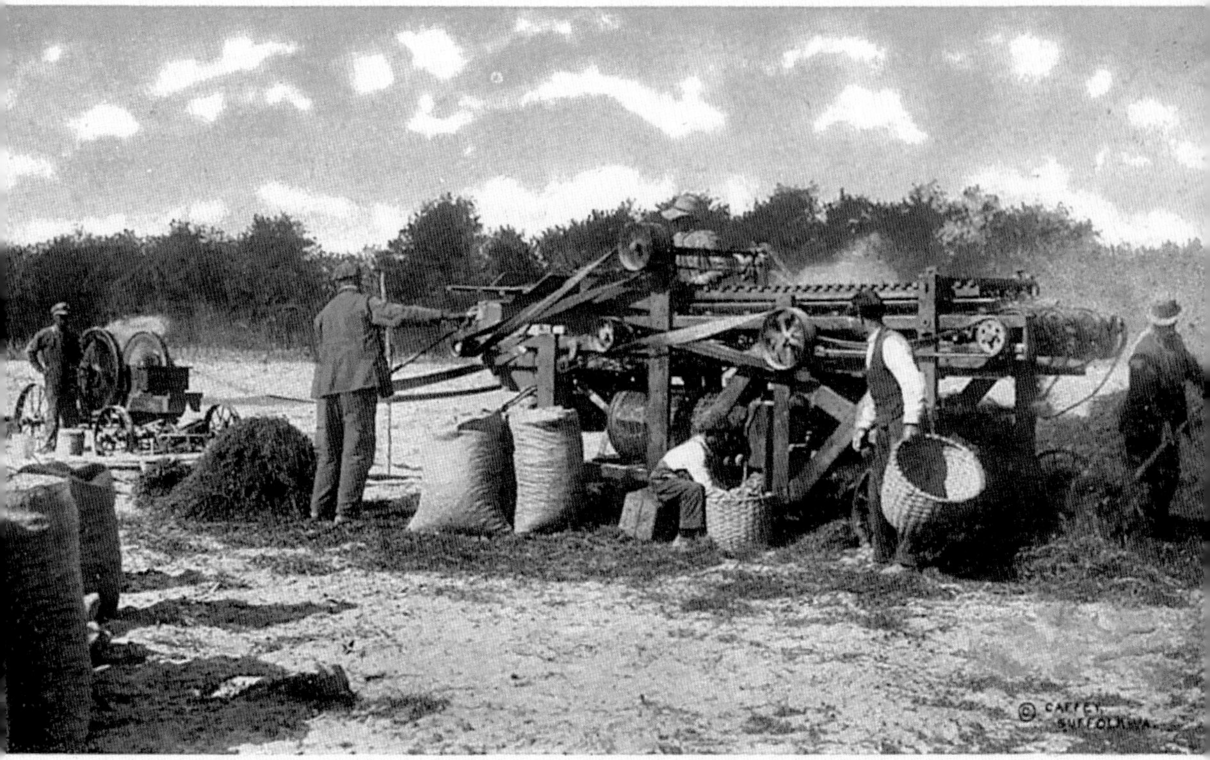

MACHINE IN OPERATION PICKING PEANUTS FROM THE VINES, NANSEMOND CO., SUFFOLK, VA.

A great improvement in peanut harvesting technology was the invention of the Peanut Picker in 1905. The dried peanut vines were fed onto a platform at the right end of the machine shown here, and the picked peanuts rolled out into a basket held by the man at the center of the picture. The empty vines were conveyed out the back of the machine.

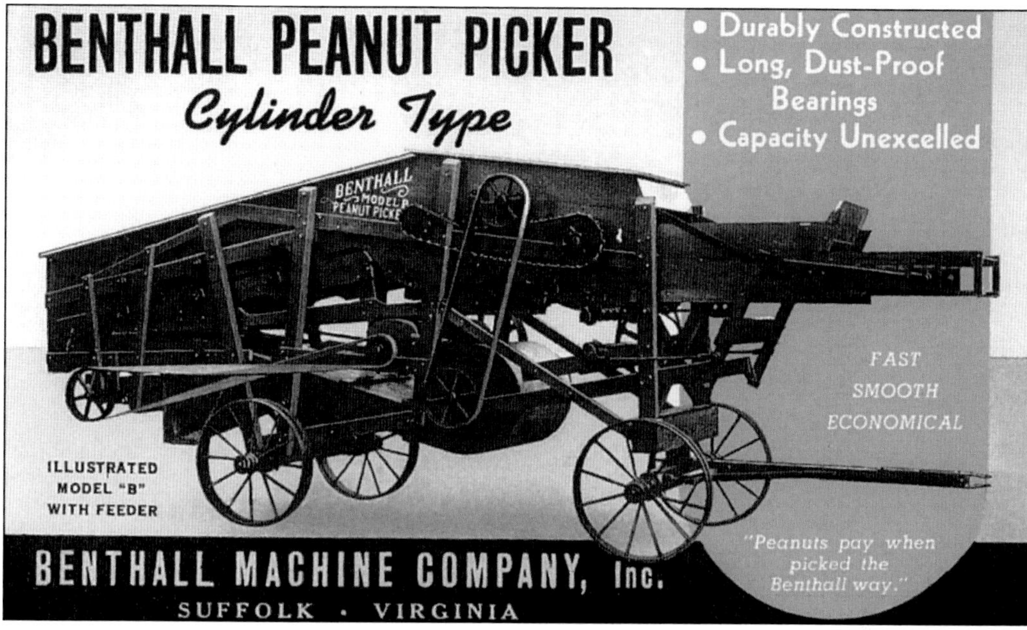

Benthall Machine Company of Suffolk was organized by Jesse T. Benthall, one of the inventors of the peanut picker. This manufacturing business thrived in Suffolk until the 1960s. This postcard/advertisement from the 1940s touts the more efficient "cylinder" system of peanut picking that replaced the earlier "chain" system. Picking peanuts was a notoriously dusty operation, hence the reference to the machine's "dust-proof bearings."

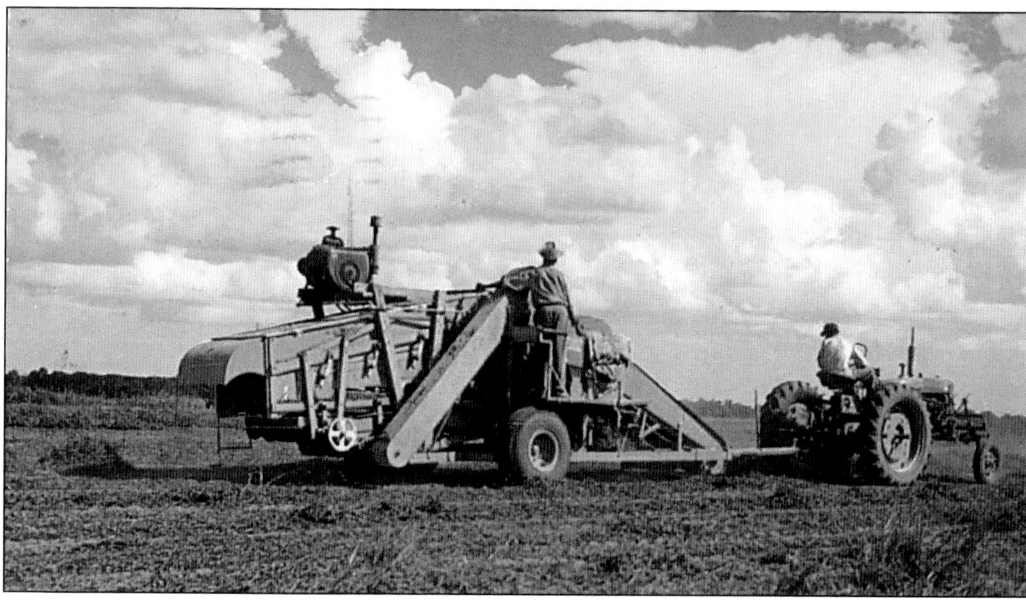

The peanut "combine" performed the operations of both pickup and threshing of the peanut vines. In this picture an inclined conveyor has been added to the front of a peanut picker to take dried vines directly from the ground into the machine. The man standing on the platform beside the machine directed the picked peanuts into burlap bags, which he dropped beside the row as the machine moved along.

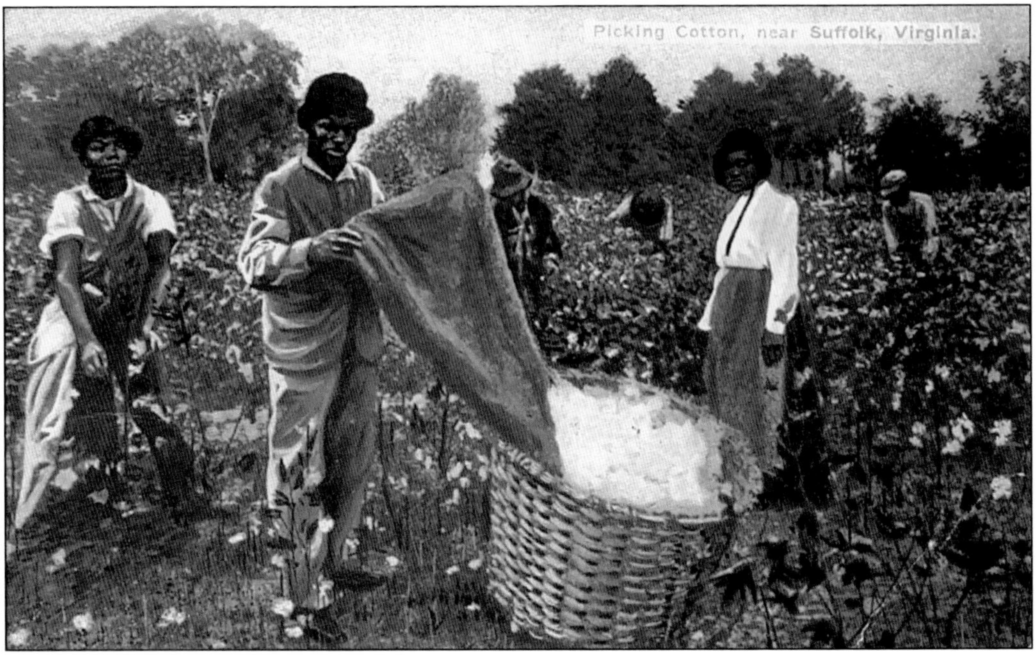

Like nearly all of the labor on a farm 60 or 70 years ago, cotton picking was done by hand. Much of the labor was provided by African-Americans. The basket in this scene was likely made in Suffolk or Nansemond County. A variety of containers were made locally as another facet of the agriculturally-based economy.

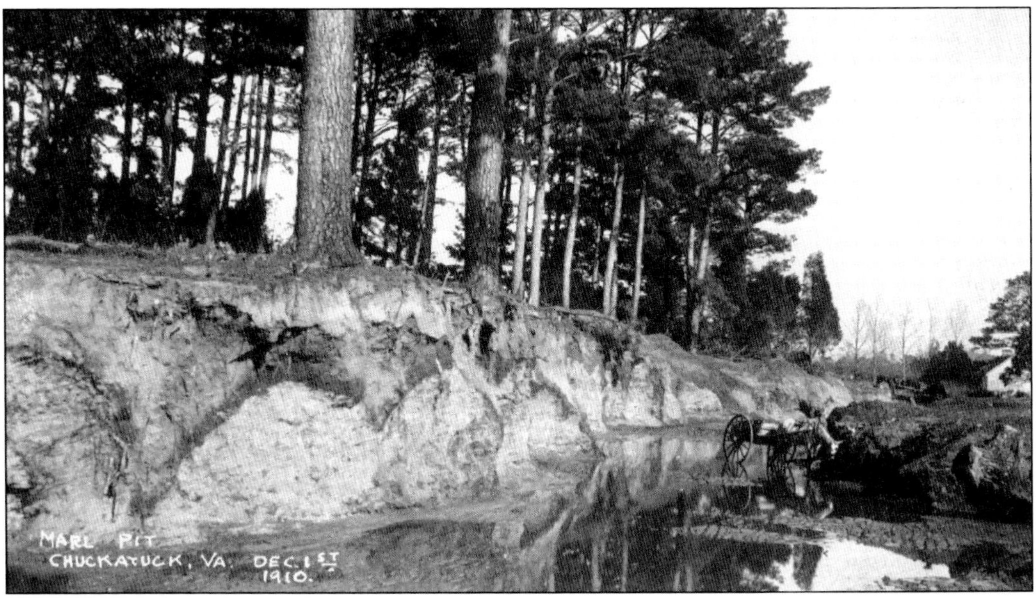

This early marl pit in Chuckatuck was dug using manpower, horses, and wagons. The Chuckatuck area had heavy deposits of marl, showing signs of early marine life. The Lone Star Cement Company operated in Chuckatuck from about 1925 until 1972. A dragline placed the marl in train cars, which delivered the material for processing and placement on barges on the Nansemond River. This property is now Lone Star Lakes.

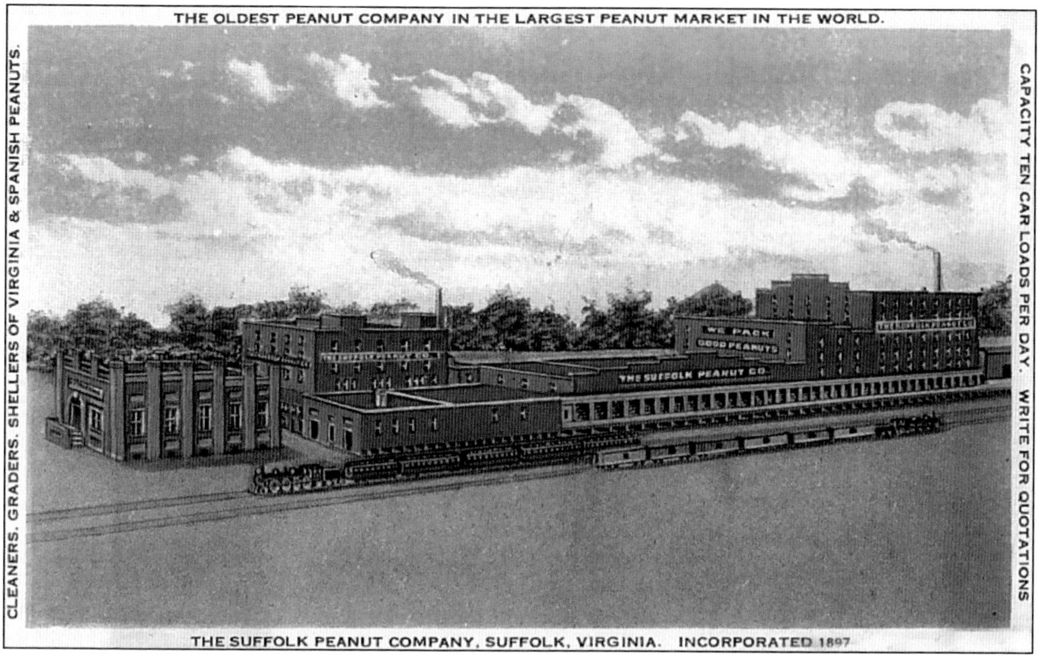

The Suffolk Peanut Company was the first successful peanut processing business in Suffolk. It was started in 1897 by John B. Pinner with John King of Windsor. In 1915 the officers were John B. Pinner, president and manager; A.T. Holland, vice president; John F. Pinner, secretary; and H.W. Phillips, treasurer. In 1915 they employed 200 to 300 people plus an office staff of 15.

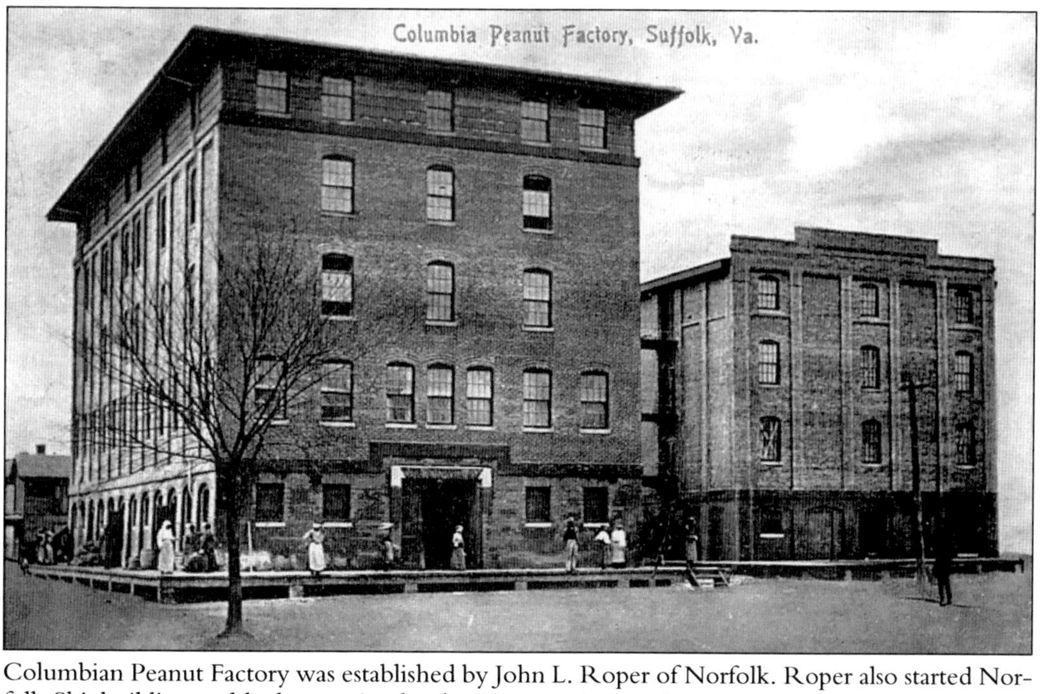

Columbian Peanut Factory was established by John L. Roper of Norfolk. Roper also started Norfolk Shipbuilding and had extensive lumber interests in North Carolina. The peanut plant here closed around 1960 and was eventually sold and demolished.

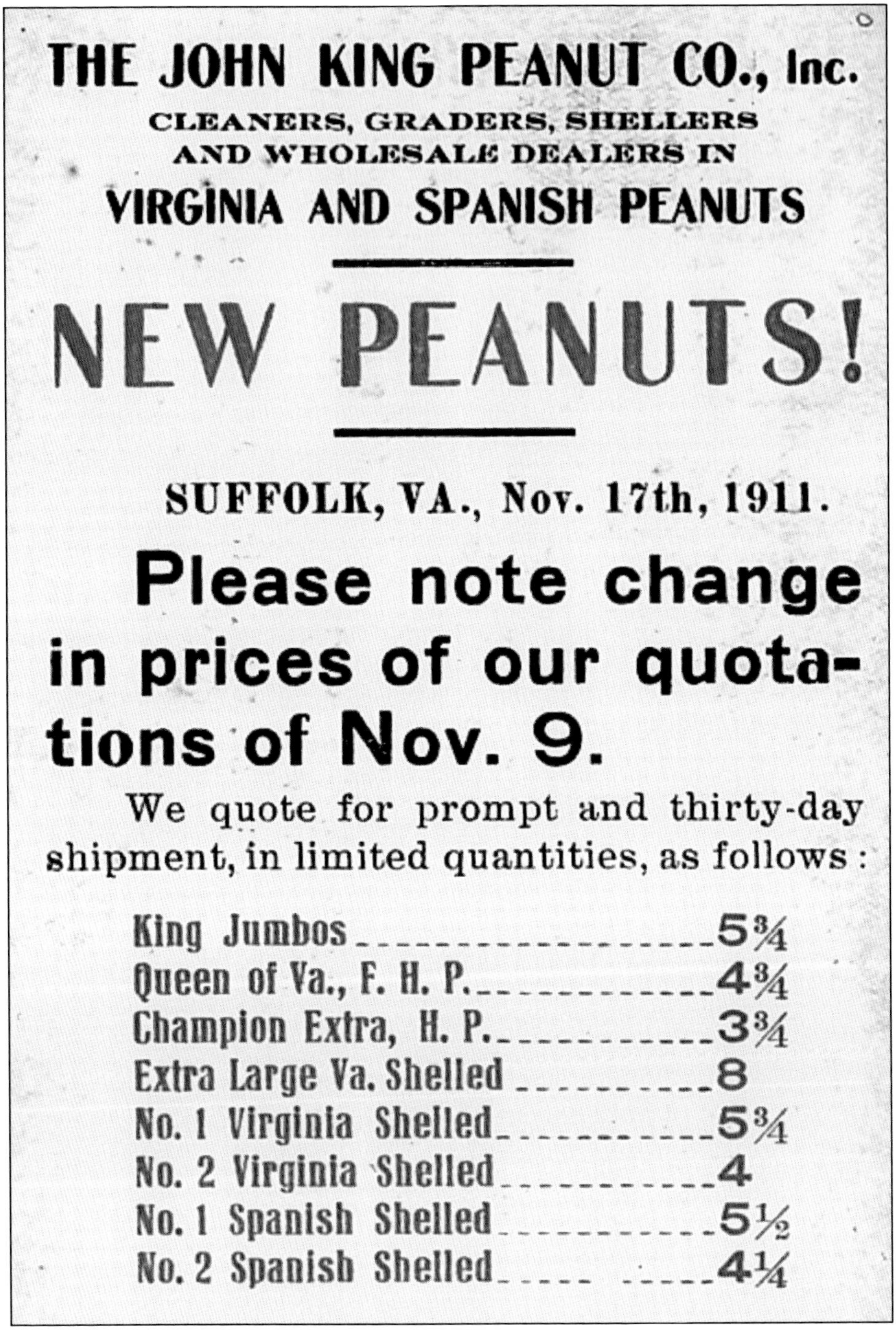

THE JOHN KING PEANUT CO., Inc.

CLEANERS, GRADERS, SHELLERS
AND WHOLESALE DEALERS IN

VIRGINIA AND SPANISH PEANUTS

NEW PEANUTS!

SUFFOLK, VA., Nov. 17th, 1911.

Please note change in prices of our quotations of Nov. 9.

We quote for prompt and thirty-day shipment, in limited quantities, as follows:

King Jumbos	5¾
Queen of Va., F. H. P.	4¾
Champion Extra, H. P.	3¾
Extra Large Va. Shelled	8
No. 1 Virginia Shelled	5¾
No. 2 Virginia Shelled	4
No. 1 Spanish Shelled	5½
No. 2 Spanish Shelled	4¼

The John King Peanut Company was incorporated in 1910 and in 1915 built a big new factory. This business dealt in cleaning, grading, shelling, and wholesaling Virginia and Spanish peanuts. In 1915 the company employed 150 people. This advertising card from 1911 would have been sent, of course, to the company's various customers. The company, located on Hall Avenue, was bought by Amedeo Obici's Planters Peanuts.

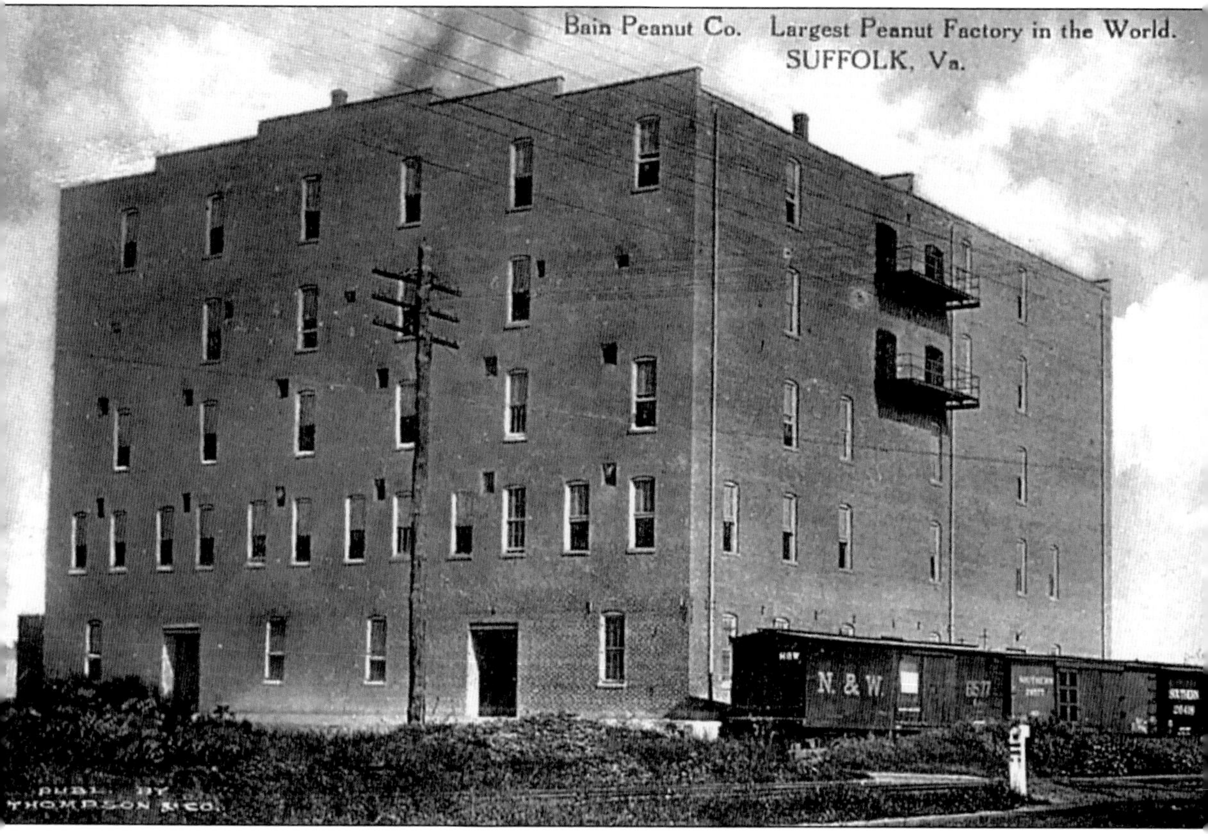

The Bain Peanut Company built their Suffolk plant in 1900 after their facility in Wakefield burned. In 1906 this became the Suffolk branch of the American Peanut Corporation. In 1907 the company added a new building that was the largest peanut factory in the world at that time. It was a modern fireproof building five stories high.

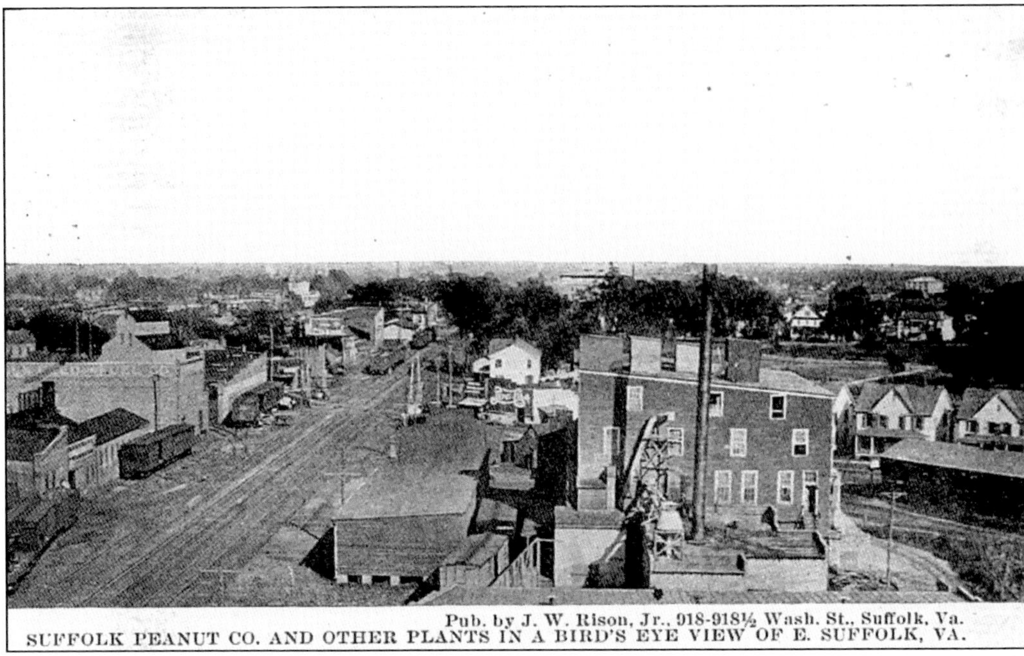

This *c.* 1907 view is of the Saratoga Street crossing of the Norfolk and Western Railroad. The Suffolk Peanut Company is the large building to the right of the tracks. Over its roof we can see the trees of Hall Place. Suffolk Feed and Fuel is the large white building to the left of the tracks.

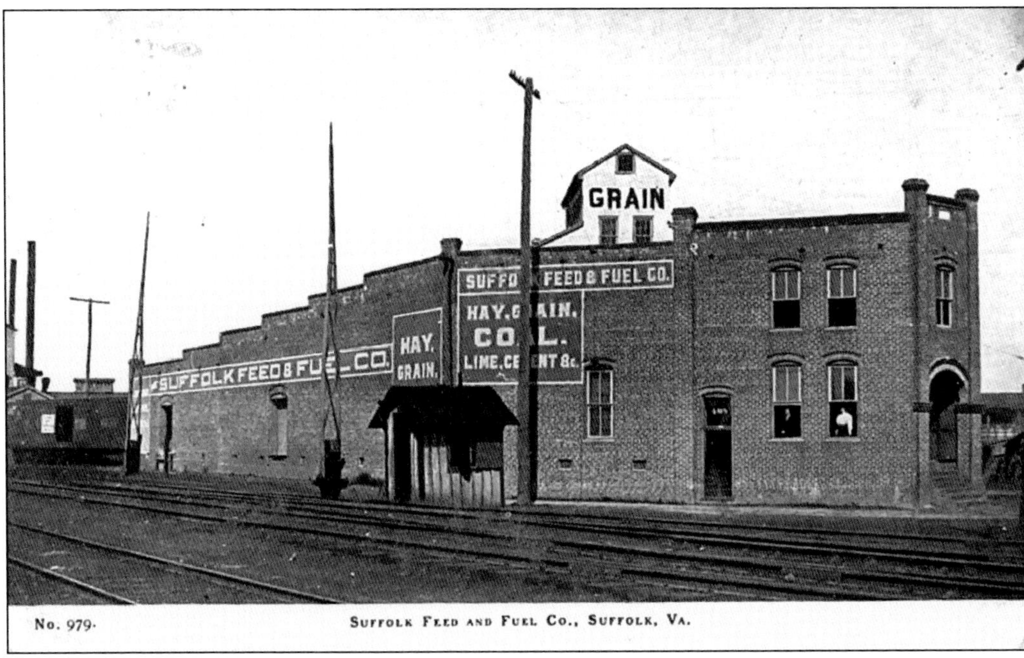

Suffolk Feed and Fuel Company was established around 1905 and provided wholesale and commission business in the handling of flour, hay, grain, lime, plaster, cement, and coal. The plant, run by G. Lloyd Bell, was on South Saratoga Street beside the Norfolk and Western Railroad. In 1915 the delivery service included 12 wagons and "an automobile truck."

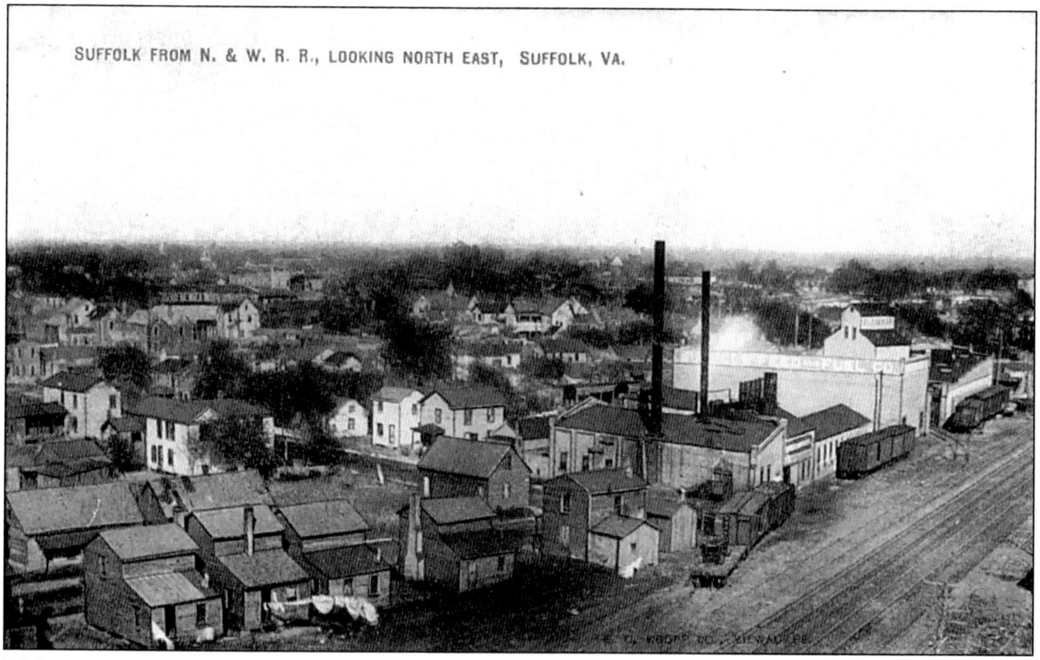

This *c.* 1907 view looks at the rear of Suffolk Feed and Fuel and its siding. The street that approaches the back of the building is Lee Street. The houses in the foreground face Wilson Street. This was an African-American neighborhood and many of its inhabitants worked in the nearby factories.

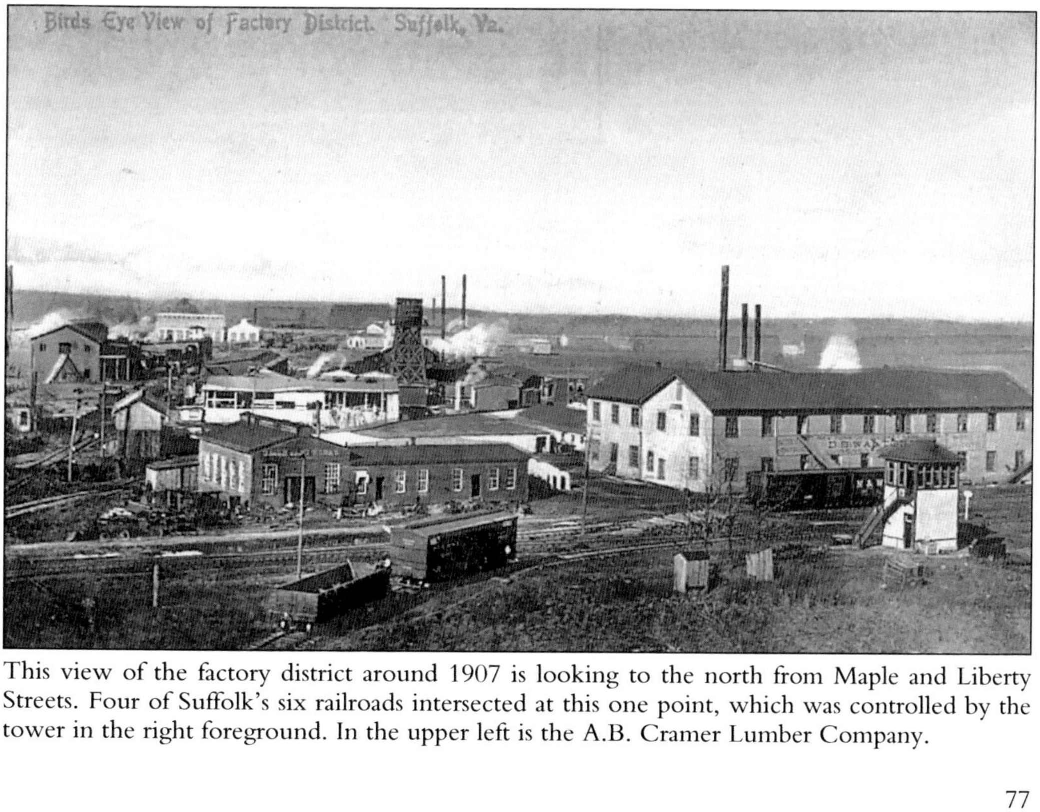

This view of the factory district around 1907 is looking to the north from Maple and Liberty Streets. Four of Suffolk's six railroads intersected at this one point, which was controlled by the tower in the right foreground. In the upper left is the A.B. Cramer Lumber Company.

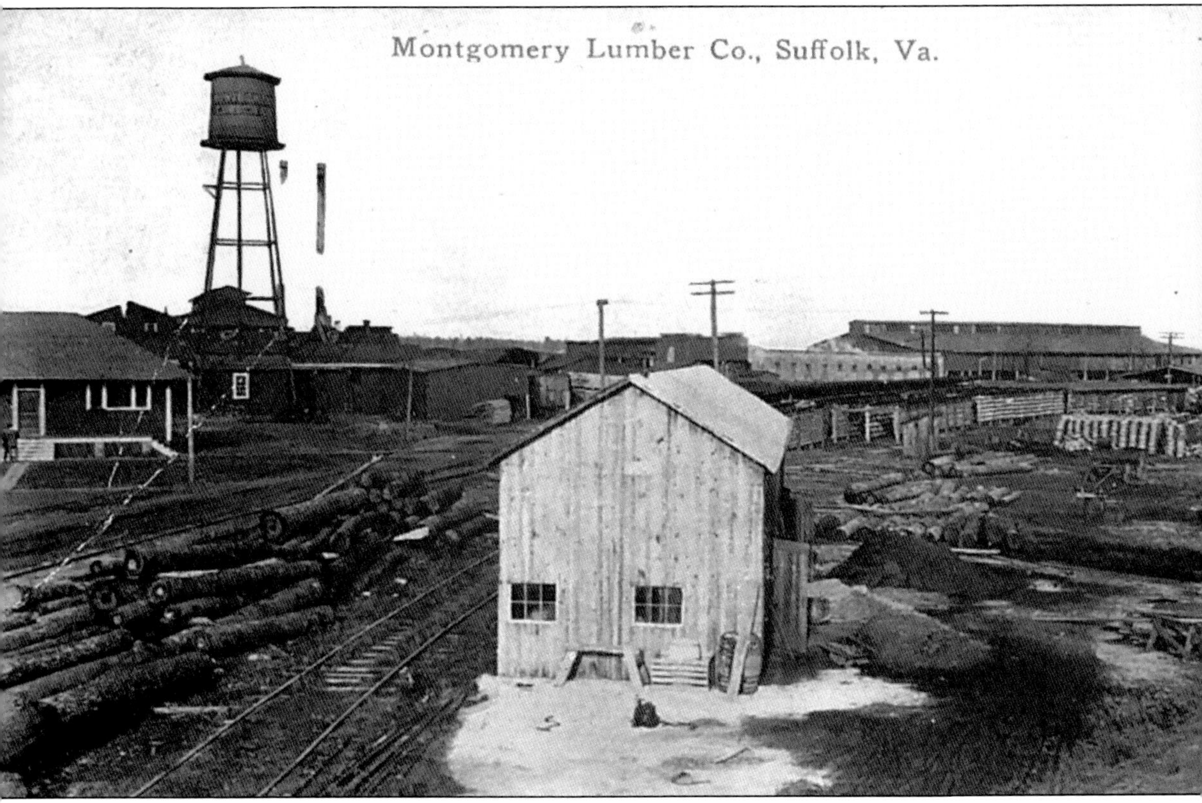

Montgomery Lumber Company was one of the many lumber businesses that came to Suffolk in the late 19th century. As a 1915 publication describes it, "This company has very extensive lumber interests and gives employment to a small army of workmen in their logging camps as well as in their mills." The company did a brisk shipping business from the wharf in Suffolk.

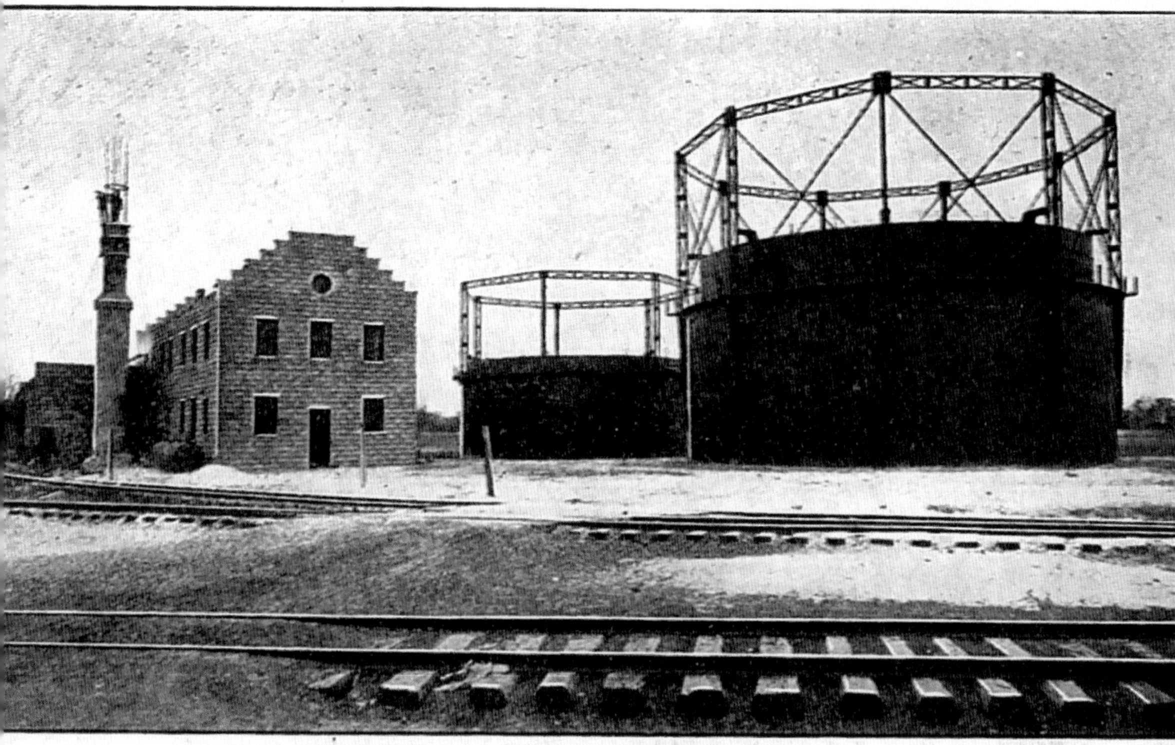

SUFFOLK GAS COMPANY, SUFFOLK, VA.

The gas plant was between Cedar Hill Cemetery and the Seaboard Railroad near Hill Street. The plant used coal to manufacture gas for lighting the town. The date of construction is unknown but it was under the Kingsboro Bridge in 1907. Suffolk had gas lights in the 1880s. The building has been demolished in recent years.

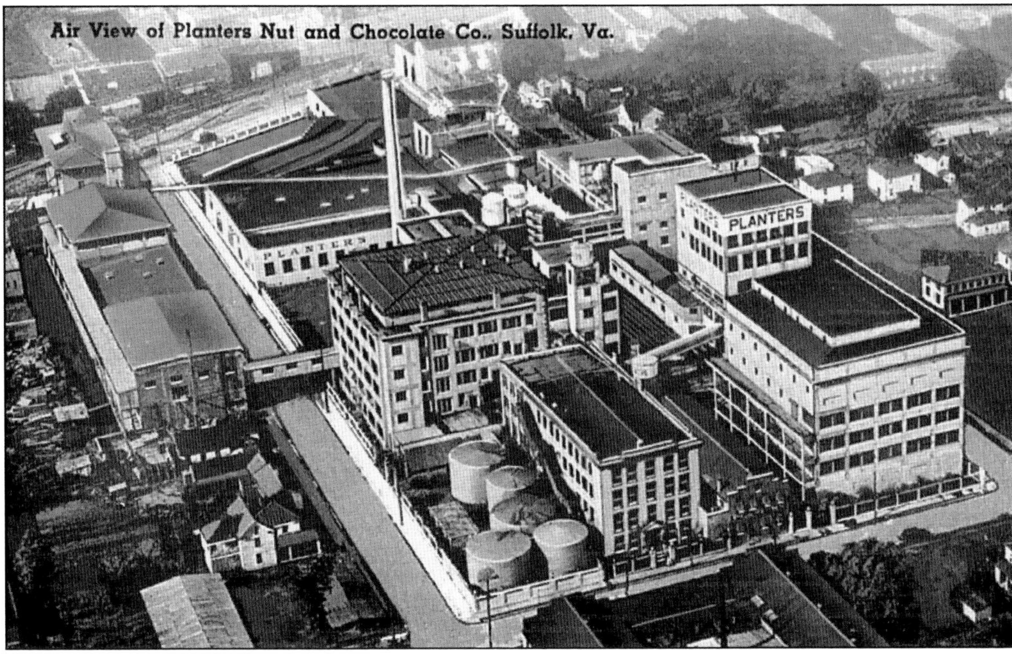

In 1913 Amedeo Obici, the little Italian with big ideas, came to Suffolk to build his Planters Nut and Chocolate Company. Soon Planters had 36 buildings on 38 acres of land in Suffolk. Obici later opened factories in San Francisco and Toronto. The Planters symbol, the monocled Mr. Peanut, was born in Suffolk with an idea from a schoolboy.

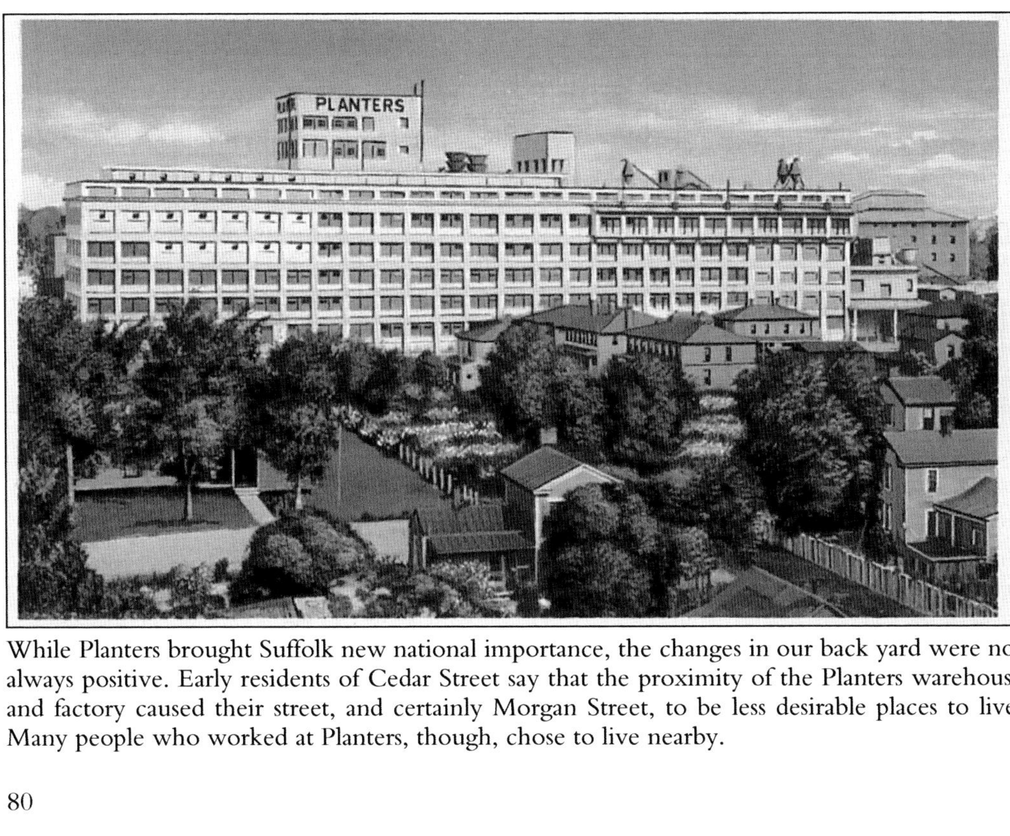

While Planters brought Suffolk new national importance, the changes in our back yard were not always positive. Early residents of Cedar Street say that the proximity of the Planters warehouse and factory caused their street, and certainly Morgan Street, to be less desirable places to live. Many people who worked at Planters, though, chose to live nearby.

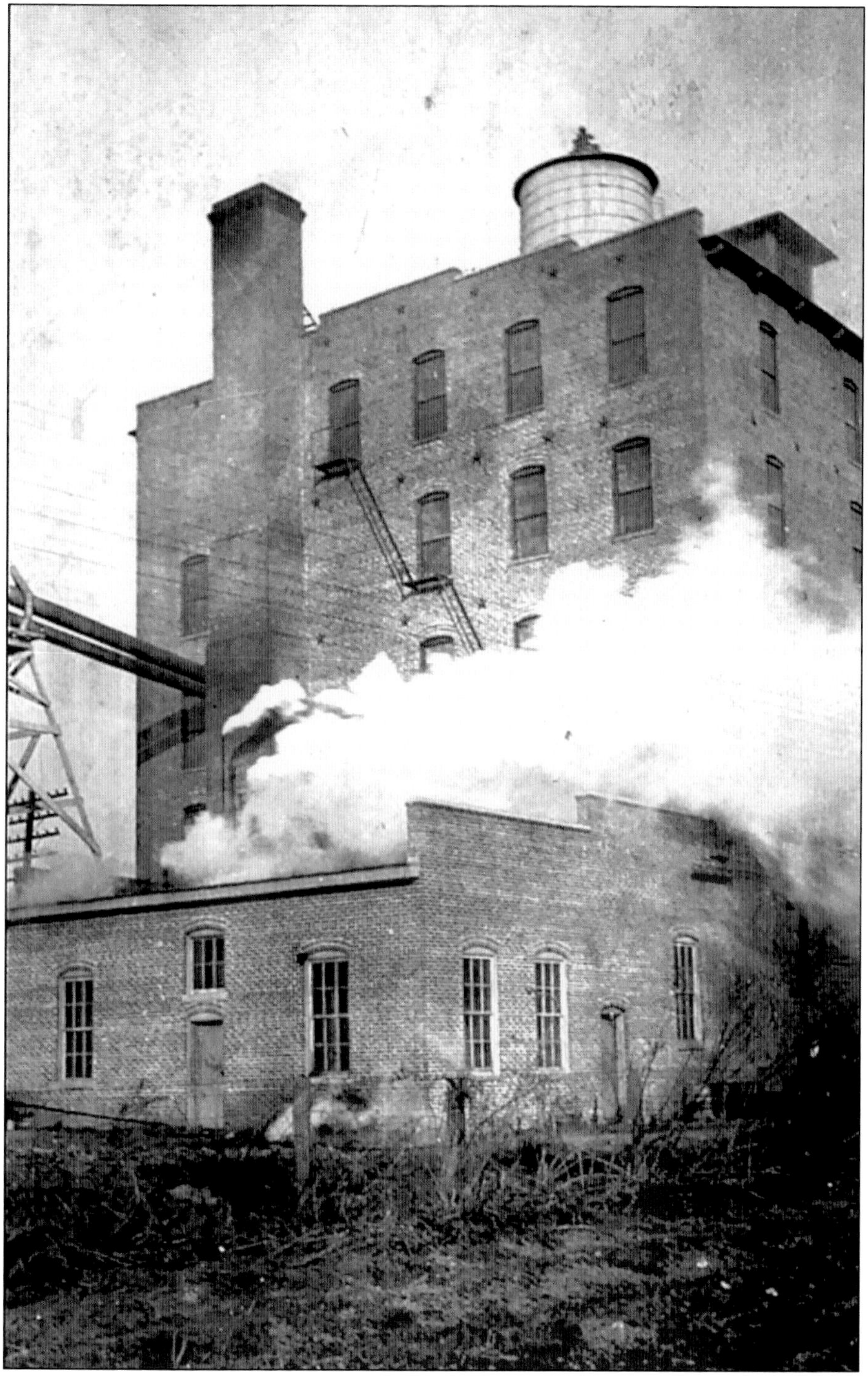

What a difference 50 years made! The Suffolk Peanut Company was built early in the century in the factory district where "out of sight, out of mind" seemed to be the motto. Smoke generally hung over the industrial area in most pictures from that period. About 50 years later, Lipton Tea (next page) presents a much brighter picture. Today it still noted for its manicured grounds.

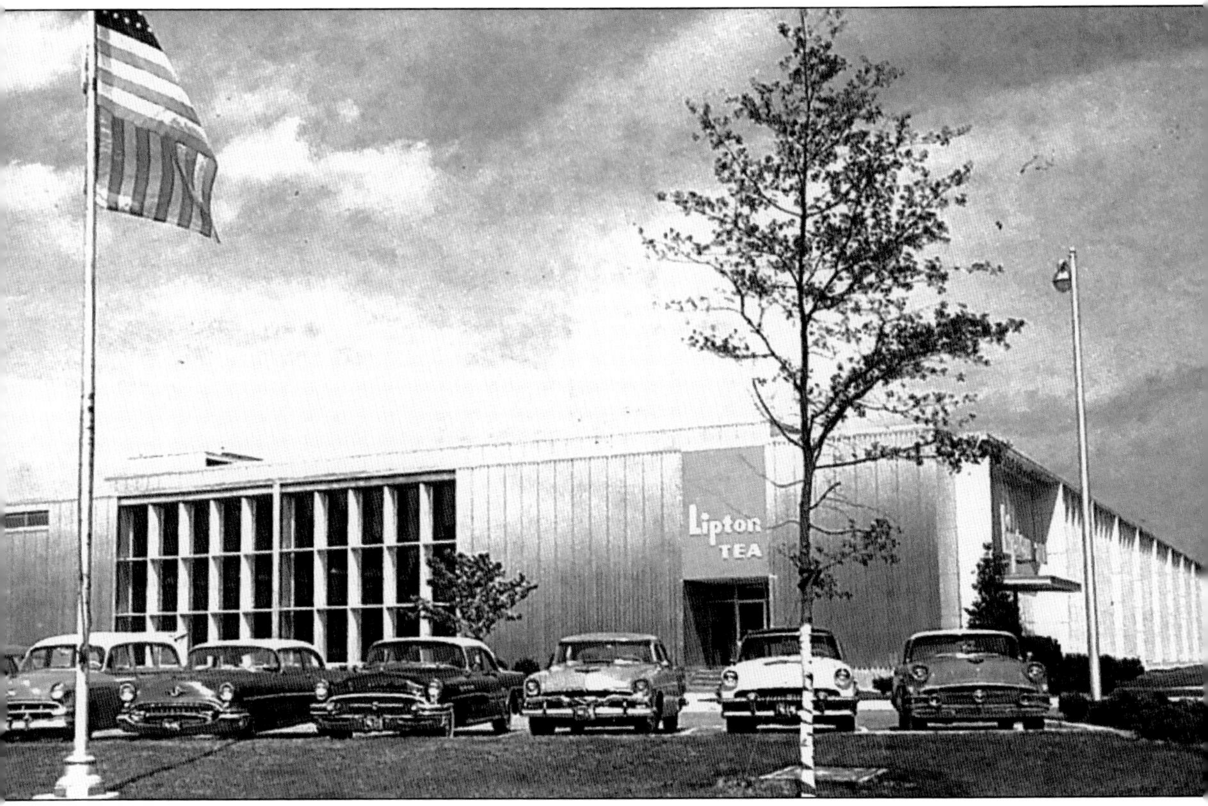

Lipton Tea, the English company started by Sir Thomas Lipton, came to Suffolk in the early 1950s. In 1955 this new plant opened, built across Washington Street from the waterworks. For many years an English tea taster was part of their staff. When this plant opened it was one of four in the country. It has expanded and is now Lipton's only tea manufacturing plant in the United States.

Five

Travel and Leisure

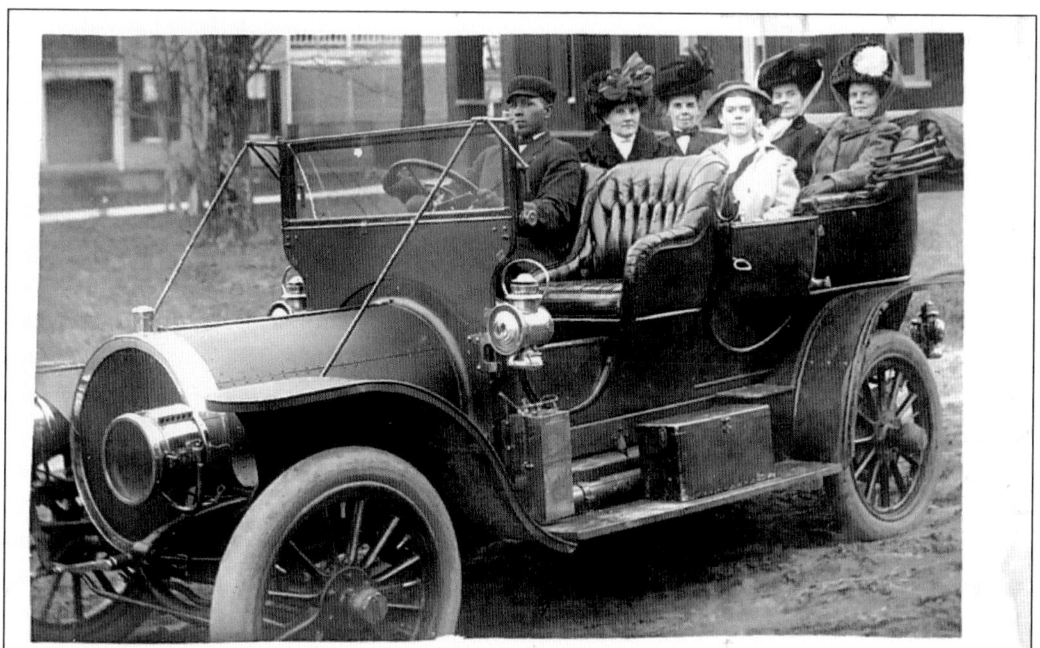

The West family heads out for a drive with a chauffeur at the wheel, hats tied on, and dusters covering their clothing. The automobile was certainly for the wealthy early in the 20th century, but all of that would change, of course, by the century's end. It was not unusual in this day of letter writing for postcards to be made from personal pictures.

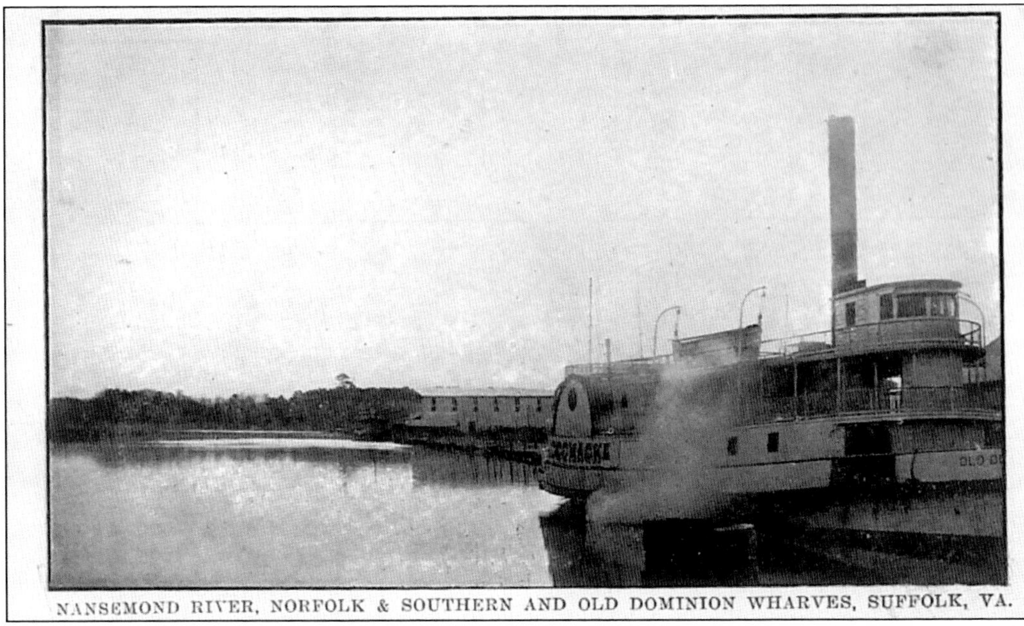

The Nansemond River was Suffolk's first highway, taking goods and travelers to all of the Chesapeake region and beyond. The Old Dominion Steamship Company made regular stops at the wharf in Suffolk in the late 19th and early 20th centuries. Beyond are the wharves of the Norfolk and Southern Railroad, originally the Suffolk and Carolina. That line was built to move lumber from Nansemond County and nearby Gates County, North Carolina, to the wharf in Suffolk.

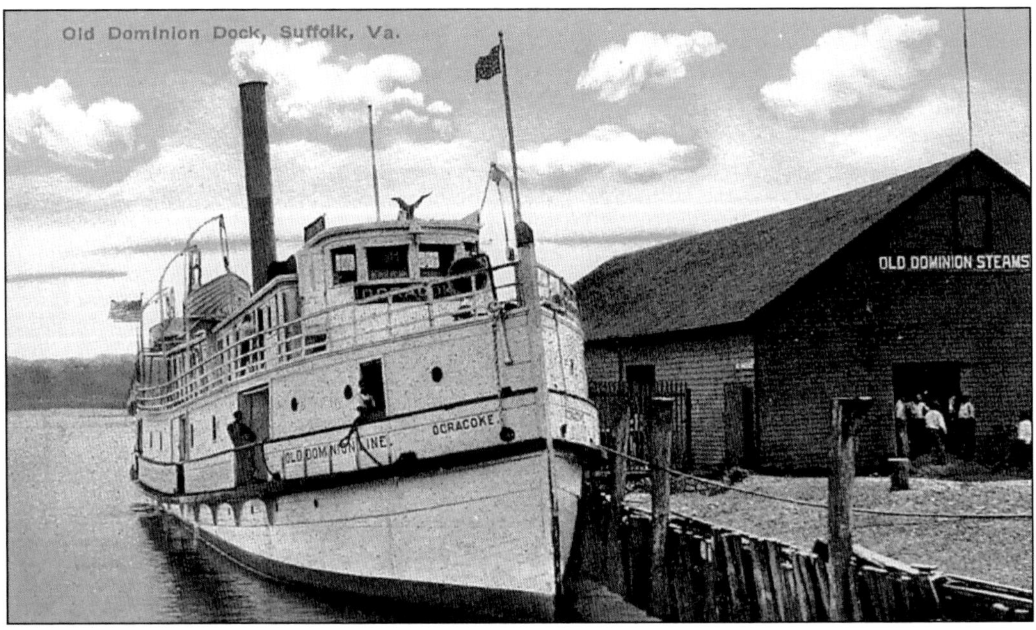

The *Ocracoke,* shown above, was one of the boats that stopped here regularly. Another was the *Virginia Dare*. This company made connections up and down the east coast carrying passengers and freight.

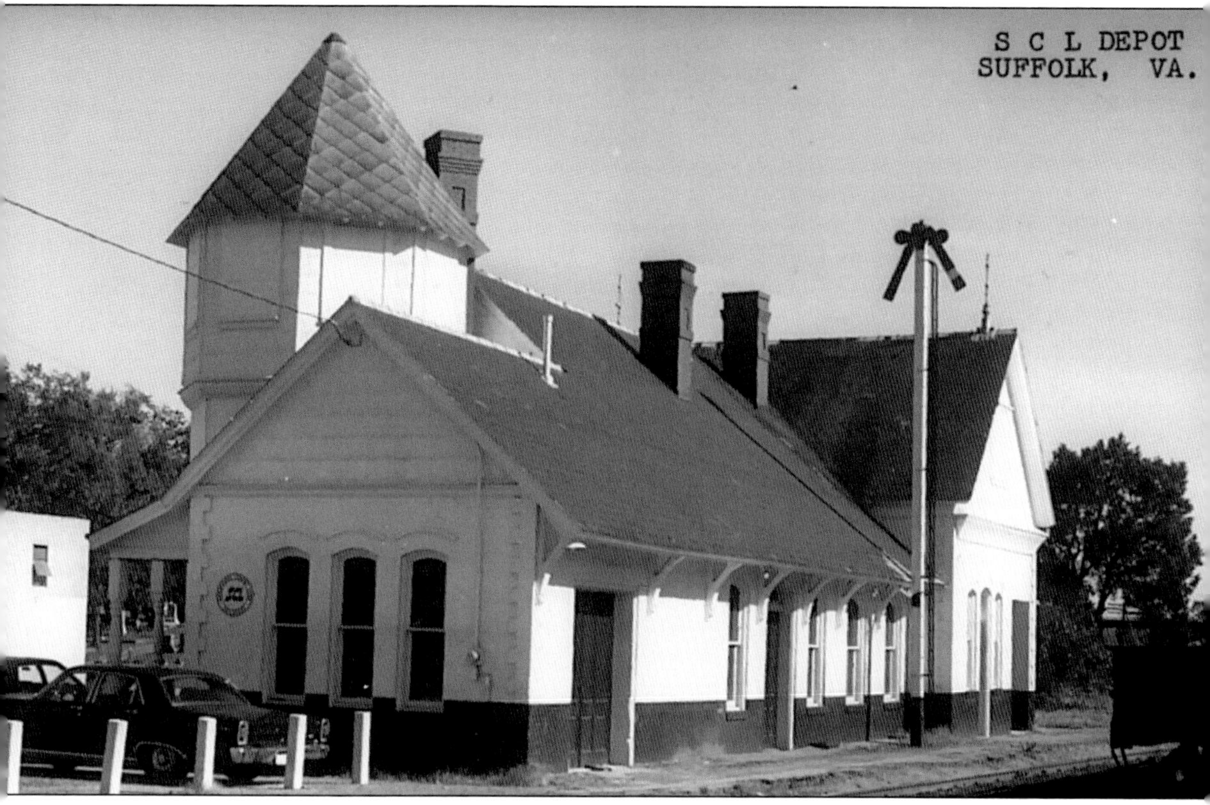

The line that would eventually become the Seaboard Railroad first came through Suffolk in 1834 as the Portsmouth and Roanoke. This depot was built in 1885 to replace an earlier one. It was used as a passenger station by the Seaboard Coastline (as it came to be called) until 1968. From about 1906 to 1956 the building also served Virginian Railroad passengers. This is now a railroad museum.

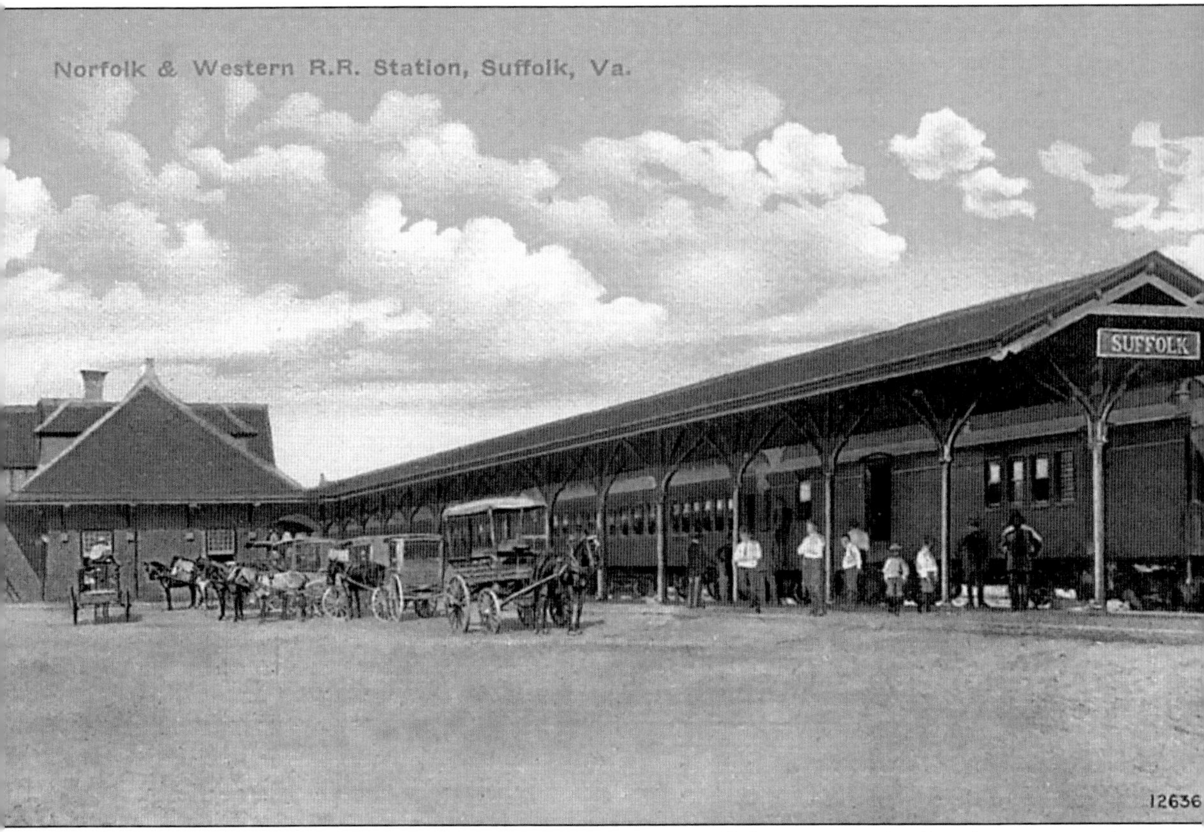

The Norfolk and Western Railroad first came through Suffolk in 1857. The first depot was at the south end of Main Street, and a new depot was built around 1910 near the end of Pinner Street in the heyday of passenger travel. Union Station, as it was called, served passengers for the Norfolk and Western, the Atlantic and Danville, and the old Norfolk and Southern lines. In 1928, 34 passenger trains a day ran on the 6 rail lines that came through Suffolk.

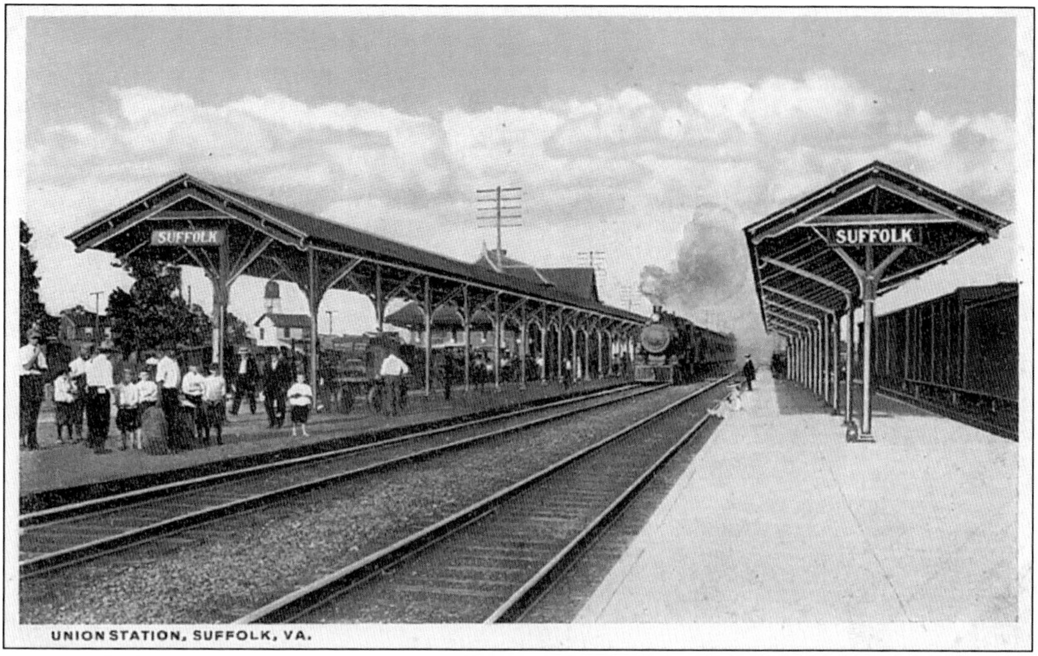

Many Suffolk people recall leaving from this station to go to college. We heard one story of a would-be college boy who left Suffolk on the train and got off in Windsor. Lady Bird Johnson stopped here on her Whistle Stop campaign for her husband in the 1960s. The canopy was still in place then.

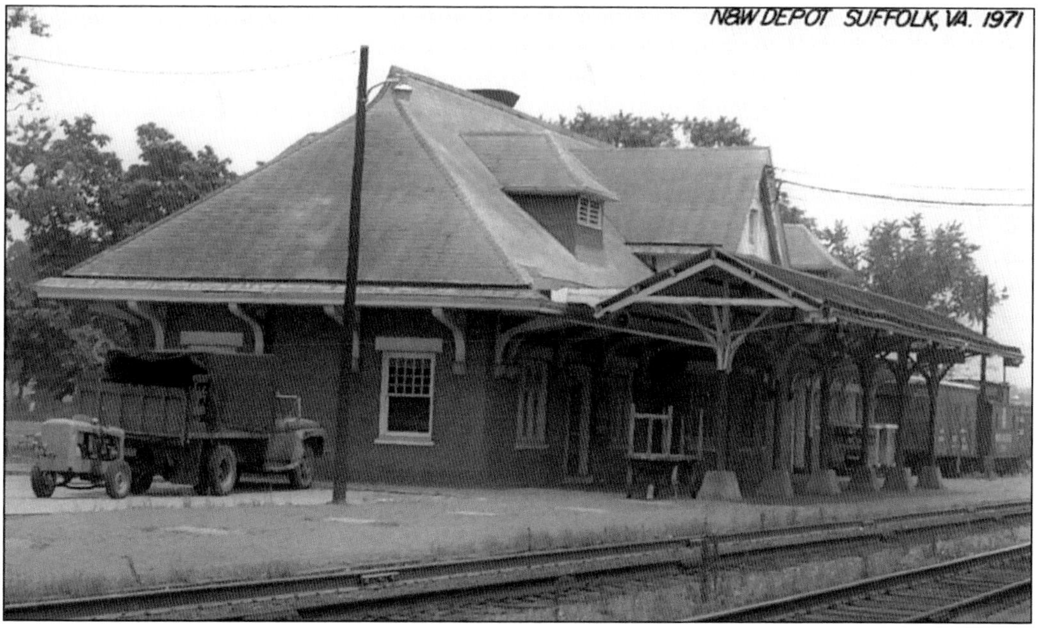

By 1971 passenger service was almost over for Suffolk. Amtrak stopped at this station for a short time but was soon gone. The passenger platform that had once been so busy was reduced in size accordingly. For a while this was used as a freight agency. Now it is a locker room for railroad crews.

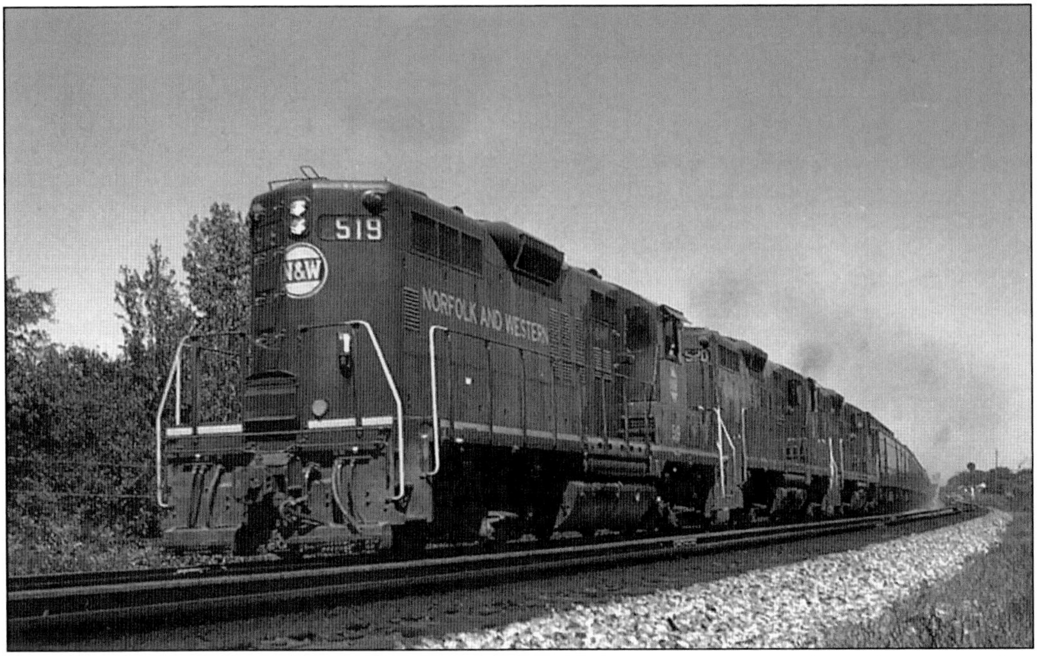

The Norfolk and Western Railroad used steam power longer than any other Class 1 mainline railroad and ran passenger service until 1971 when Amtrak took over. Here these three diesel units power a west bound passenger train at Lake Kilby. Diesels took over from steam in 1957 and 1958. By this time the passenger service was beginning to wane.

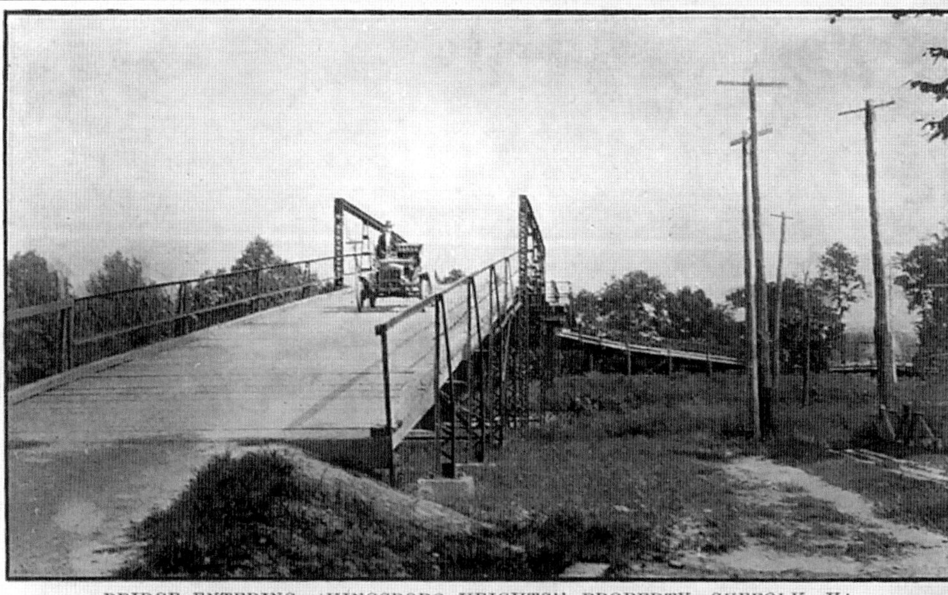

BRIDGE ENTERING "KINGSBORO HEIGHTS" PROPERTY, SUFFOLK, VA.

The Kingsboro Bridge was built *c.* 1900 to take Pinner Street over two, and later three, railroads. The riveted steel bridge was replaced during the Depression by a wooden one. In the 1980s, a concrete and steel replacement was built. The Kingsboro area was developed on the former Rose Hill plantation land.

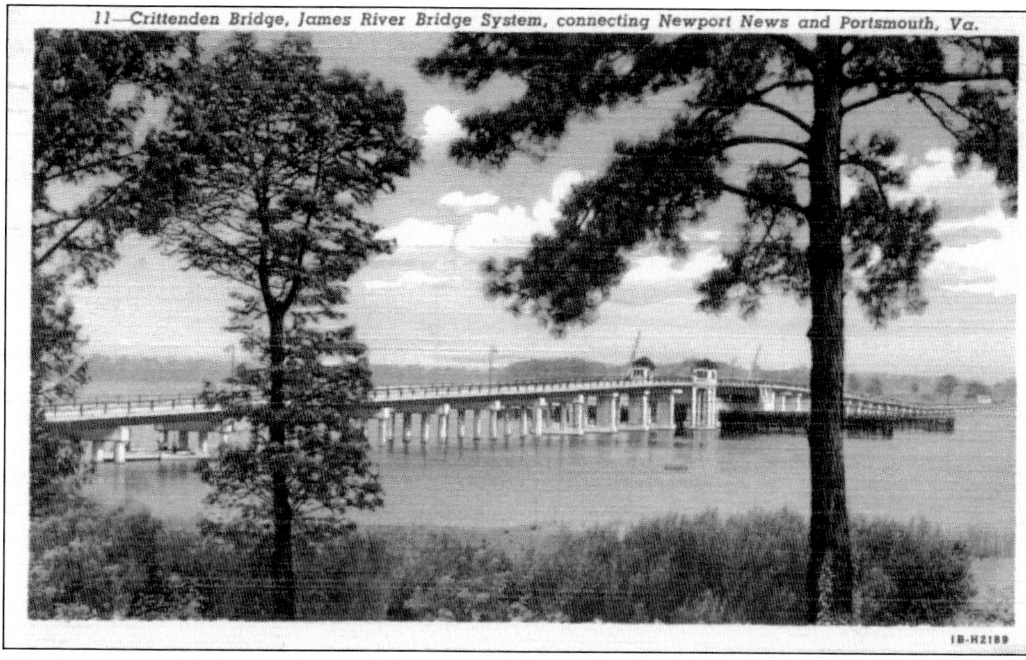

The Nansemond River Bridge and the Crittenden Bridge were both opened on July 4, 1928, as part of the James River Bridge System. These two toll bridges in the northwestern part of Suffolk were built for the private James River Bridge Corporation and connected Portsmouth and Newport News by way of the current Virginia Route 17. The James River Bridge, a third bridge in the system, opened on November 17, 1928. The Crittenden Bridge, also known as the Chuckatuck Creek Bridge, connected the Crittenden area to Isle of Wight County. Many inhabitants of the area were once employed as fishermen, oystermen, and boat builders. The highway and bridge system was a catalyst for growth when it replaced the ferries.

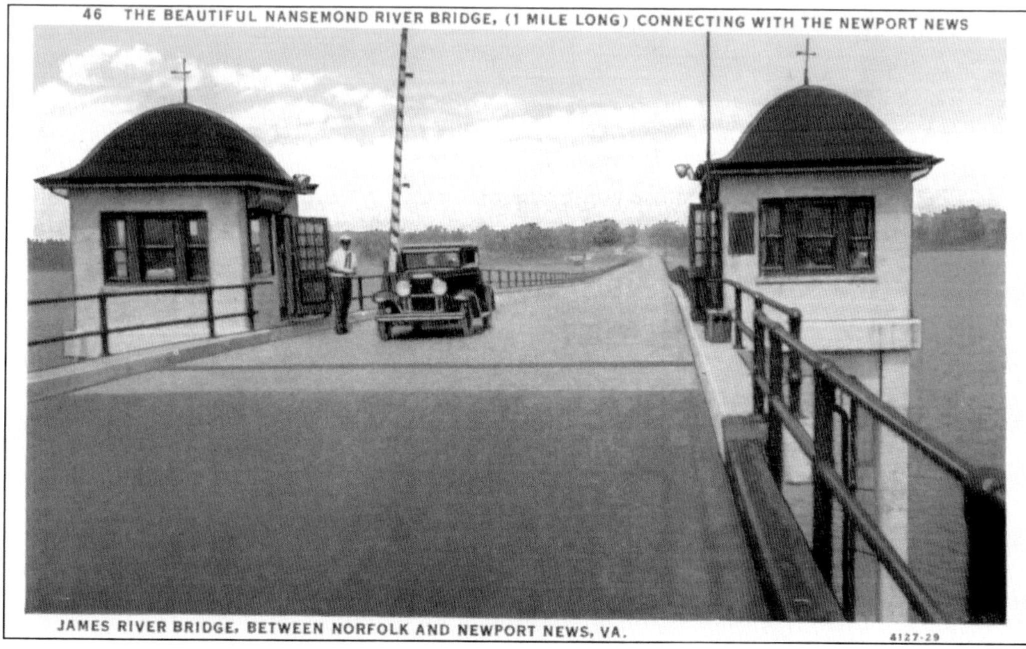

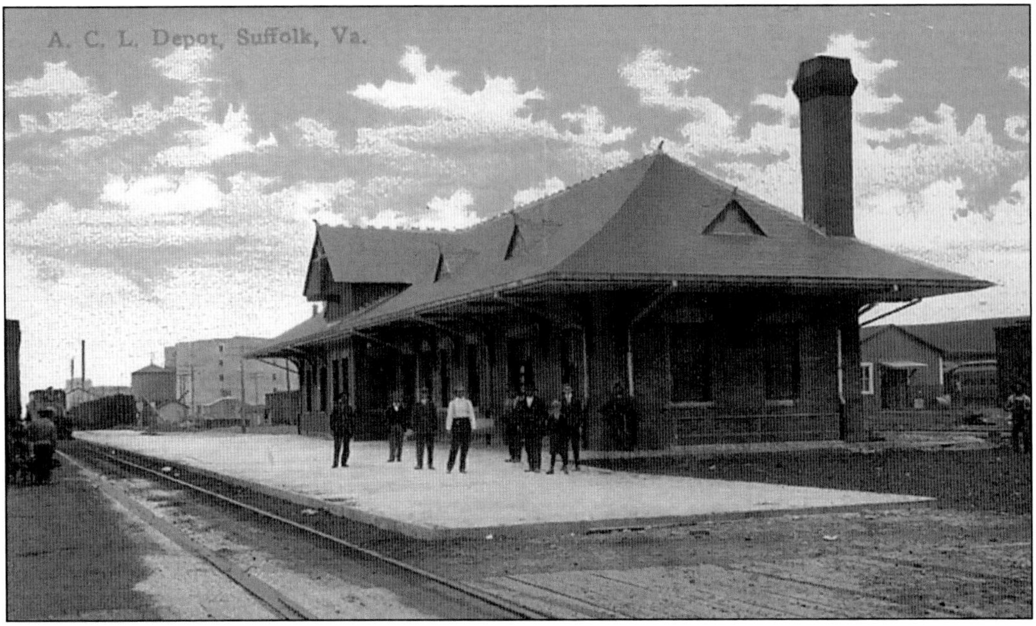

The Atlantic Coastline Railroad was the fourth rail line to come through Suffolk around 1889. This station stood on East Washington Street and was very busy around the turn of the century when Suffolk boasted "six railroads and deep water to the sea." The railroads and the river were wonderful for commerce in Suffolk.

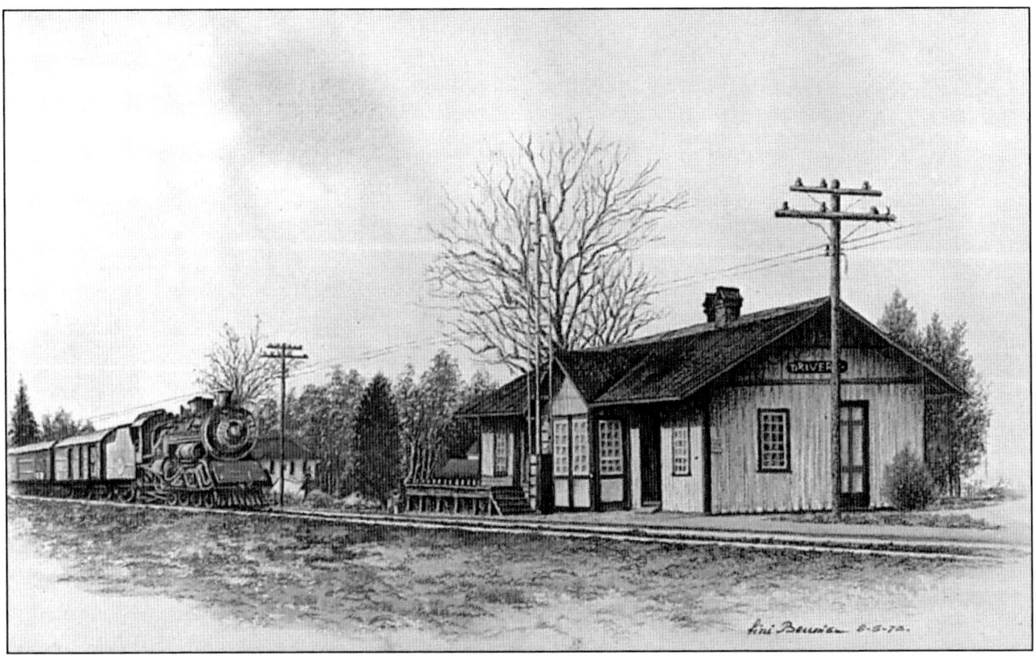

The Atlantic Coastline Station in Driver was built in the late 1800s. The Driver community was surrounded by truck farms. With the railroad, Driver potatoes, spinach, strawberries, or kale could reach a larger market in record time. The station now houses a feed and seed store.

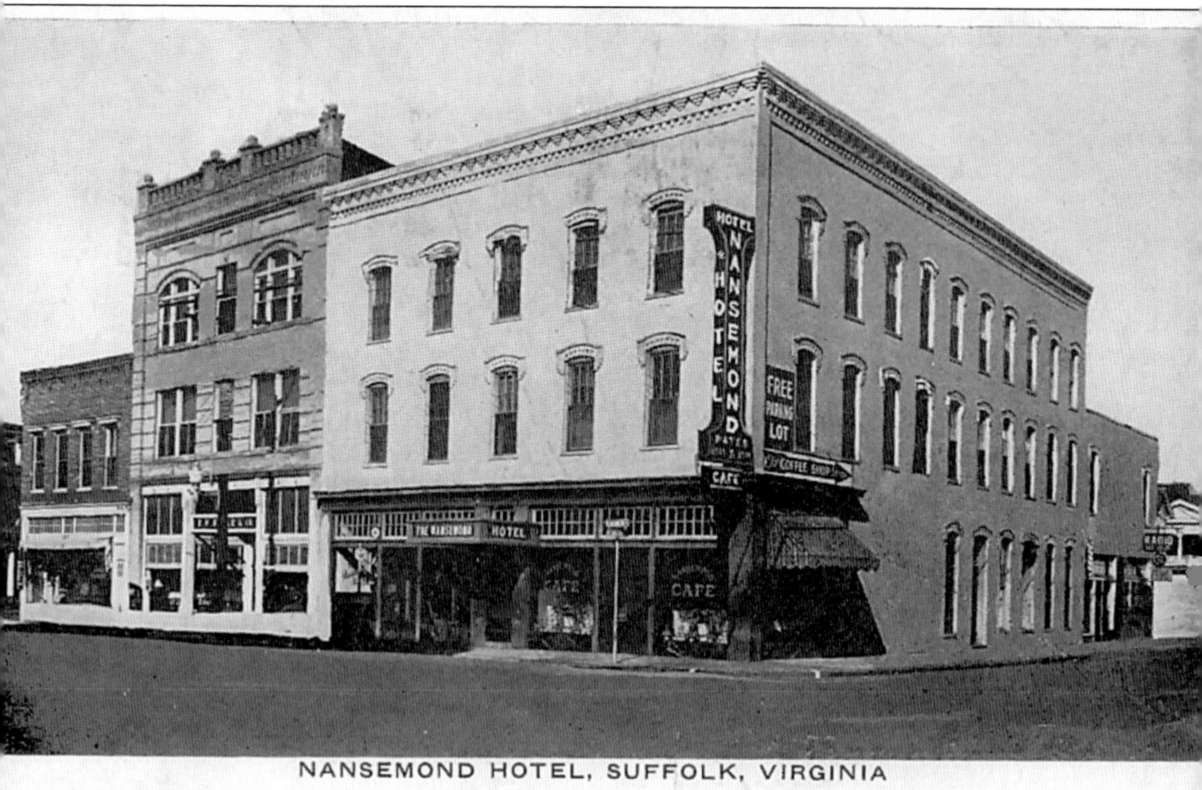

The Nansemond Hotel stood at the corner of West Washington and Saratoga Streets. Built in the late 19th century, it primarily served business travelers. It was known as the Hill Hotel for a while before becoming the Nansemond. Baker Furniture Store and Bowden's Florist (center and left) shared the block with the hotel.

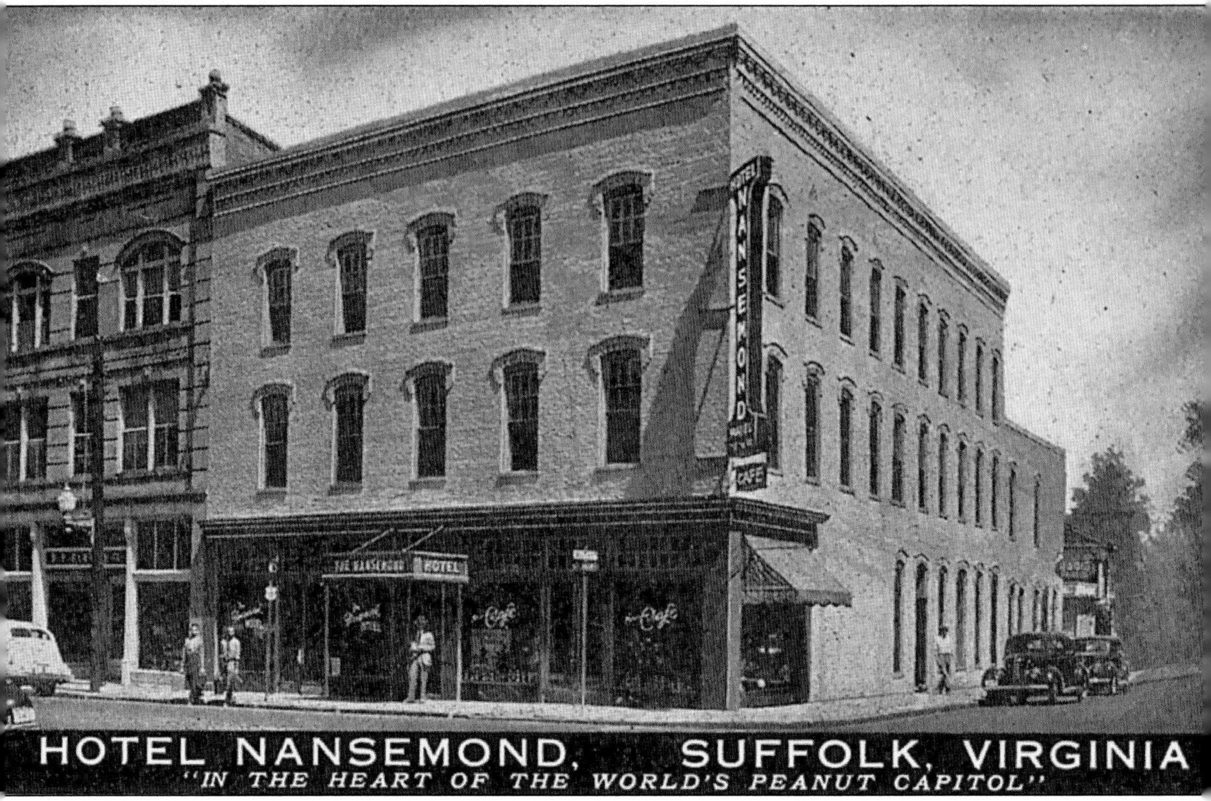

Like the Elliot Hotel around the corner, the Nansemond had a café on the street level. R.W. Baker Furniture Store occupied the building to the left of the hotel. The row of buildings was demolished in the 1960s and the National Bank built its new facility there.

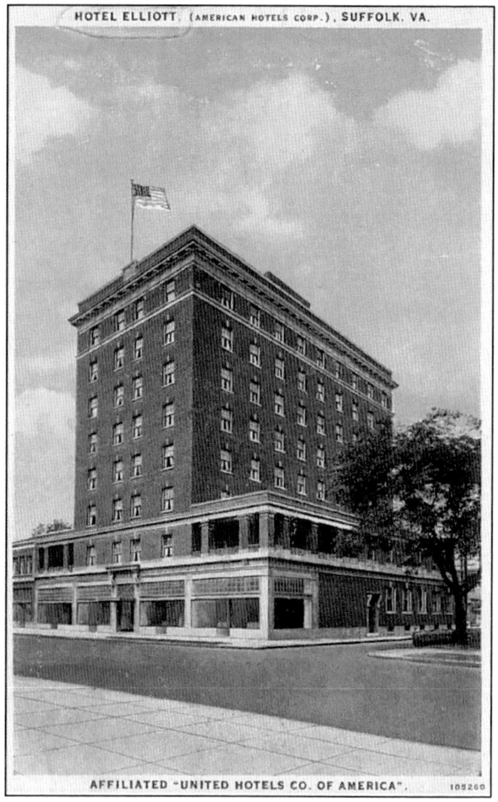

The Elliot Hotel opened in 1925 at the corner of North Main and Market Streets. It had two ballrooms and, in the early days, an open-air dining room known as the Palm Court. There was also a coffee shop and a fine dining restaurant. This was the location of many social gatherings throughout the mid-20th century. In its later years, this establishment was known as the Hotel Suffolk. In the late 1960s or early 1970s it became the Suffolk Towers apartments.

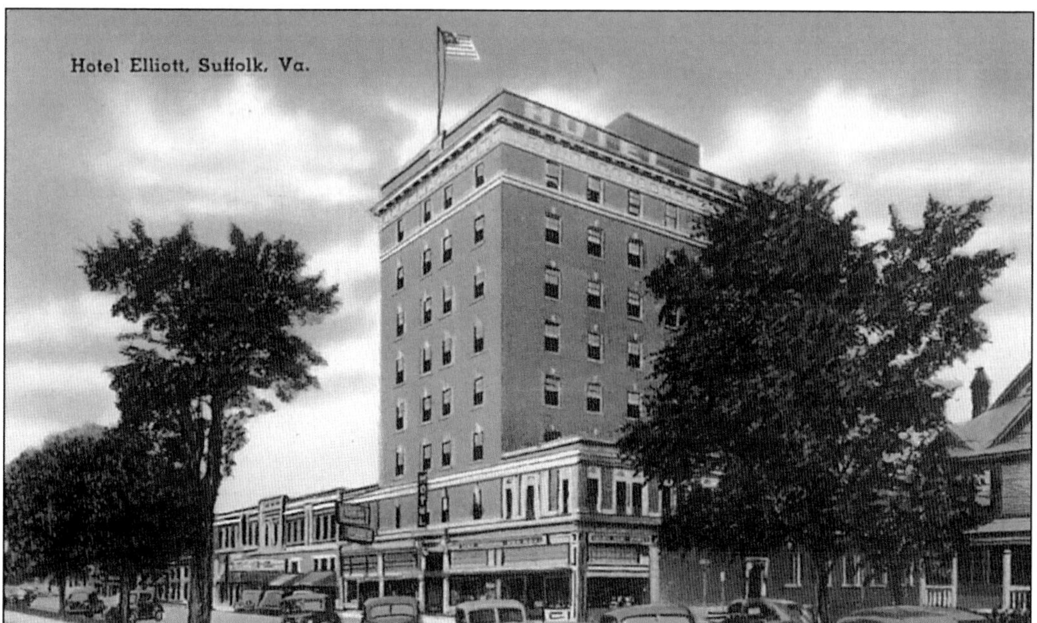

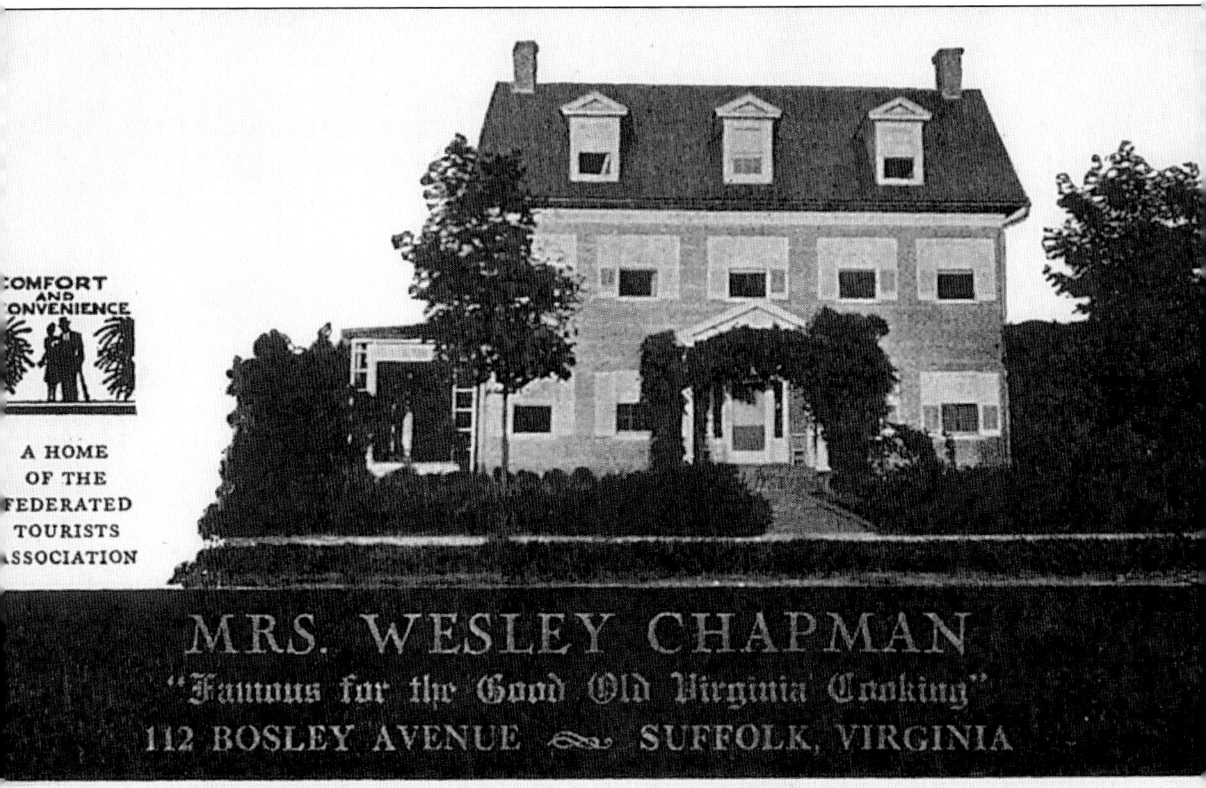

This beautiful home was built in 1917 on Bosley Avenue near Lakeview Hospital. Perhaps young residents from the hospital stayed here. It would also have been convenient for out-of-town family members of patients at Lakeview. The house was bought by M.A. Cross *c.* 1941 and became a private residence.

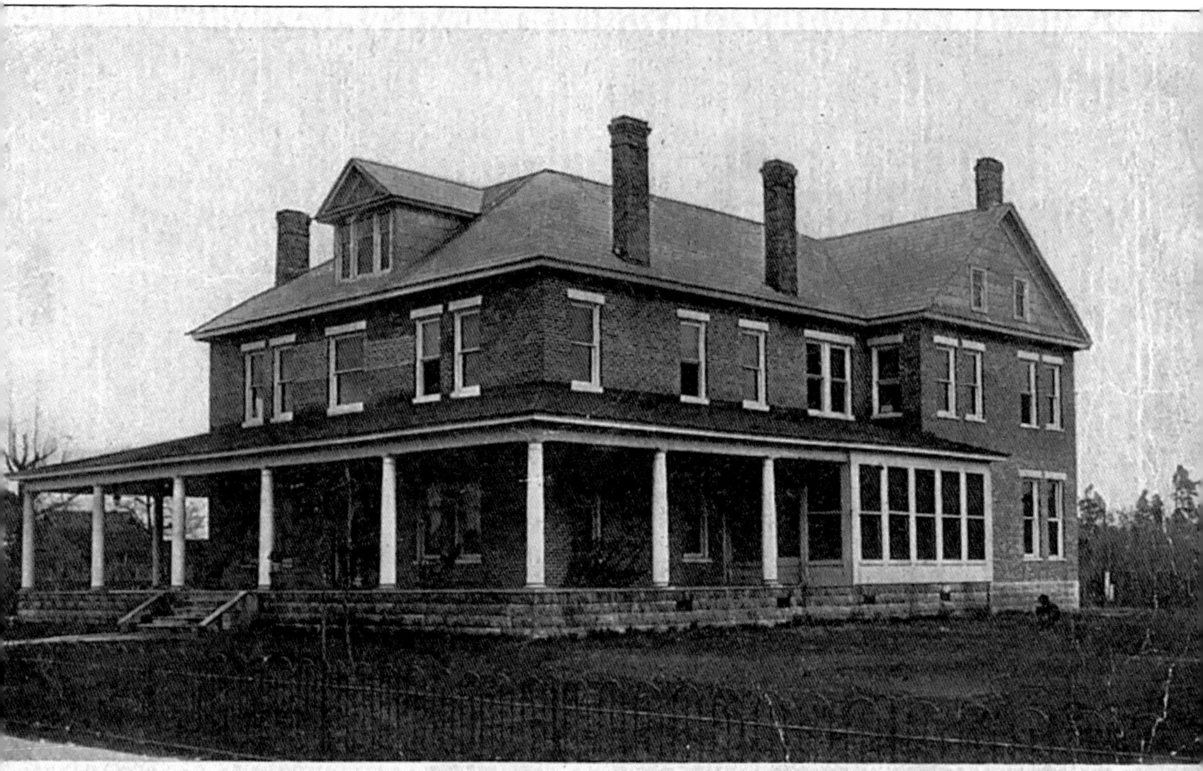

HOLLAND HOTEL, Holland, Va.

The Holland Hotel, built after the great Holland fire of 1910, was in the center of downtown Holland. Its proximity to the railroad must have made it very attractive to travelers. It was here in 1928 that a group of businessmen held a meeting that led to the formation of the first Ruritan Club in the country.

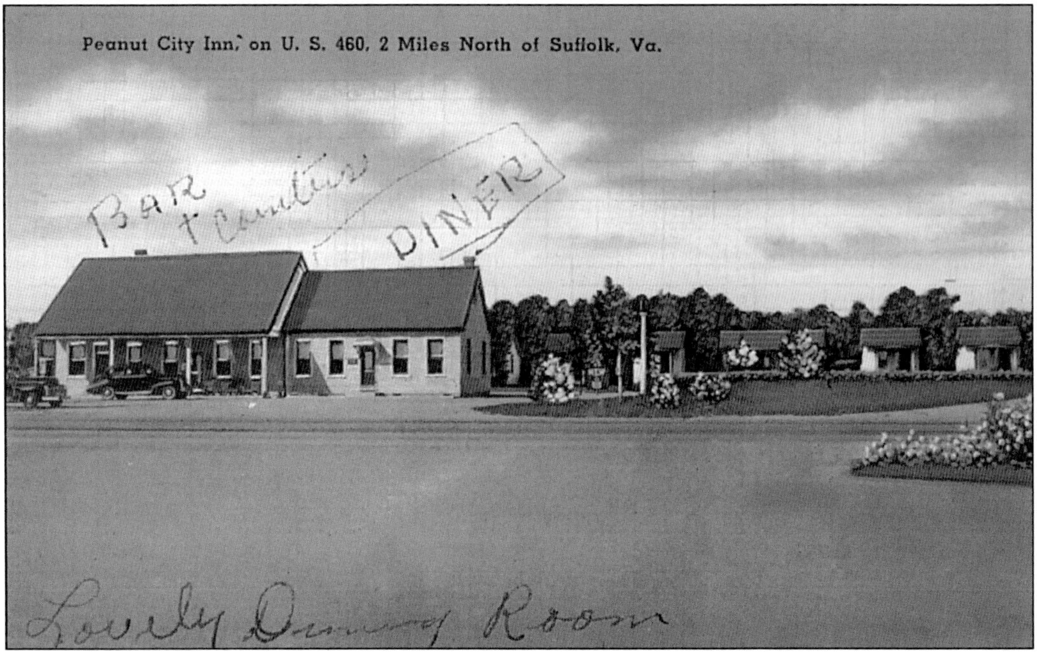

On Route 460 north of Suffolk at Elephants Fork was another motor court, the Peanut City Inn. The inn was near Lover's Lane (Murphy's Mill Road). Opened in the 1940s, the tourist cabins had become weekly rentals by the early 1950s, and the restaurant continued operation until the late 1950s.

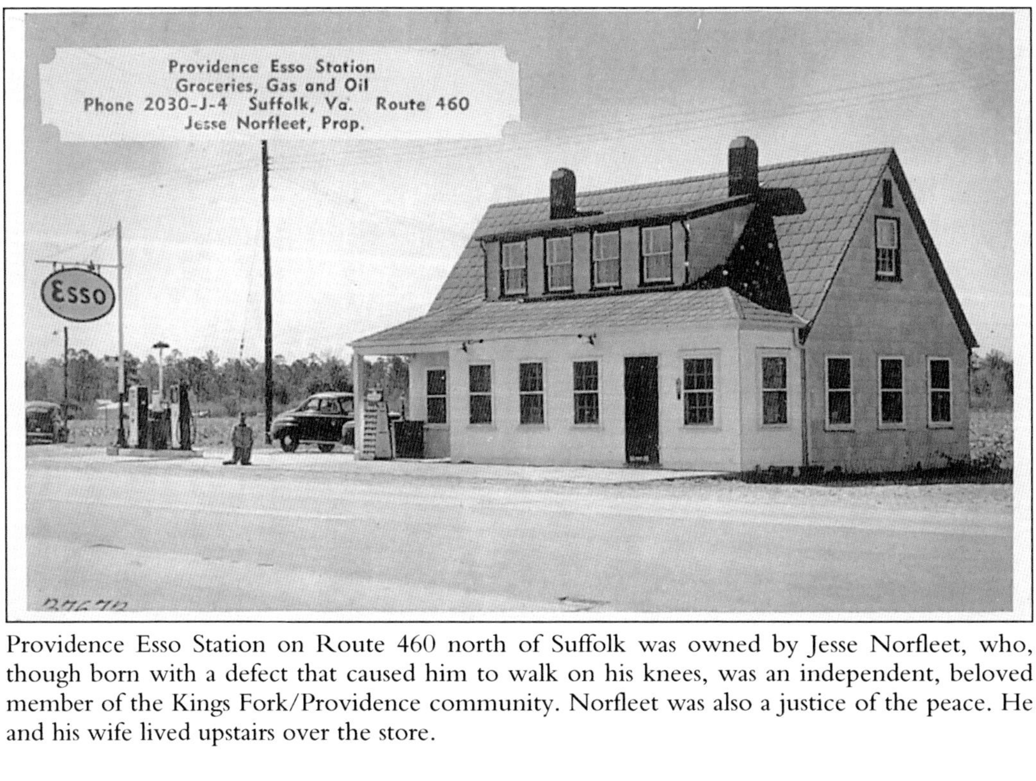

Providence Esso Station on Route 460 north of Suffolk was owned by Jesse Norfleet, who, though born with a defect that caused him to walk on his knees, was an independent, beloved member of the Kings Fork/Providence community. Norfleet was also a justice of the peace. He and his wife lived upstairs over the store.

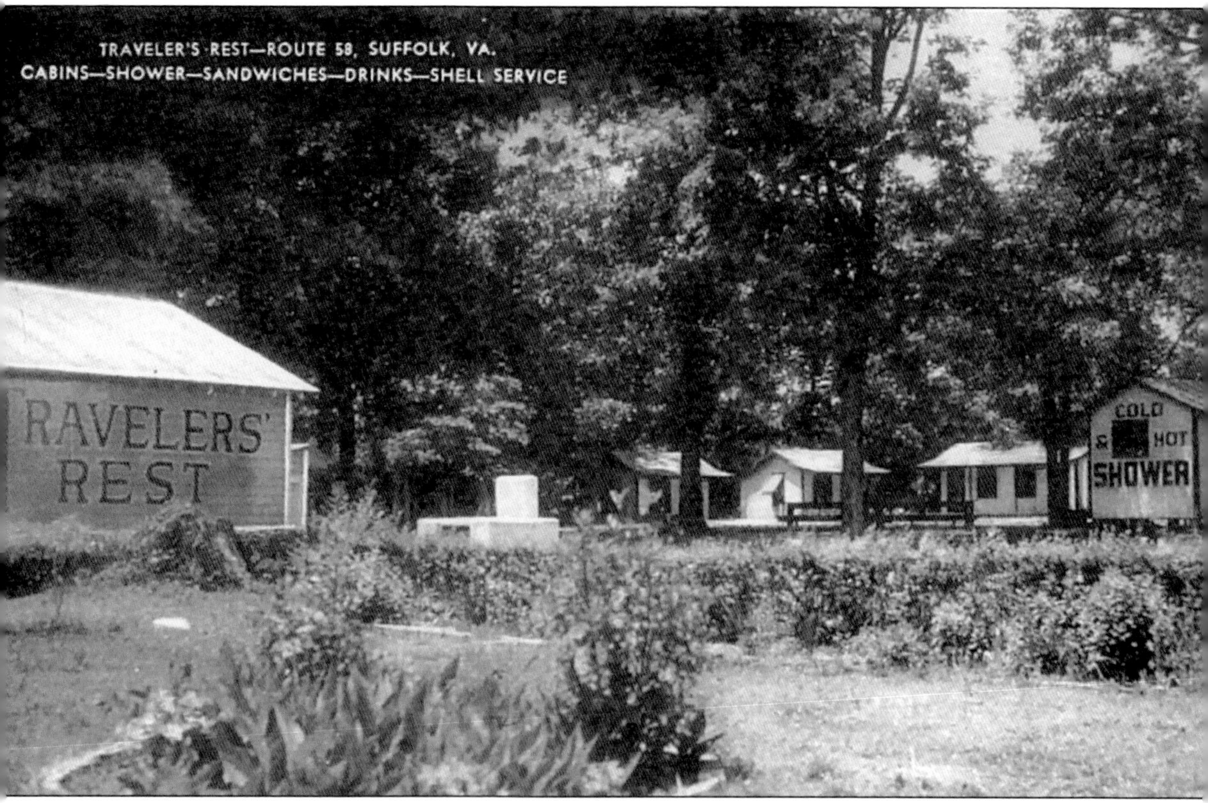

In the 1920s and 1930s Americans were just beginning to take to the road in automobiles. Some roads were paved, making travel easier. Cars did not travel very far very fast and towns were more contained. Motors courts such as Travelers Rest (above) on Route 58 east of Suffolk (East Pinner Street today) were an economical alternative to the pricier downtown hotels.

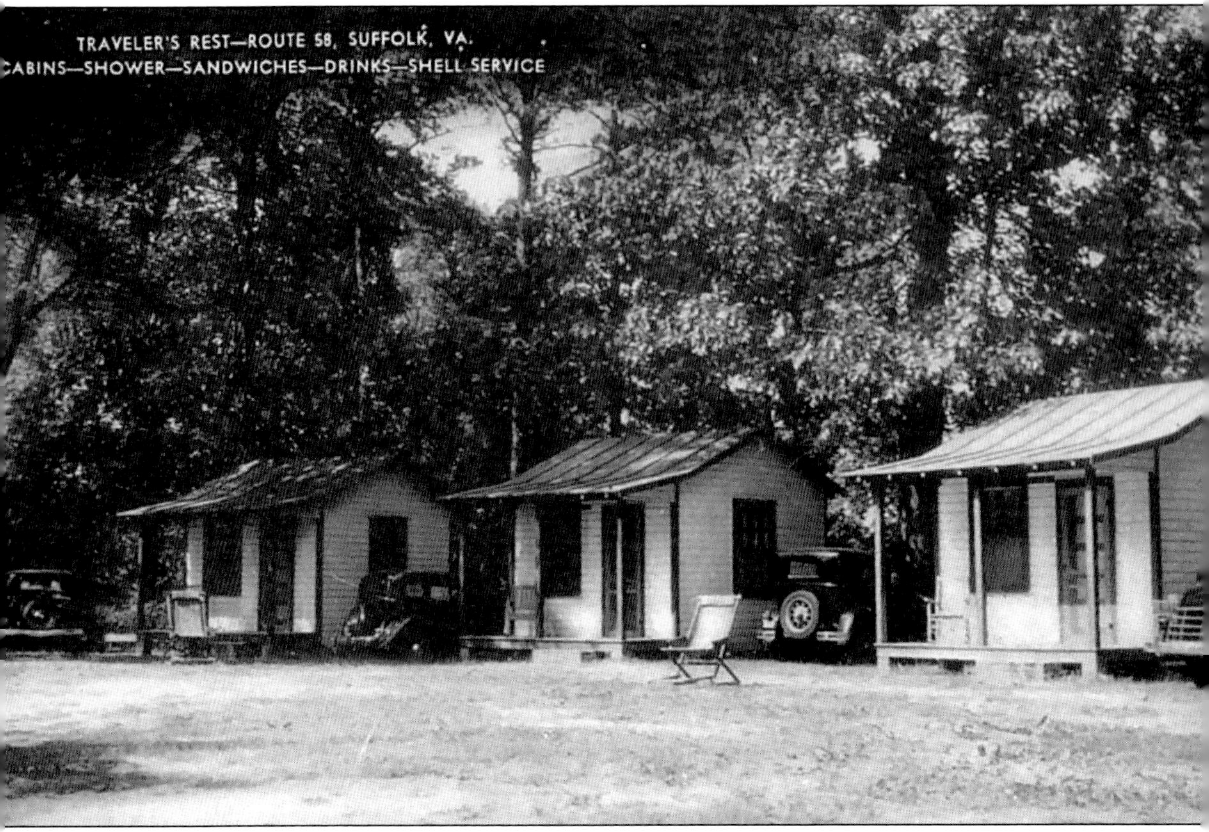

From 1950 to 1952 the Traveler's Rest was operated by the Barrett brothers, Earl and Harold. The buildings were owned by Jimmy Ward. Eventually there was only a restaurant on the site, and it is now known as the Dining Room.

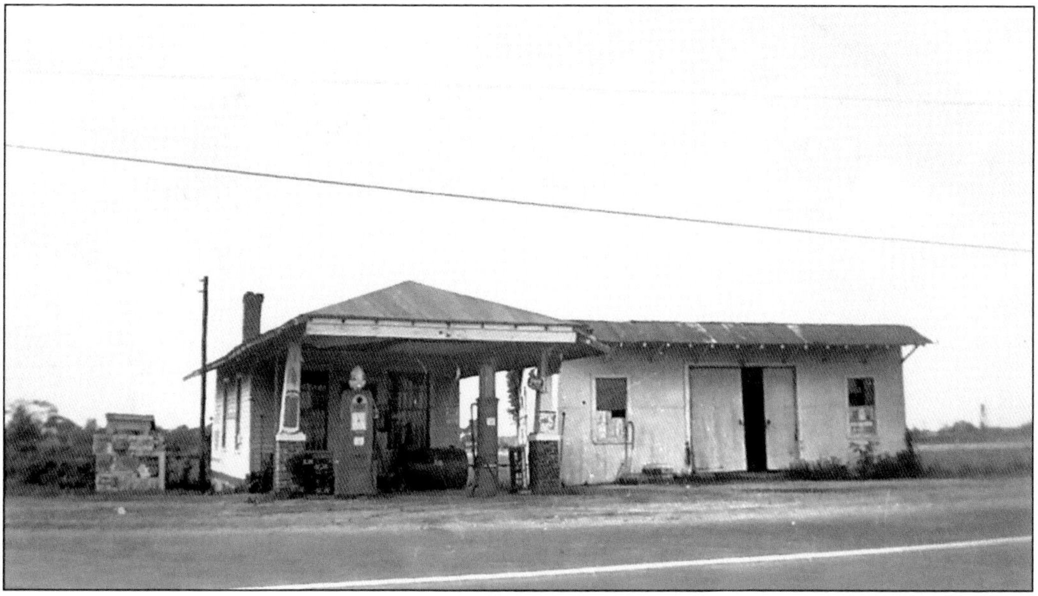

This unidentified service station/country store in the early 1920s is typical of those that were once prominent. One example is the one that was at the intersection of Route 10 and Kings Fork Road. The station was demolished years ago but the neighborhood is still identified on city maps by the name of the old store—Red Top.

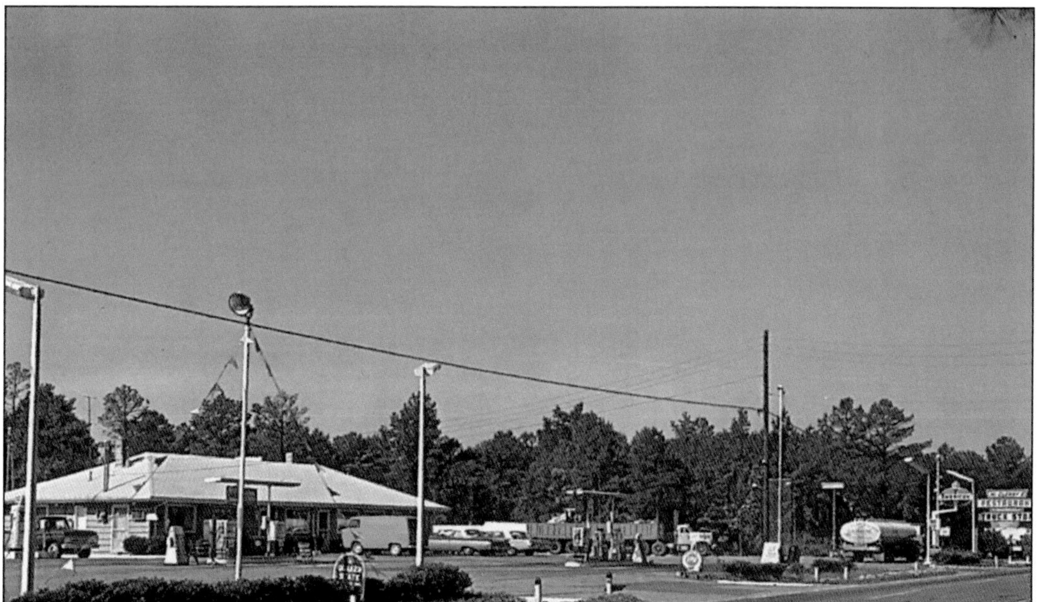

This building constructed in the 1950s on Route 58 West of Suffolk was originally McClenny's Truck Stop. Small truck stops like this one were soon beaten out by larger full service facilities. Though the building still stands, it is vacant and the site has been abandoned.

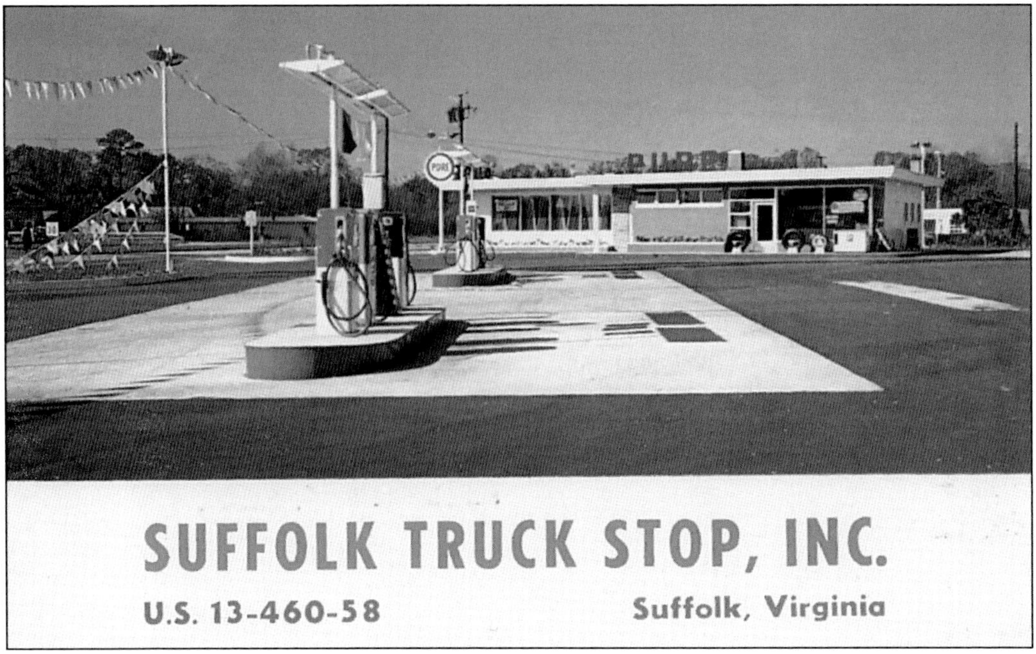

Suffolk Truck Stop was probably built after Constance Road opened in the early 1950s. It is on Constance between Myrtle and Elm Streets. Visible not far away to the left, in typical 1950s fashion, is another gas station catering to automobiles. This building now houses Suffolk Food Mart and Henry Trucking.

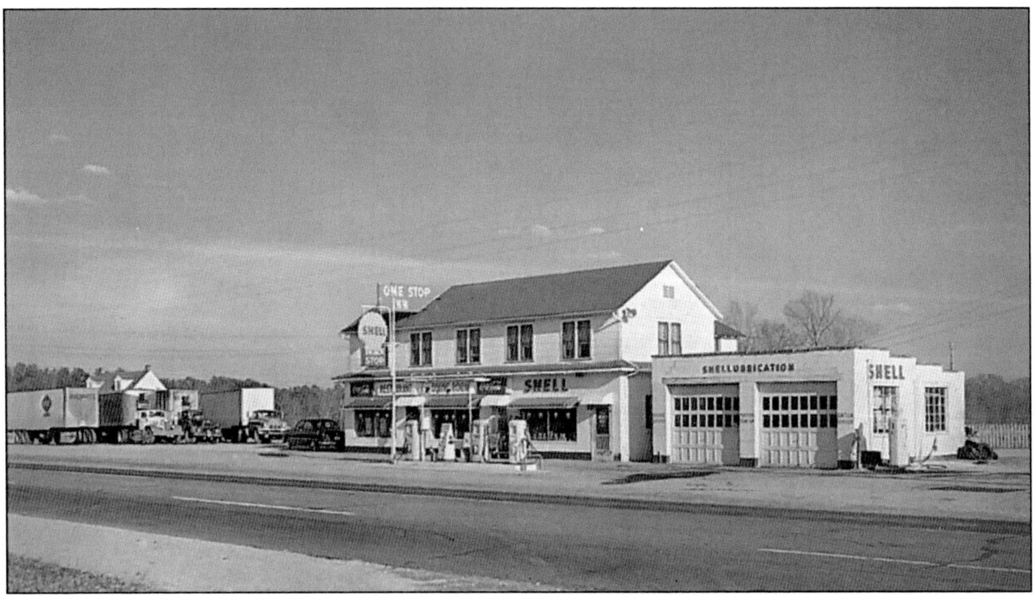

The One Stop Inn opened on Route 58 West around 1950 near the present-day Forrest Glen School entrance. It was originally called Lee's Esso and the proprietor was Southgate Lee. It was later the Cricket Inn then Dianne's Grill before it was given the name shown here. The bunk rooms with showers upstairs were rented to truckers. The place closed in the 1970s and has been demolished.

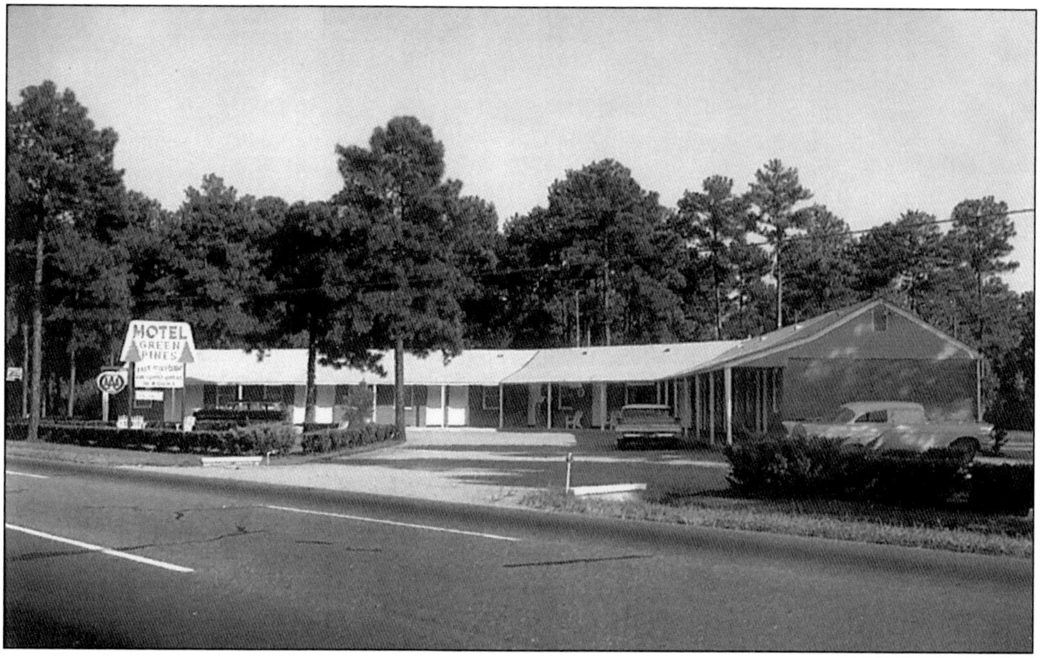

The Green Pines Motel (above) was built on Route 58 West between Suffolk and Holland around 1960. At roughly the same time the Jon Del (below) was built on Route 58 East near Magnolia. They were designed to give the traveler an economical, convenient stop. Many of the small motels have now been abandoned (as is the case for the original Green Pines) but the old Jon Del is still open and has adopted a new name—Green Pines!

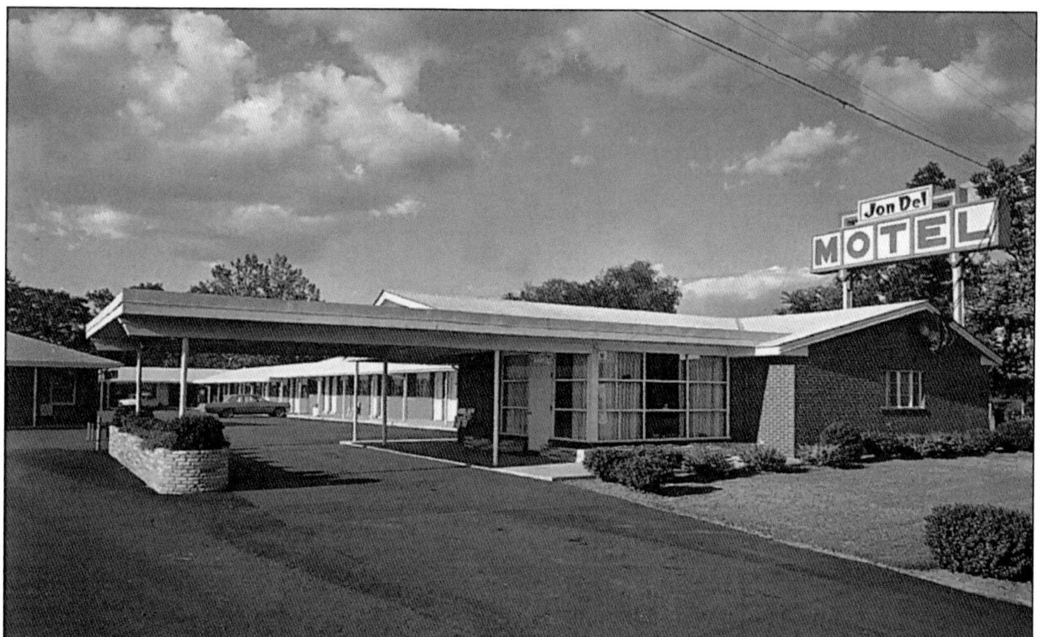

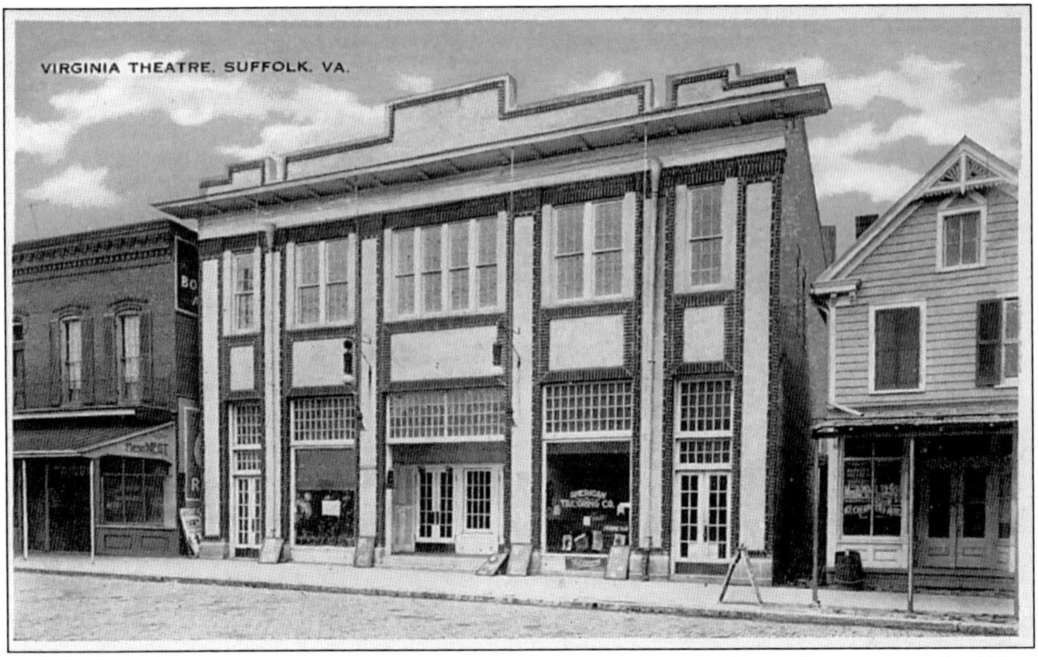

In the second decade of the 20th century, the Virginia Theater was located on present-day West Washington Street. It offered traveling shows and silent movies. D.W. Griffith's *Birth of a Nation* was shown here. By the 1920s more modern movie theaters were built. This building was demolished several years ago.

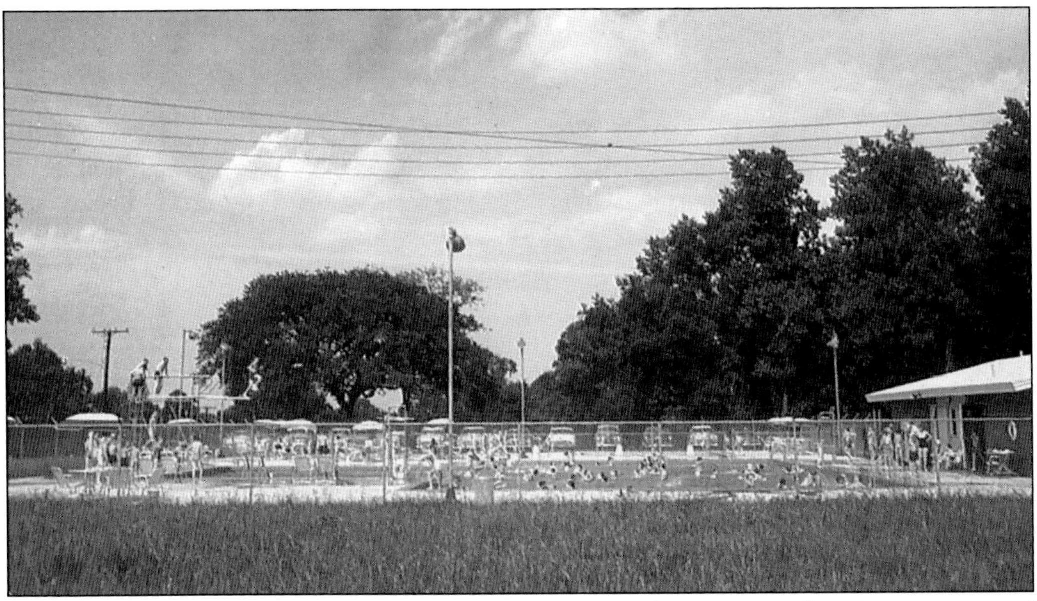

The Suffolk Swimming Pool was built in the early 1950s from private donations encouraged by radio station WLPM. The pool, which was segregated like most of daily life in Virginia in its day, was for members only but the vast majority of middle class white children in Suffolk who were born after World War II went to the pool regularly. The Suffolk Swimming Pool closed in the 1990s.

Six

THE WATERWORKS

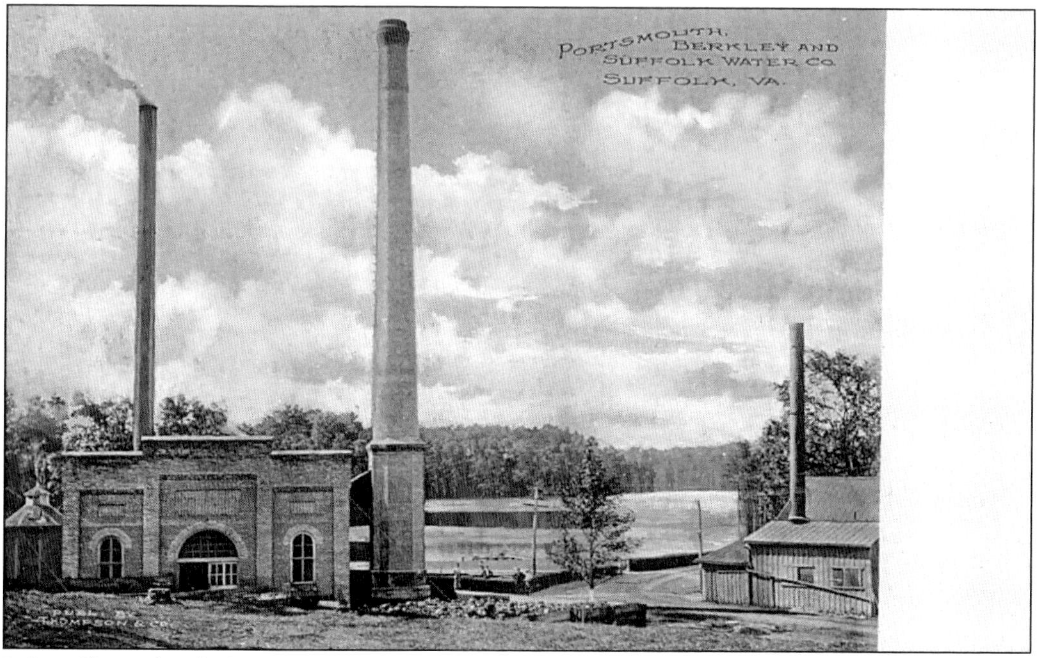

Lake Kilby and Kilby's Mill had been on the South Quay (Holland) Road since colonial times but with different names as ownership changed. In the early days the mill and the water to run it were the property of the Meade family. In 1885 the enterprise was bought by the Portsmouth, Berkley, and Suffolk Water Company and furnished water to those three locations.

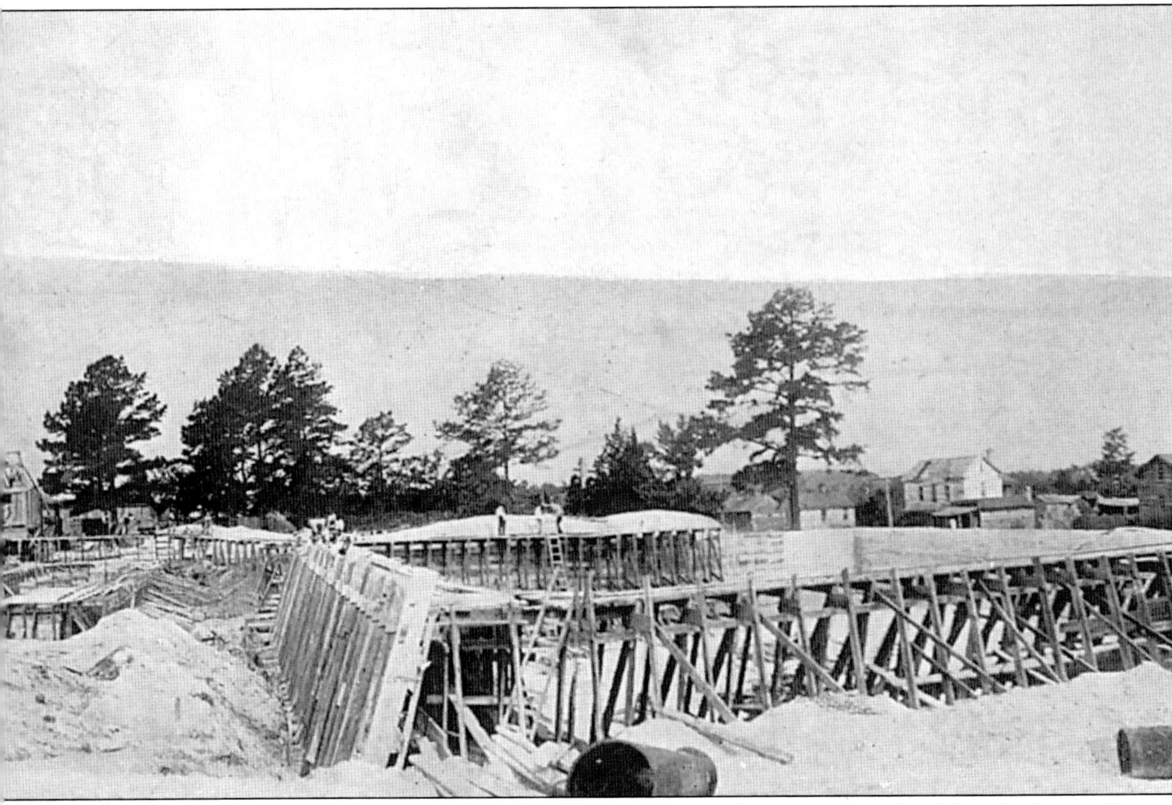

It has been suggested that the popularity of the waterworks as a postcard subject is due to its having been such a mammoth undertaking. These *c.* 1900 views might support that theory. The late W.E. Maclenny, a historian, said that the water is "as pure as any in eastern Virginia as it is supplied by good springs." When the plant was first built, untreated water was pumped to Portsmouth, Berkley, and Suffolk.

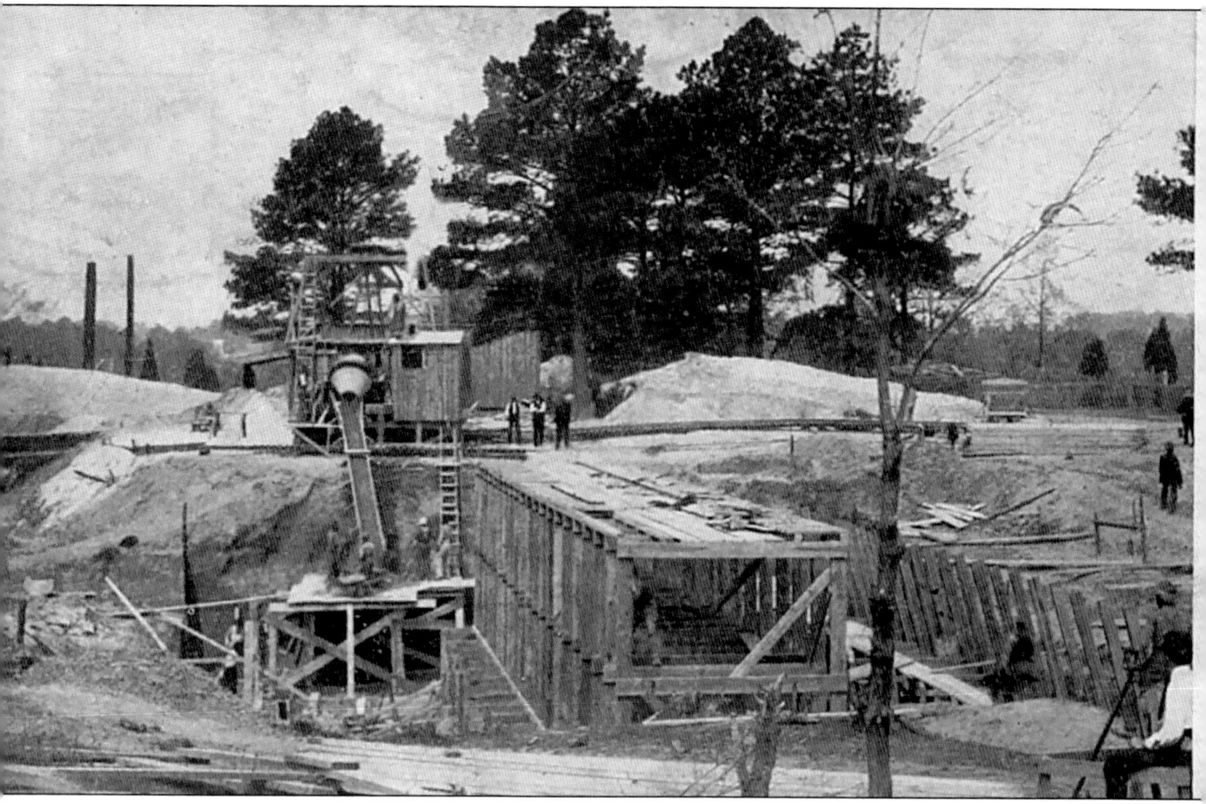

This massive undertaking was impressive considering that it used so much manual labor. The filtration plant, under construction here and on the opposite page, was a later addition. The water was piped straight from the lake in the earliest days. The primary use of the water at first was for extinguishing fires.

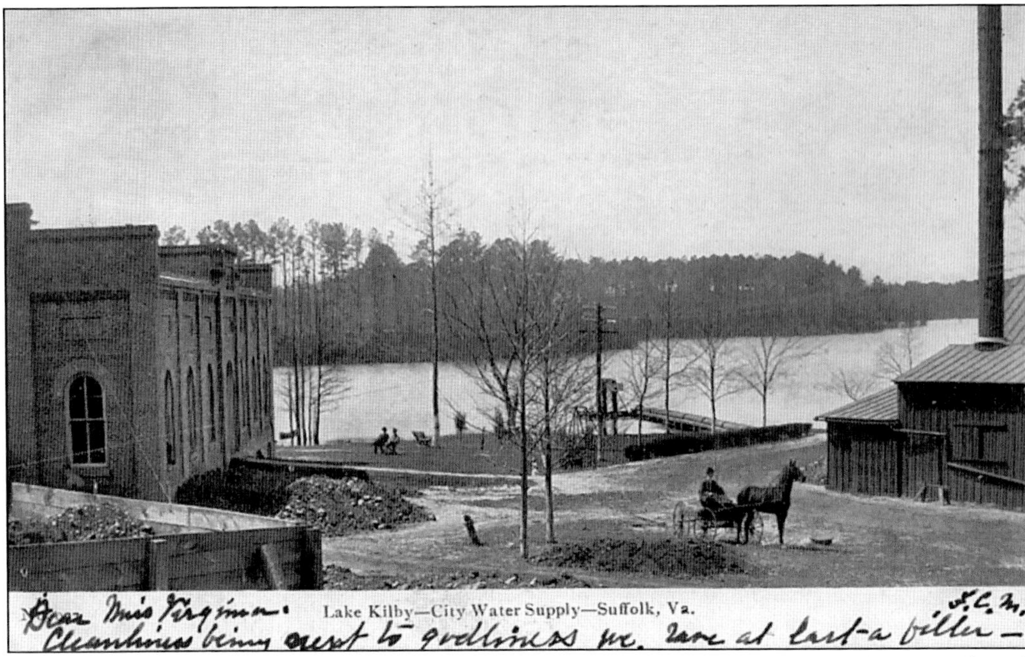

The waterworks seems to have been considered a park. One reads of friends taking Sunday afternoon walks to the waterworks. One young Suffolk lad around 1906 reported in a letter to his brother that "Daddy couldn't sleep and he and mama walked all the way to the waterworks last night!" In this view the gentleman in the conveyance might be about business or pleasure, but the people on the bench seem to be taking in the sights.

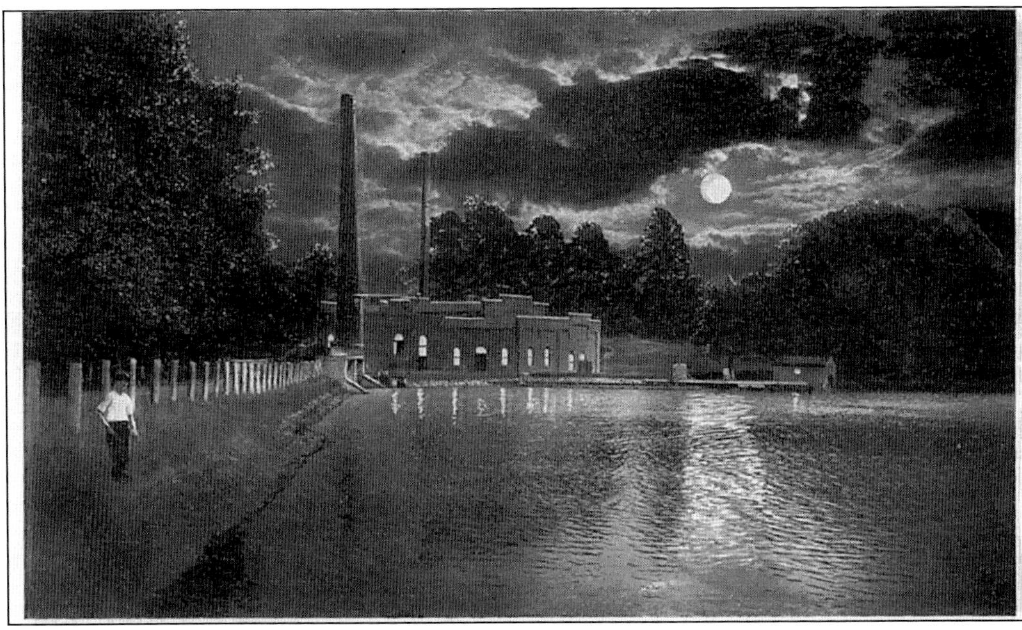

The waterworks was an exceedingly popular subject for postcards early in the century. The tall black standpipe provided water pressure. The pumping plant—an obvious essential—is shown here. Eventually the waterworks came to be the property of the city of Portsmouth.

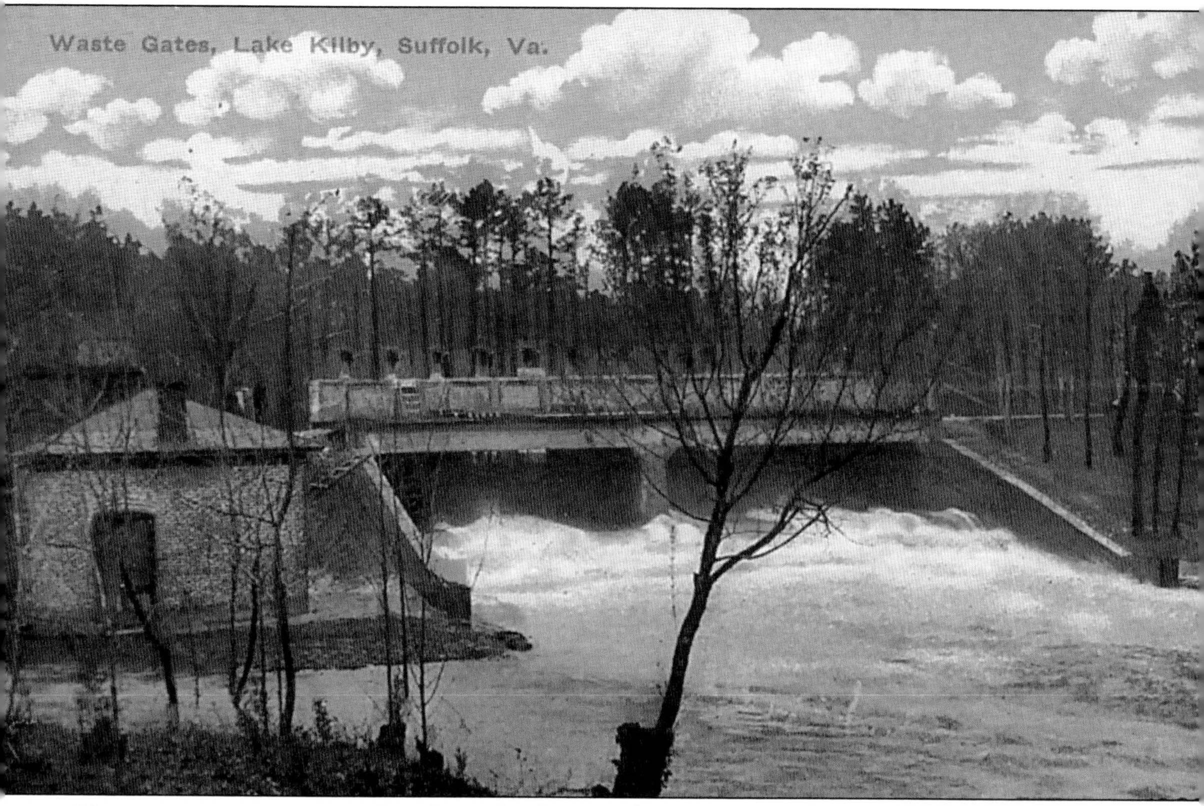

The waste gates present another dramatic picture. The property in the background on the west side was purchased in preparation for building the waterworks. It belongs to the City of Portsmouth today and, for the last 50 years, has been the site of the Suffolk Golf Course.

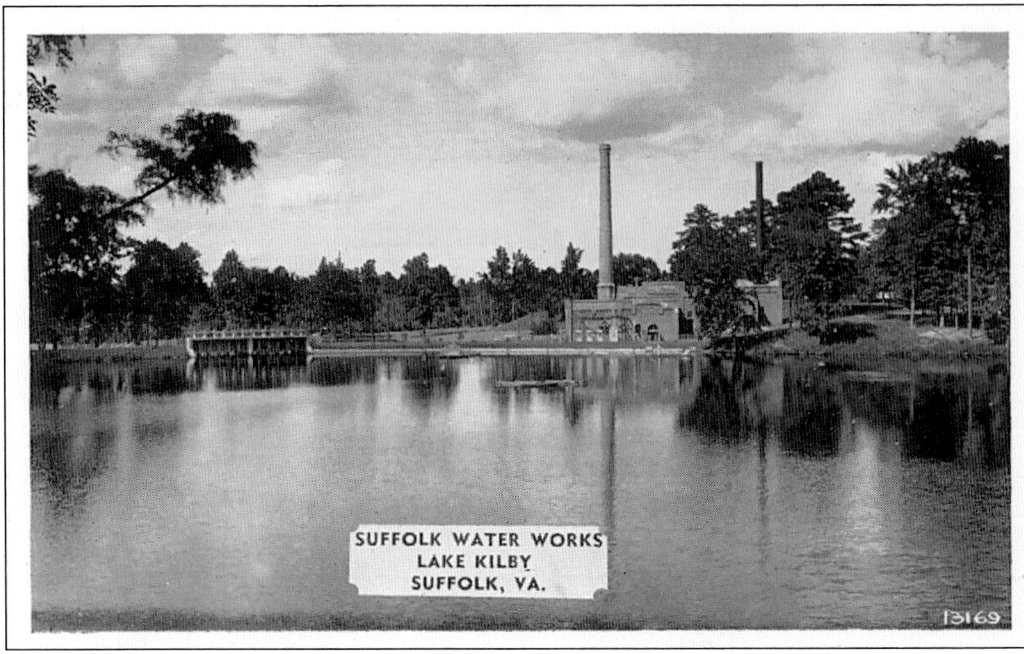

The card above was published by the Starkey Mathews Company of Suffolk, which was located on East Washington Street at the time. The card was mailed in the 1940s. One writer of another card noted that thousands of dollars were spent to make the place beautiful. The card below shows a park-like setting with a bench and a swing beneath shade trees.

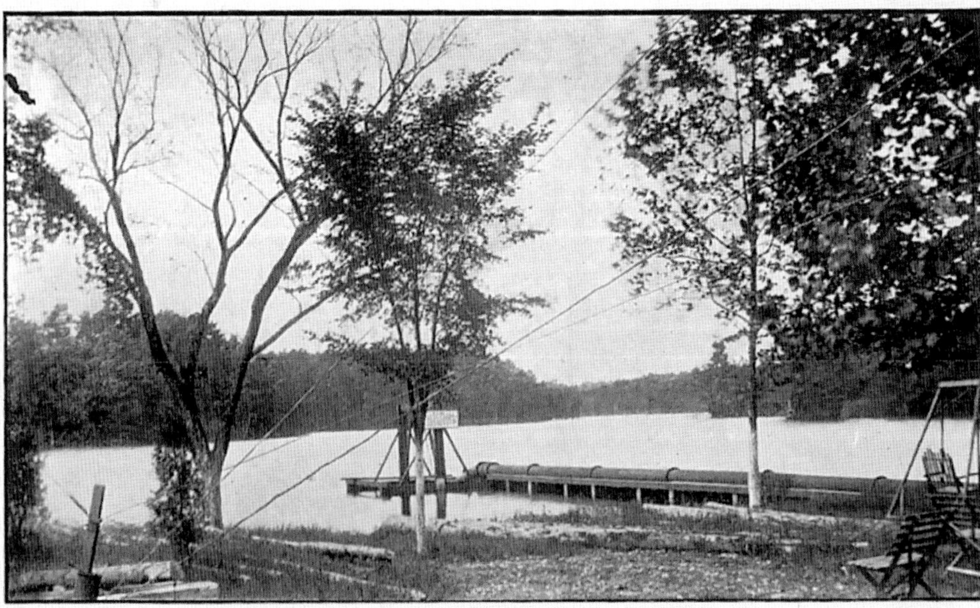

LAKE KILBY, CITY WATER SUPPLY, SUFFOLK, VA.

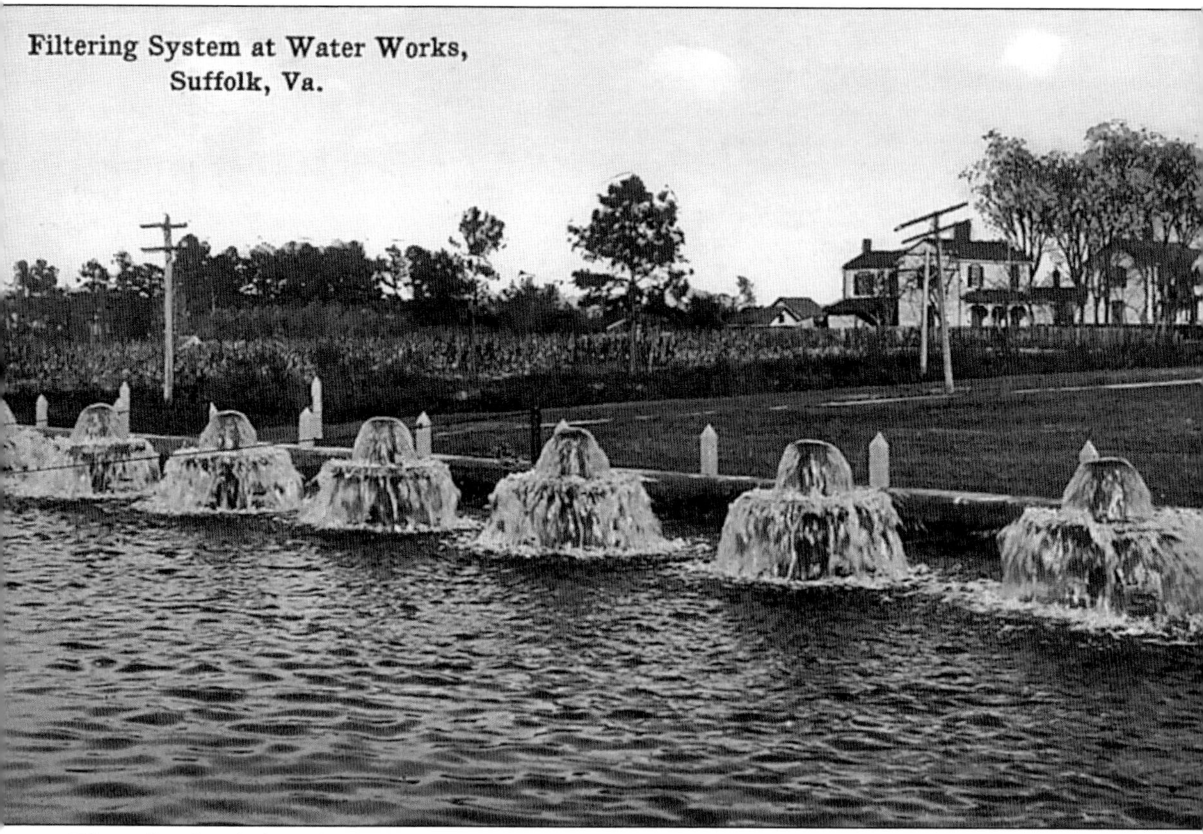

The Kilby family bought the lake and the mill from James R. Saunders after the Civil War. Perhaps the house shown in this view was the Kilby home. Several family members are buried in a small cemetery on the waterworks property. The main feature of the view here, however, is the filtration system. This card was published by J.D. Dickerson of Suffolk.

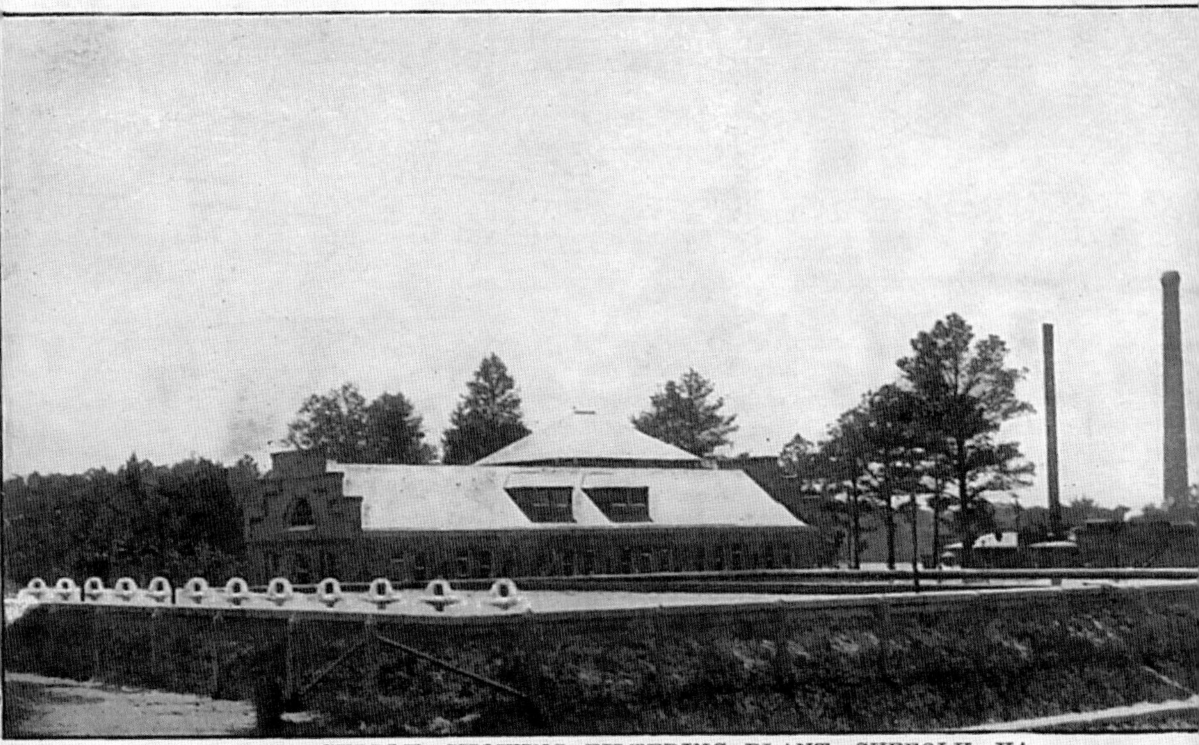

CITY WATER SUPPLY, SHOWING FILTERING PLANT, SUFFOLK, VA.

The filtering plant, shown here after completion, provided clean drinking water. This picture was taken around 1907, soon after the first filtering plant was built. With many additions and improvements, the plant was used until an entirely new treatment facility was constructed late in the 20th century.

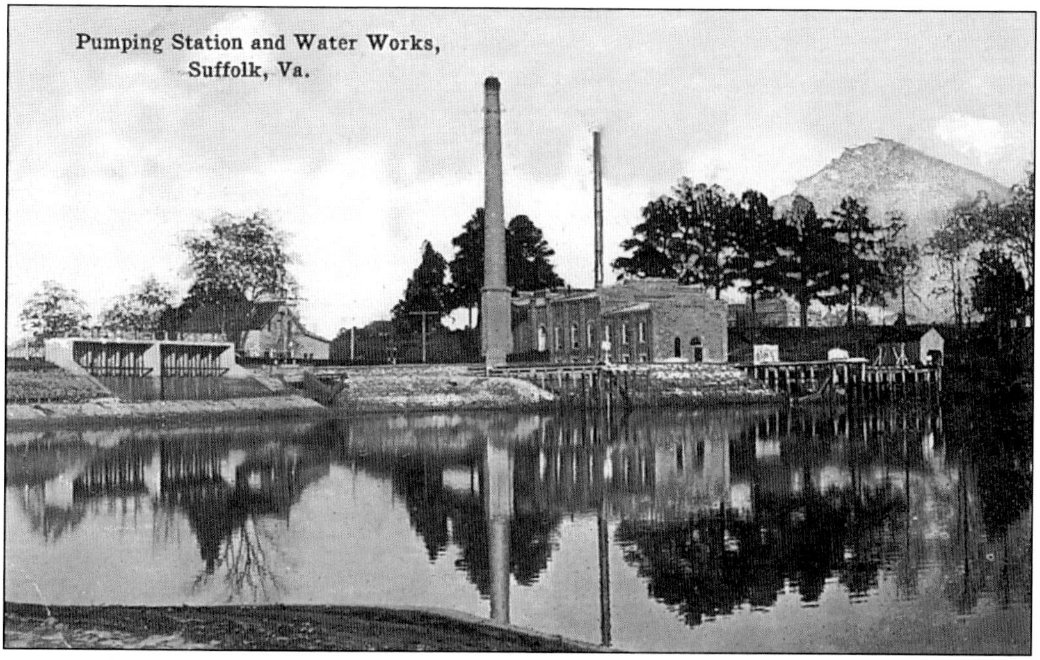

West Washington Street (the Holland Road) originally ran very near the steam-powered pumping station and over the waste gates. This must have provided a dramatic view for travellers.

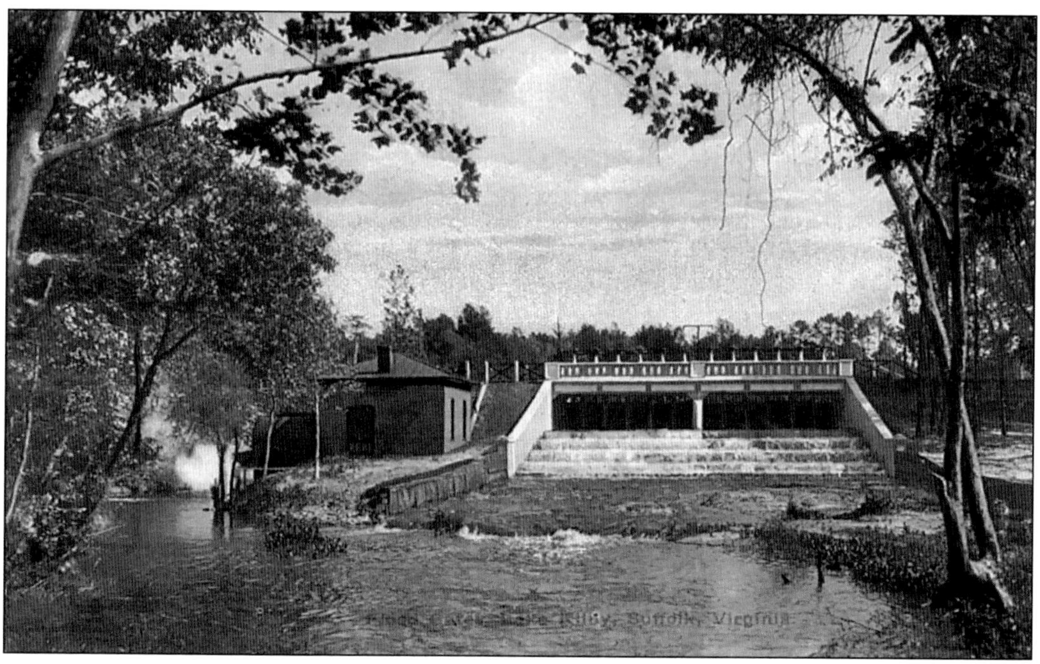

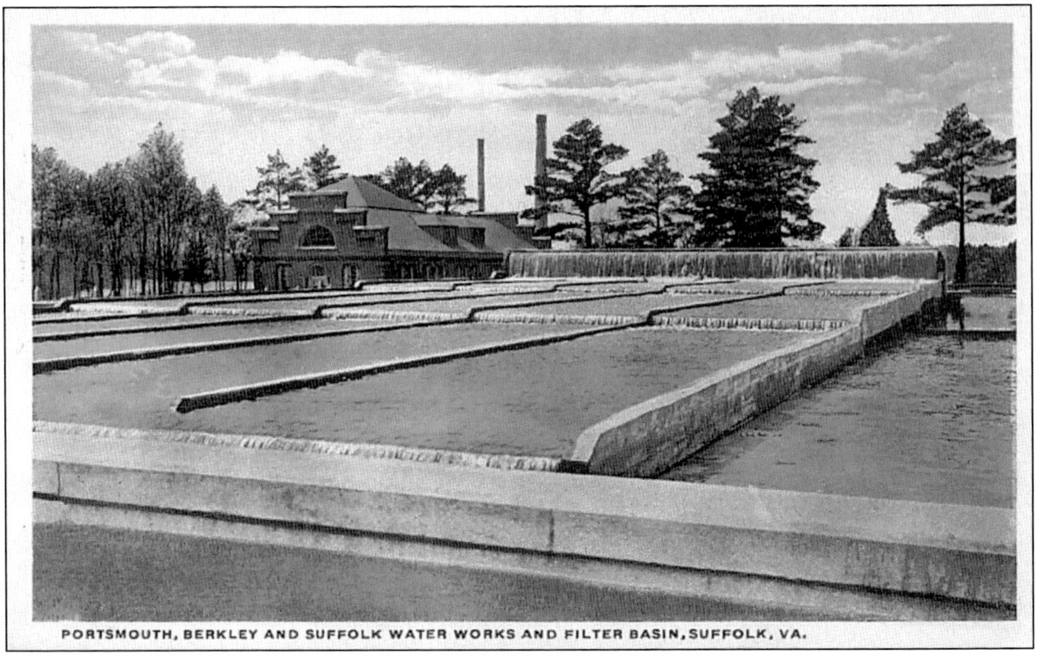

The original filtration system was built by the privately owned Portsmouth, Suffolk, and Berkley Water Company. Around 1919 the City of Portsmouth bought the facility.

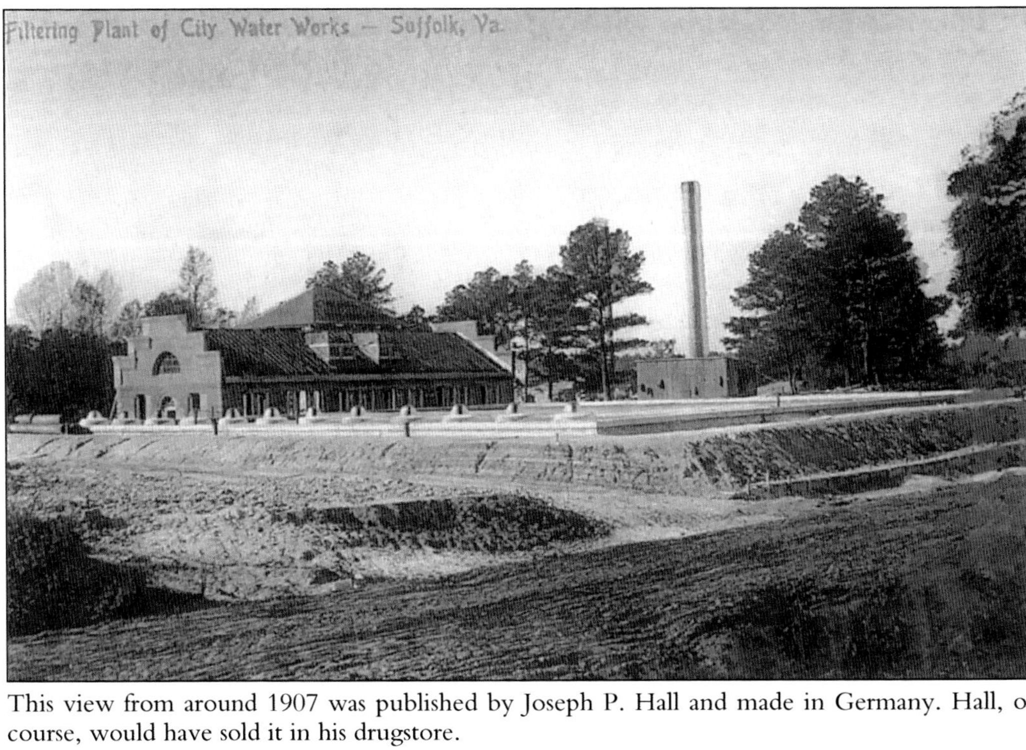

This view from around 1907 was published by Joseph P. Hall and made in Germany. Hall, of course, would have sold it in his drugstore.

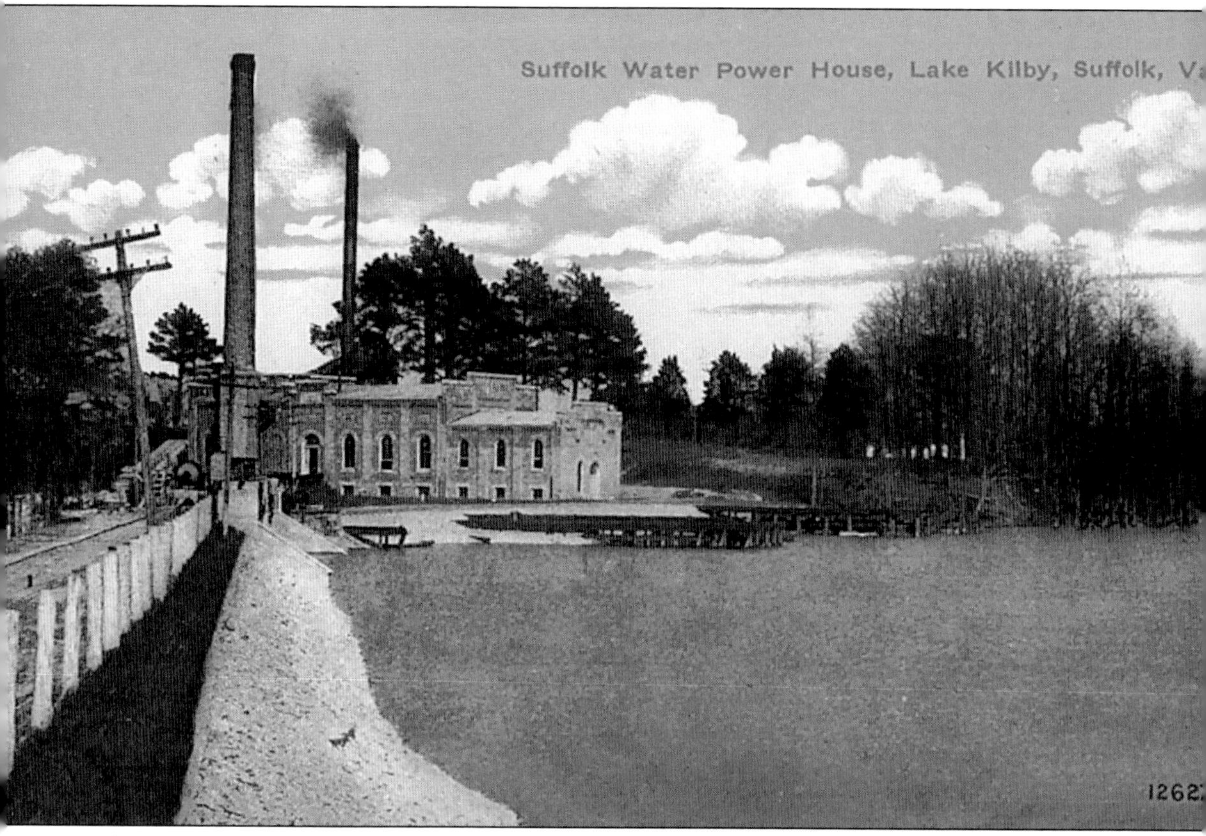

In the view here we see the Holland Road to the left of the picture. The power house had a large smokestack, also seen above, as part of its steam operation. The tall black standpipe was some distance to the east and provided water pressure.

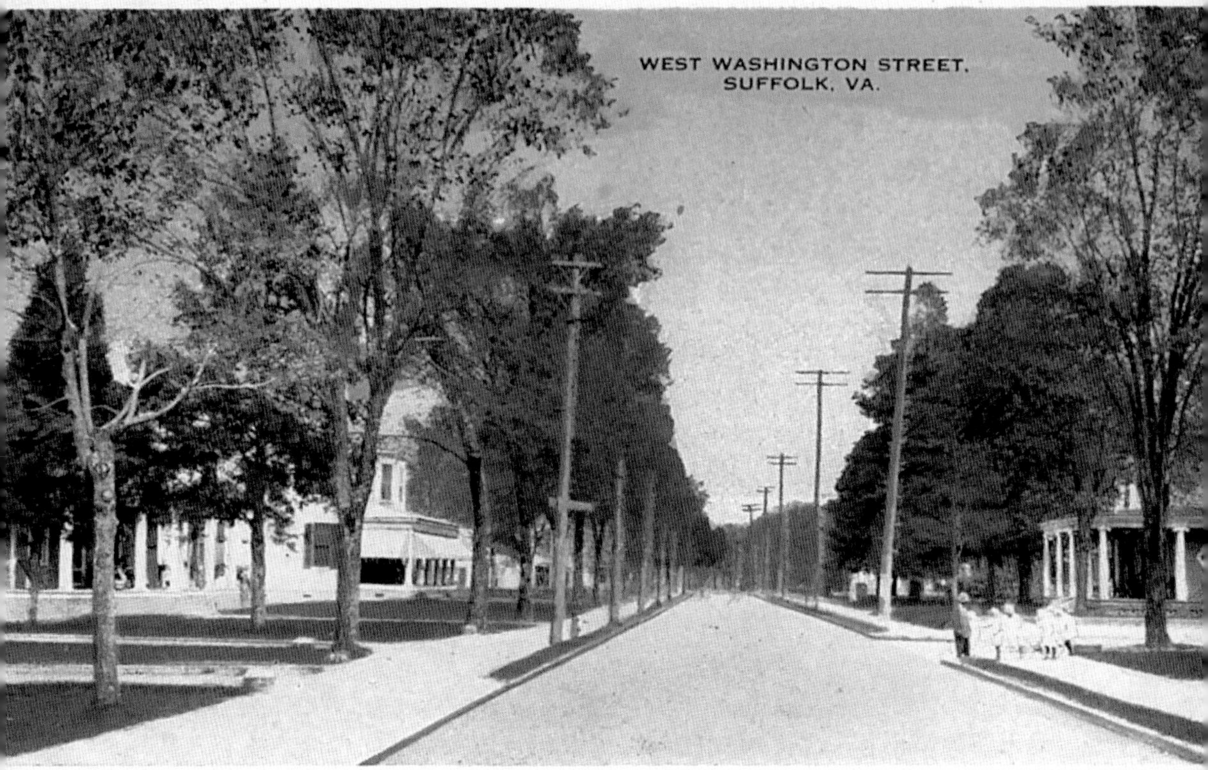

Looking west, this is the route to the waterworks. This was the perfect Sunday afternoon stroll.

Seven

Scenic Suffolk

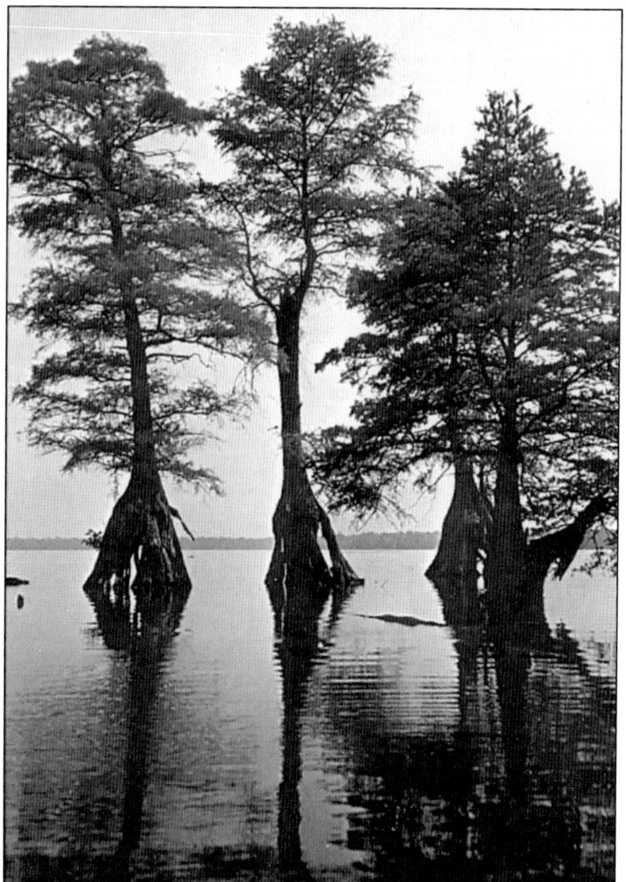

Legends about the Great Dismal Swamp, which has fascinated man throughout history, are numerous. Resting in parts of several counties in two states, the lake contains one of the two natural lakes in Virginia. Lake Drummond, which is 3.5 miles long and 2.5 miles wide, is shown here. The juniper water was once thought to have curative powers and was sold by the cask. Col. William Byrd named the swamp when he surveyed the area in 1728, and George Washington invested in it.

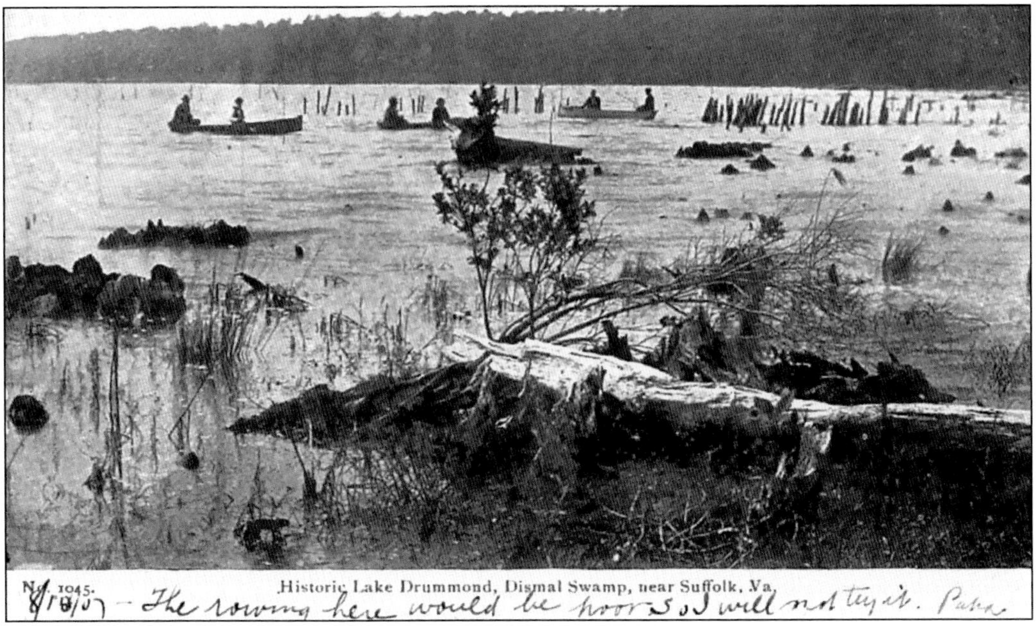

Before the Department of the Interior gained ownership of much of the swamp, people had hunting camps there. There are no more camps and there are many restrictions about when and how the swamp can be used. The purpose is to protect this rare spot from any more damage by man. The lake was named for William Drummond, who was later governor of North Carolina.

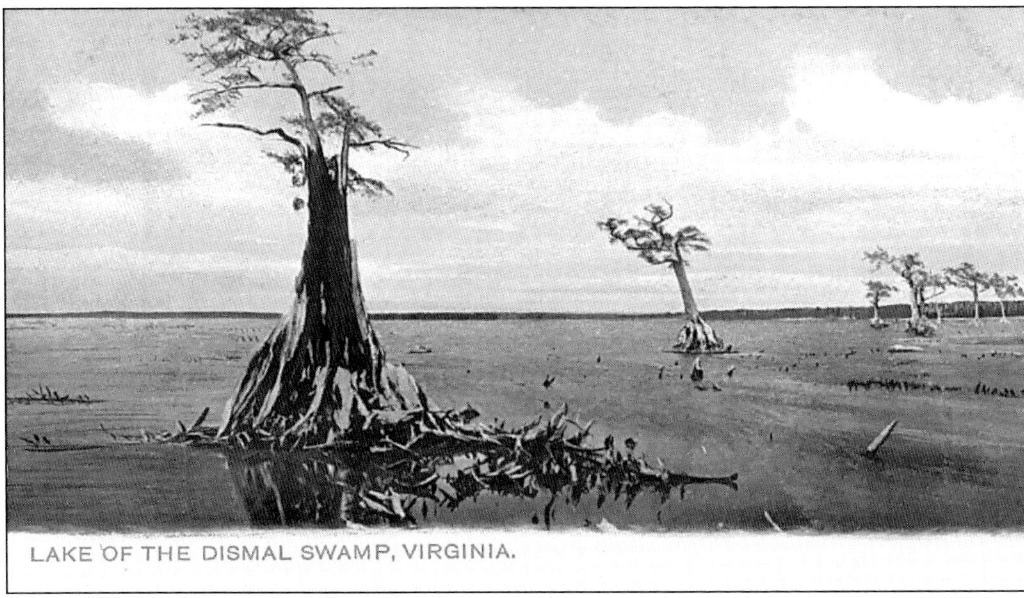

Thomas Moore wrote a ballad entitled "The Lake of the Dismal Swamp" about a pair of ill-fated lovers. Many other 19th century writers were inspired by the mysterious swamp, including Harriet Beecher Stowe, who wrote *Dred, A Tale of the Dismal Swamp*; Henry Wadsworth Longfellow, who penned a poem called "The Slave in the Dismal Swamp"; and Henry David Thoreau, who wrote in *Walden* about railroads "next in the Great Dismal Swamp scaring the owl and the fox."

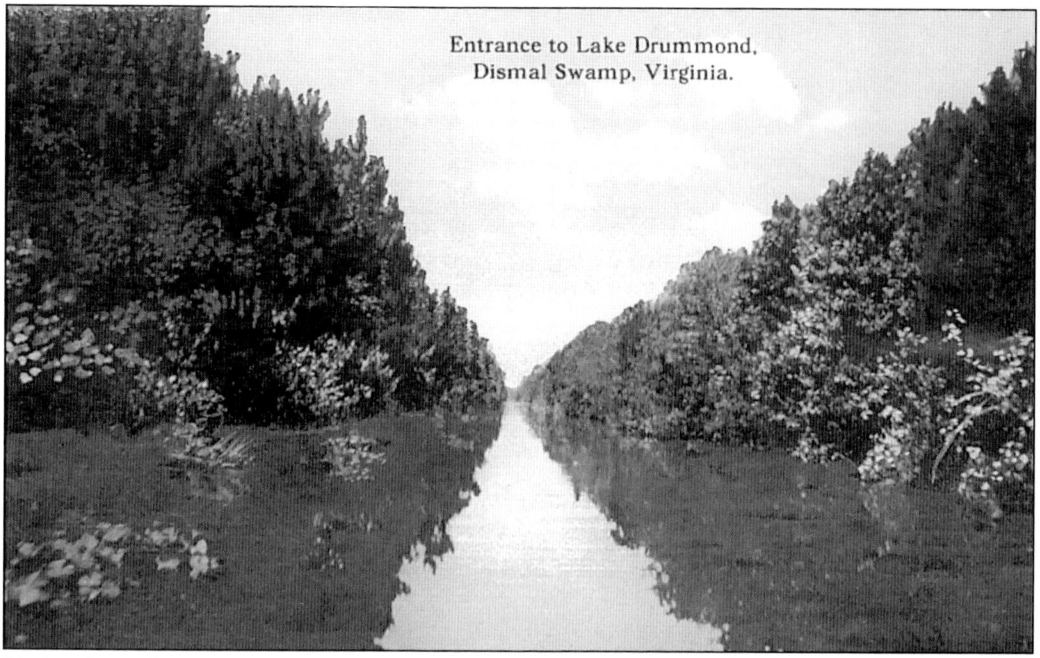

Today the only water entrance to the Swamp is through Chesapeake where the Dismal Swamp Canal runs. The only land entrance is in Suffolk. The vegetation along the canal above gives some idea of how impenetrable the swamp is. Even experienced woodsmen have been known to get lost here.

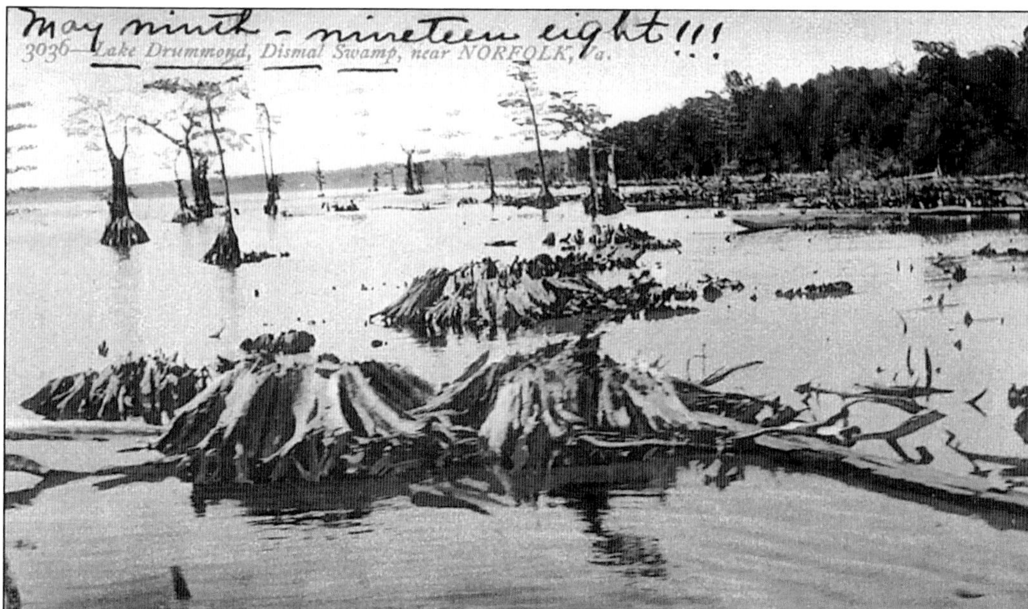

Historian Joseph Dunn wrote "The strange bald knees of the cypress rear themselves about the huge body of the parent tree, and the lifted arches of the gum, covered in hardy annual flowers, give an infinite variety of color . . . . The ferns wave along the banks, high as a man's head, and every passing breeze quickens into life the whispering reeds."

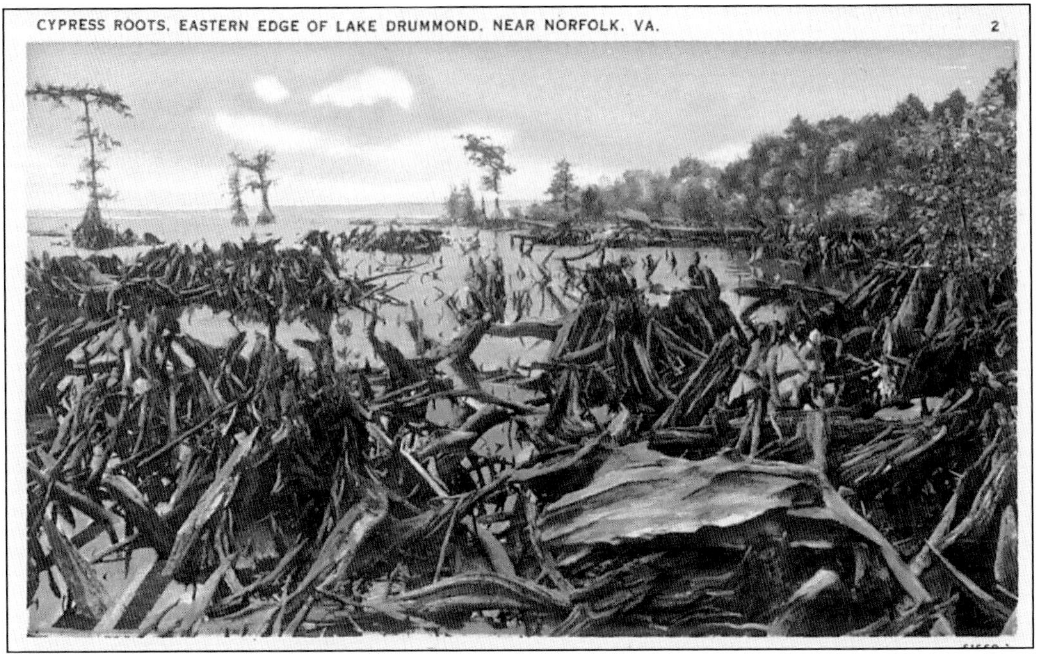

Trees were cut from the swamp for a long time. Logging and drainage ditches have changed the nature of the plant life in the swamp. Even the once plentiful cypress is not quite so plentiful any longer.

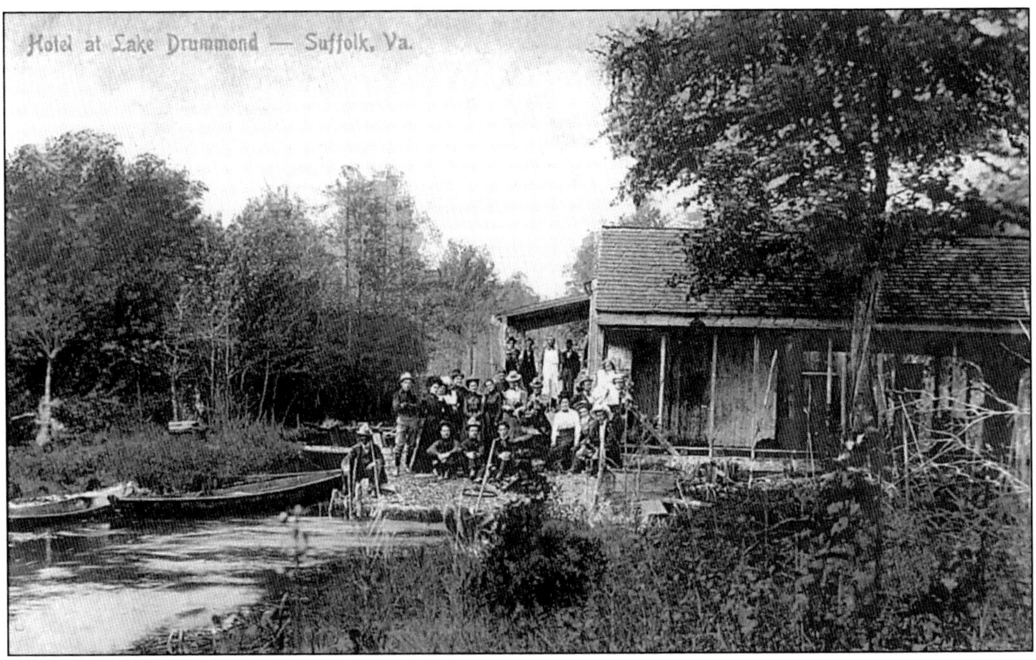

From the earliest days of English habitation of the area, the Dismal Swamp has attracted sportsmen, adventurers, runaways, lovers, and pleasure seekers. The hotel in the swamp was the site of duels and elopements as it sat on the state line in a kind of no-mans-land.

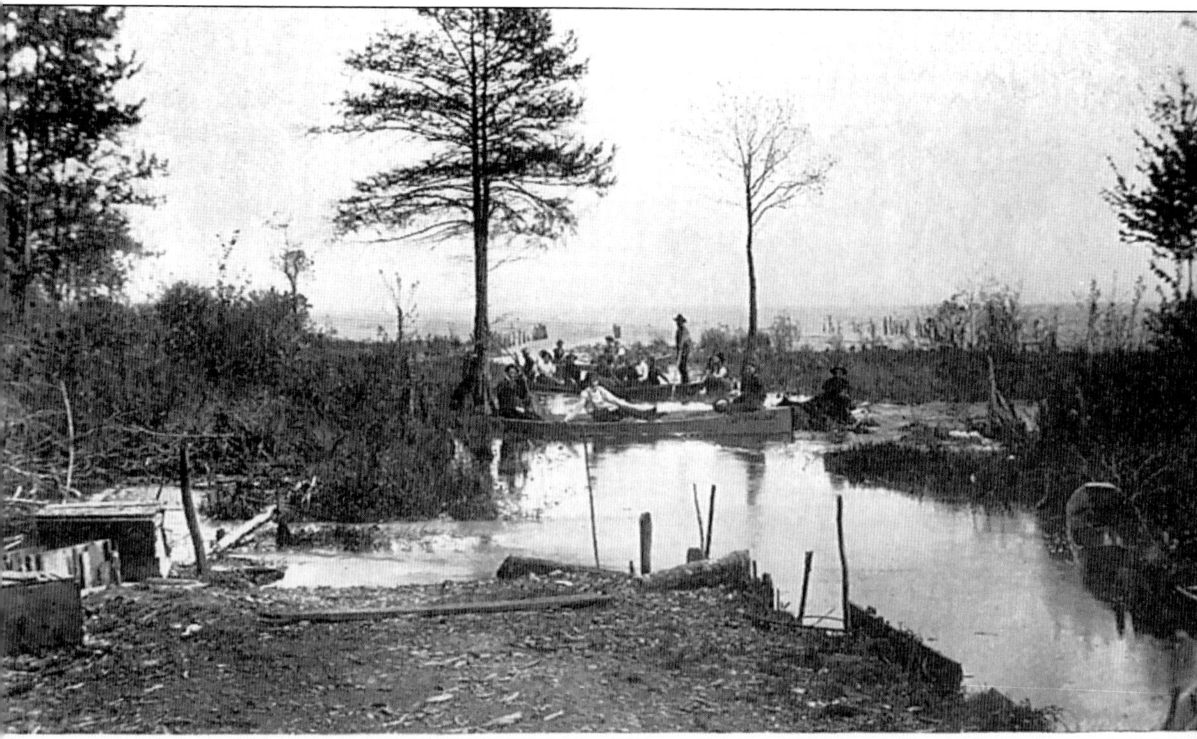

25. "LAKE DRUMMOND," DISMAL SWAMP, ACCESSABLE FROM SUFFOLK, VA.

The trees of the vast peat bog known as the Dismal Swamp attracted businessmen for at least three centuries. Of particular interest were the cypress and juniper trees. Canals were built to move forest products out of the swamp and to market. The Jericho Ditch, one of the canals, went to the Nansemond River by way of Shingle Creek—so named because of the vast number of wooden shingles that moved through there.

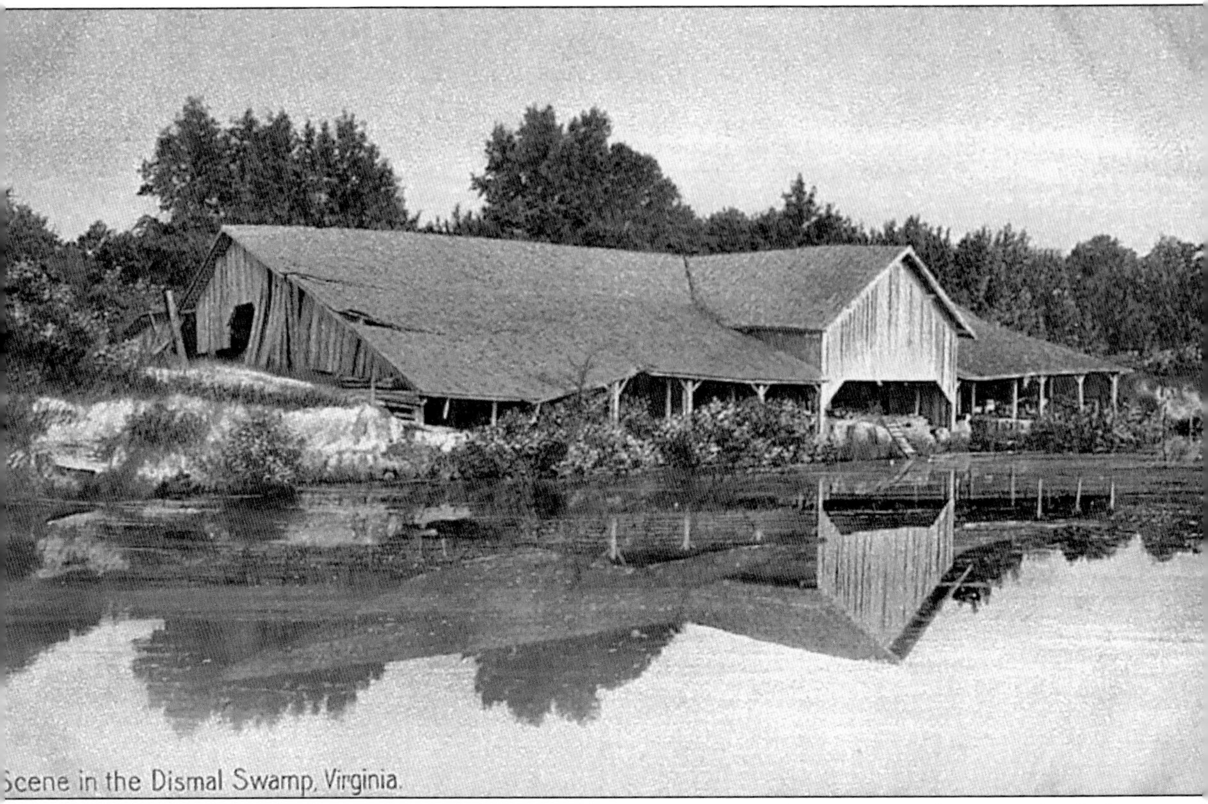

This building is probably a remnant of the big lumber days when scores of loggers mined the "gold" of the swamp. The Camp family of Franklin was among those who sought riches in the forests of the swamp. In 1973 they changed the swamp's future for the better by deeding 50,000 acres to the Department of the Interior.

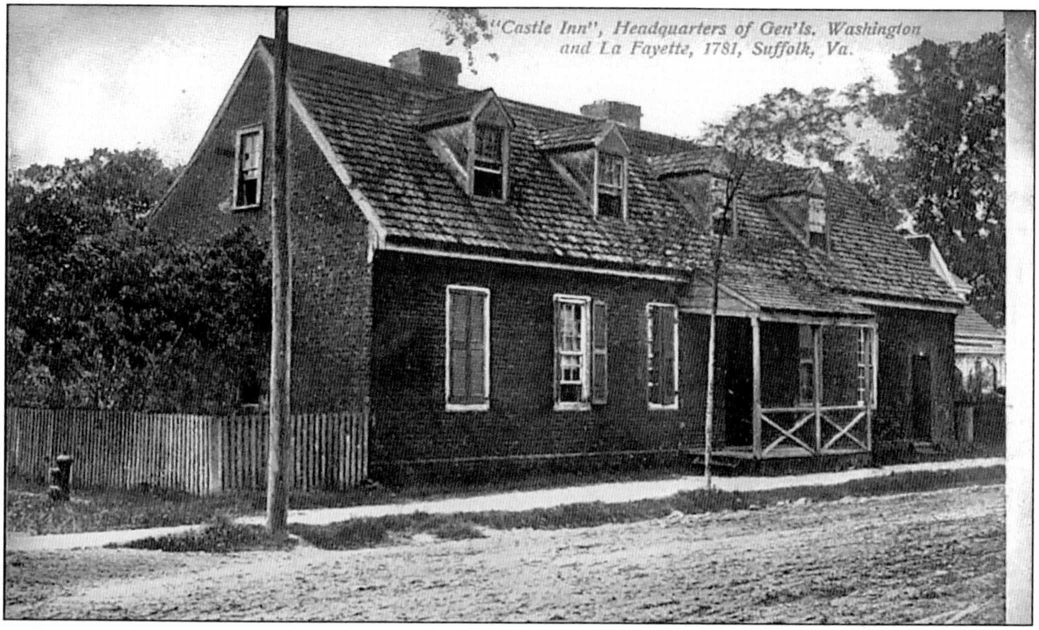

Lafayette did stay at the Castle Inn when he came to Suffolk in 1825. However, although labeled as the Castle Inn, this is actually the 1752 alms house (or poor house) that was one of the few buildings to survive when the British burned Suffolk in 1779. The house stood on the northwest corner of present-day Mahan and Main Streets but was demolished in 1912.

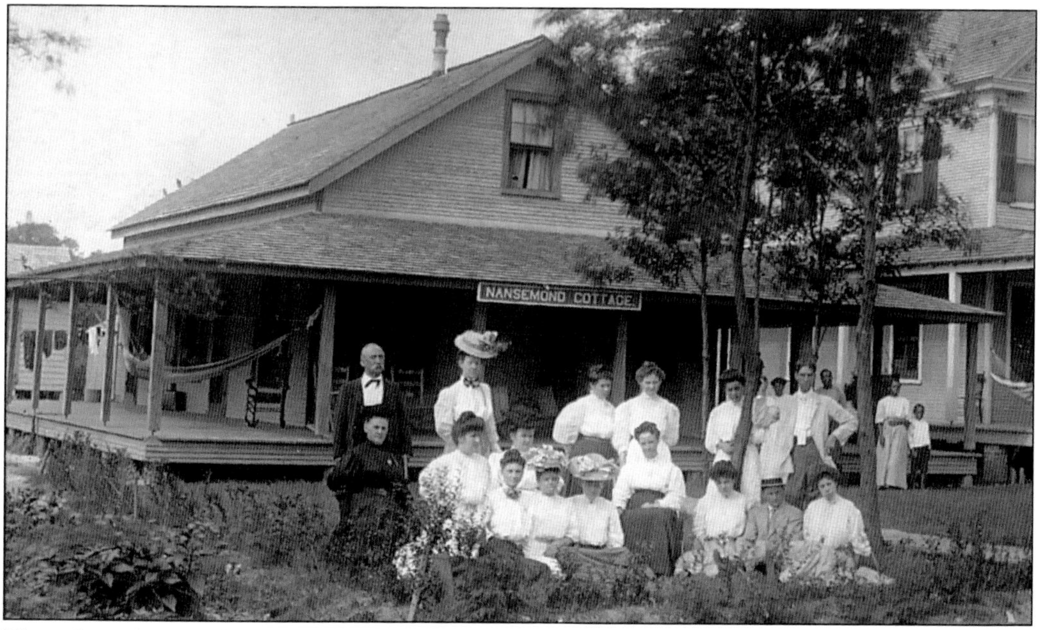

The whereabouts of the Nansemond Cottage is unknown to this writer except to say that it is beside a railroad, perhaps in the Dismal Swamp or at Magnolia Salt Sulpher Spring. The Gibson Girl attire modeled by the ladies in the foreground represented a casual summer look about a century ago. The African-American workers in the background might have traveled to the holiday spot with their employer.

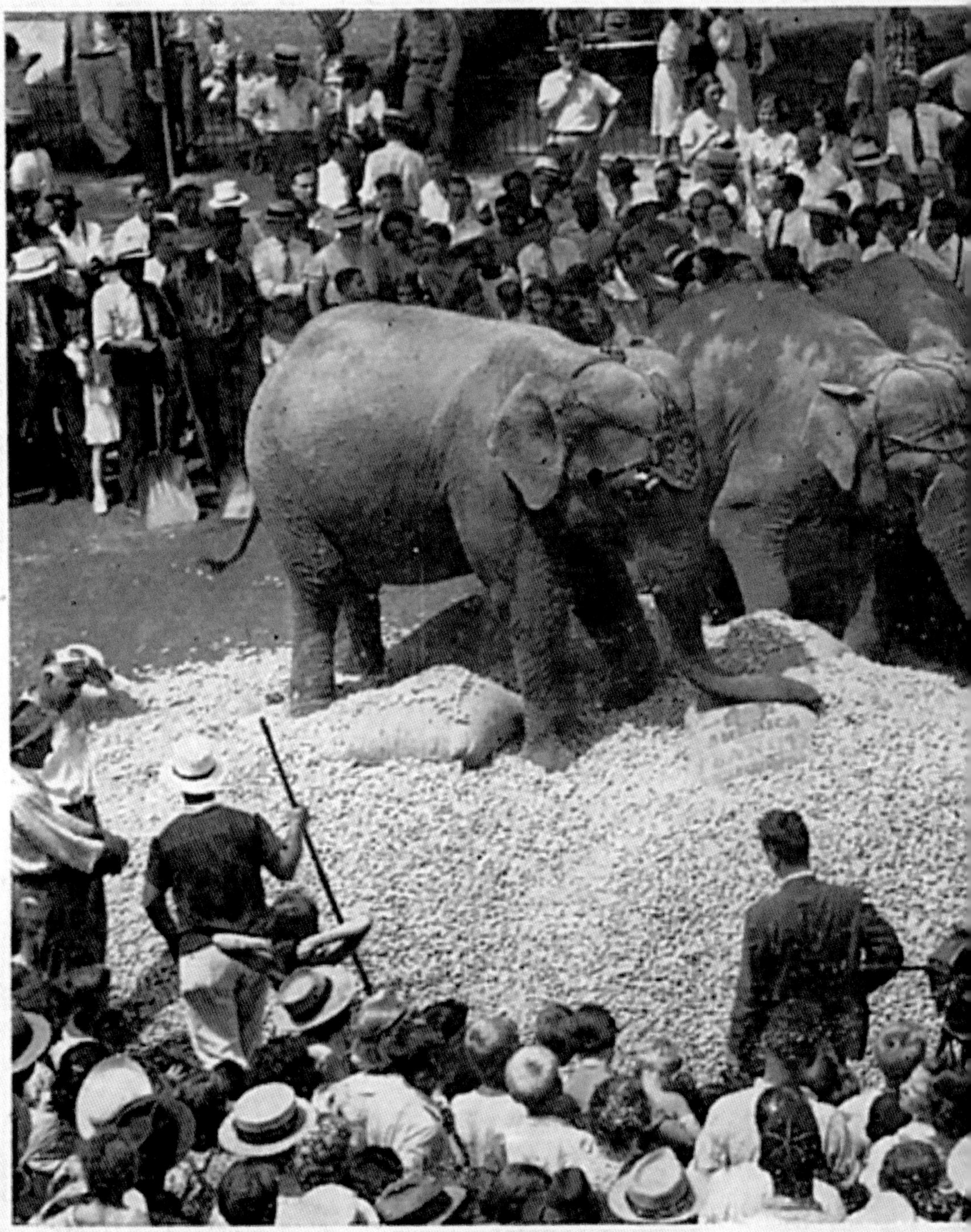

In 1941 the first peanut festival was celebrated in a very big way. As a kickoff for festival events, a load of peanuts was dumped on Main Street and elephants from Barnum and Bailey's Circus were

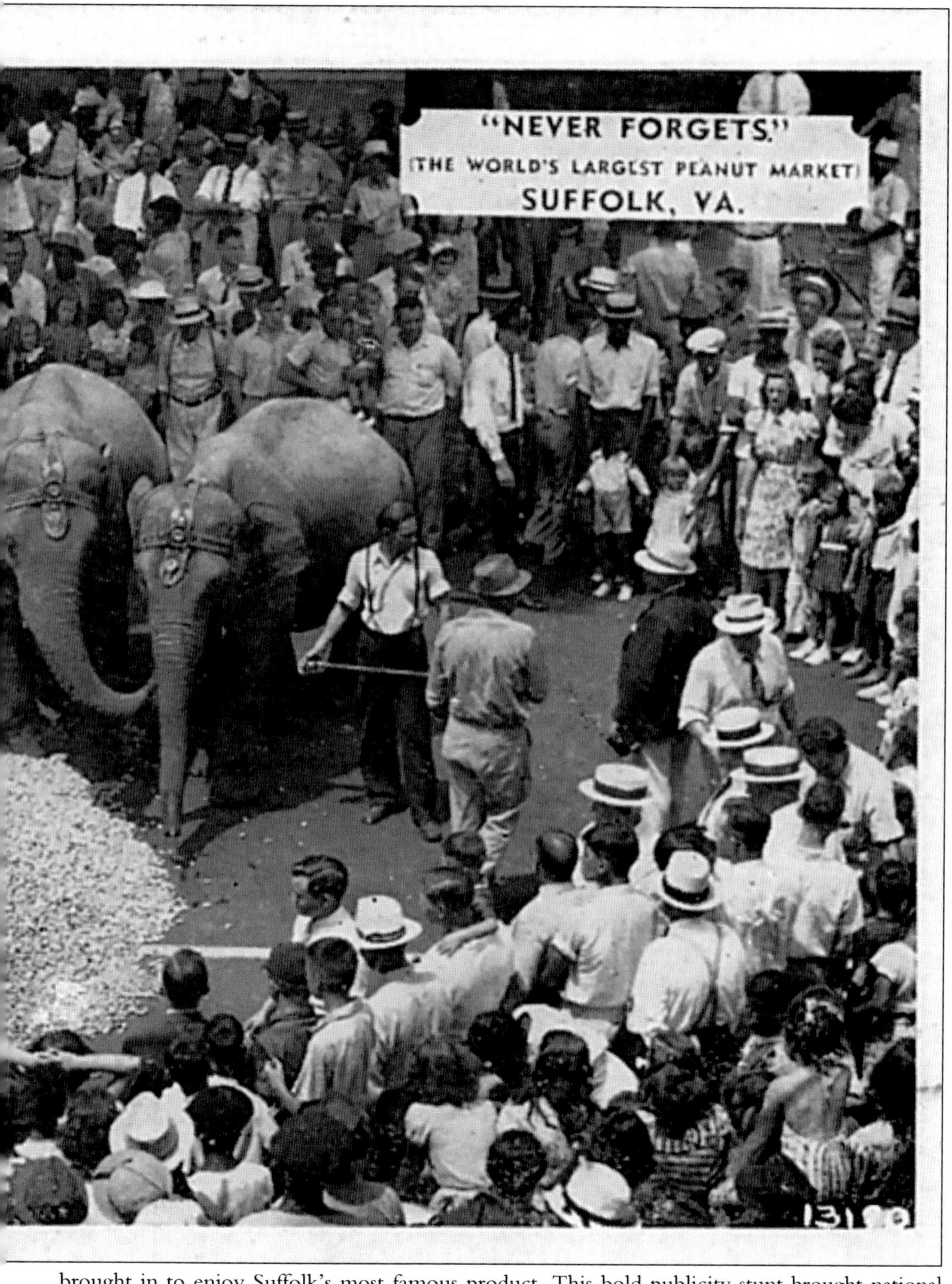

brought in to enjoy Suffolk's most famous product. This bold publicity stunt brought national attention to Suffolk as the World's Largest Peanut Market.

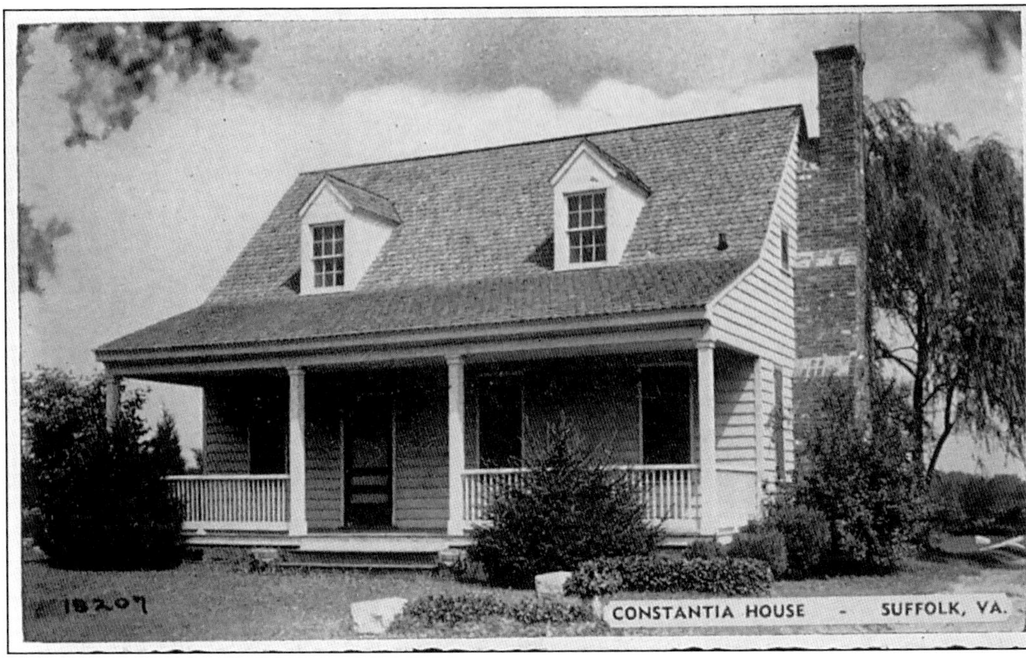

John Constant is thought to have been Suffolk's first permanent English settler. In fact, the village here was first known as Constant's Wharf. His home was built *c.* 1720 on a hill overlooking the river. In the 1920s the Constantia Chapter of the D.A.R. demolished the old house and built this replica. Cedar Hill Cemetery eventually covered what had been Constant's farm. The replica of the house has been moved to another site.

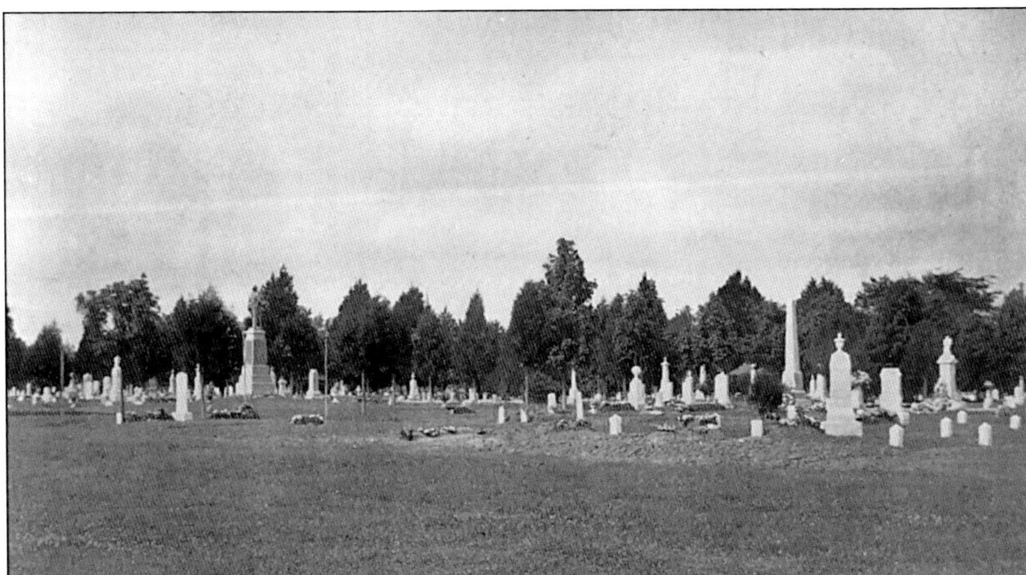

Cedar Hill began with a community chapel built on part of John Constant's farm around 1802. The area around the chapel became a burial ground and Cedar Hill grew from that. It is thought that the open space in the foreground was the site of the chapel and the earliest graves. It is likely that Wilbur J. Kilby, superintendent of Cedar Hill in the late 1800s, planted the cedars.

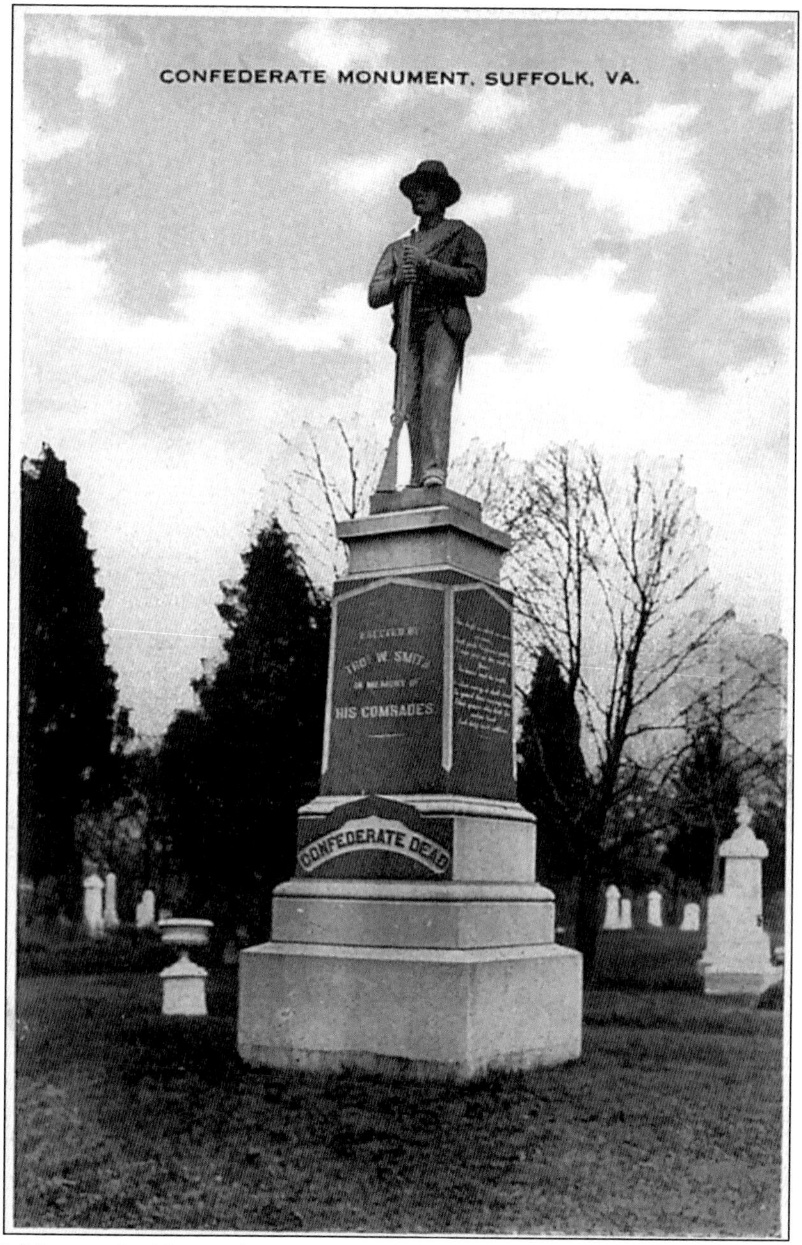

Thomas Washington Smith was born in Somerton, served in the Confederate Army, and had a successful post-war business career in Suffolk. He had this monument erected in beautiful old Cedar Hill Cemetery on November 14, 1889 in memory of his fallen comrades. The dedication was a splendid affair with a parade of dignitaries and Confederate veterans in carriages, on foot, and on horseback departing from the Smith home on Franklin Street. Numerous orations were given at the site, including one by Gov. Fitzburgh Lee. Tom Smith and his family are buried nearby. In 1878 Captain Smith had organized a militia group. He dressed them in Confederate gray uniforms and called them the Suffolk Grays. This group later became Company F of the Fourth Regiment of the Virginia Militia. They were one of two Suffolk Units to serve in the Spanish-American War.

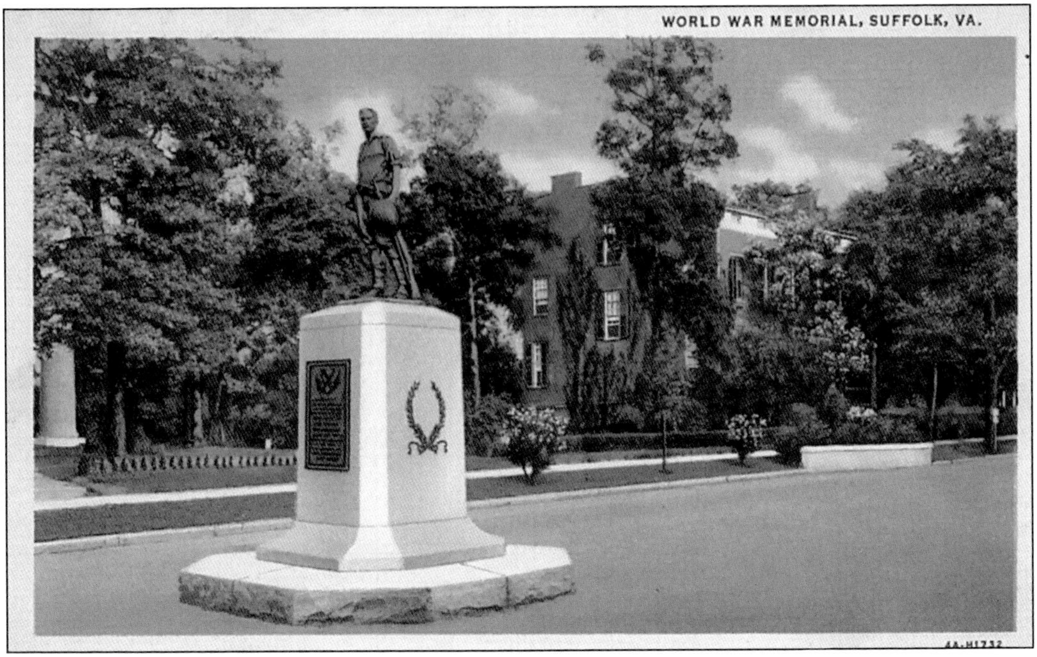

The World War I monument was erected by the American Legion in memory of men from Suffolk and Nansemond County who died in that war. It was dedicated on May 10, 1931 at its original site in the street in front of the old Nansemond County Courthouse. In the background we see the 1837 Riddick home, now a house museum.

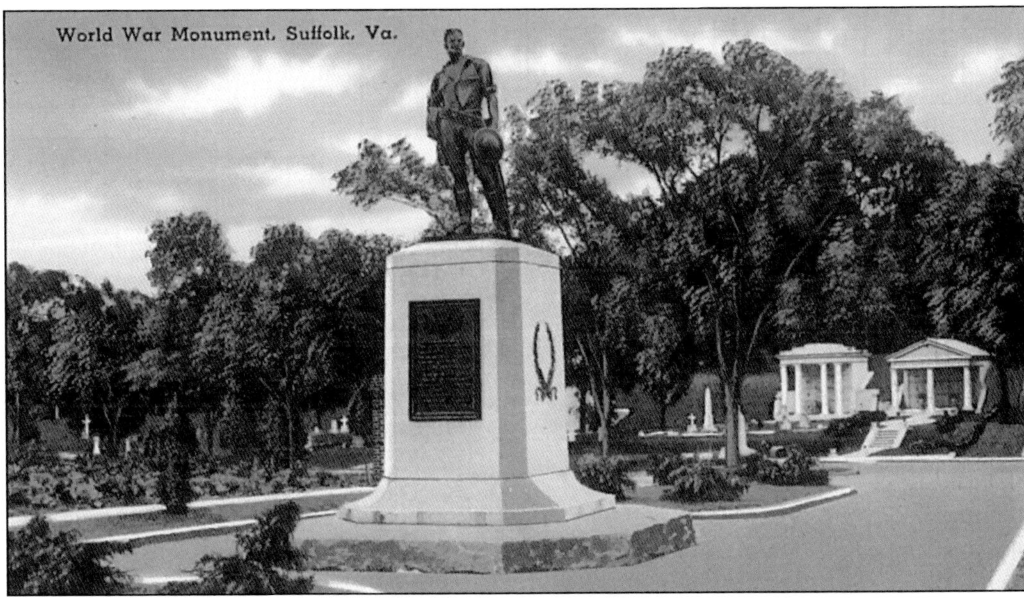

The Word War I monument was soon moved to the entrance of Cedar Hill Cemetery where it now stands with other war memorials. Dr. F. Whitney Godwin, a native of Chuckatuck, was instrumental in having the monument erected initially. He is interred in a mausoleum visible in the background. The Brewer-Godwin mausoleum is on the left and the I.O. Hill mausoleum is to the right.

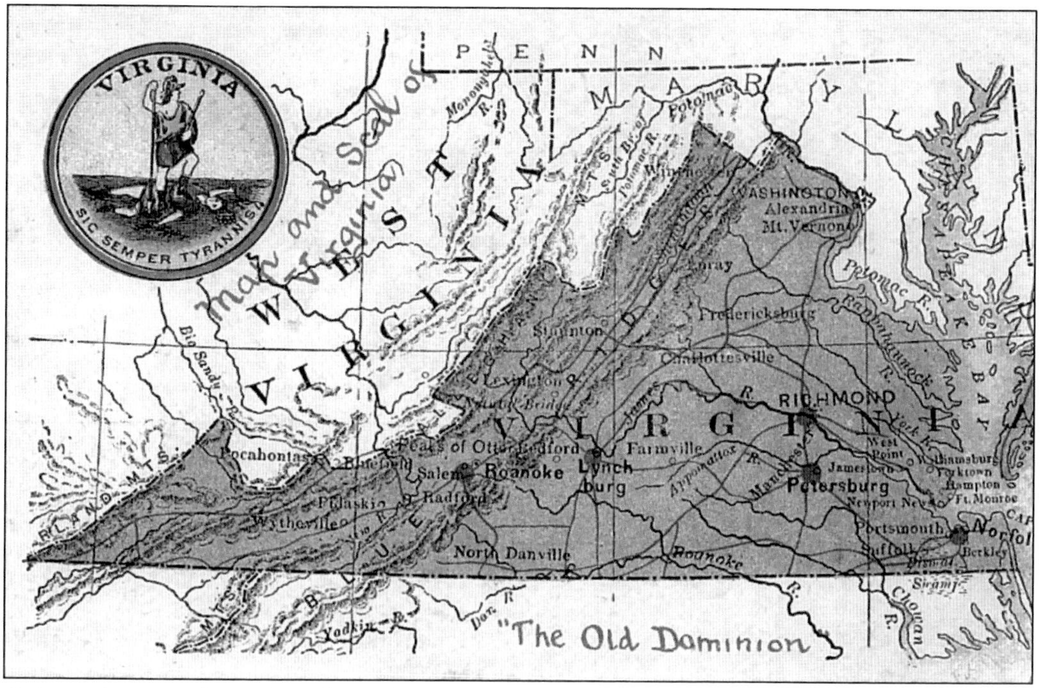

Perhaps the map above dates from the 1907 Jamestown Exposition, which celebrated the 300th anniversary of the Jamestown Settlement and the birth of the Virginia colony.

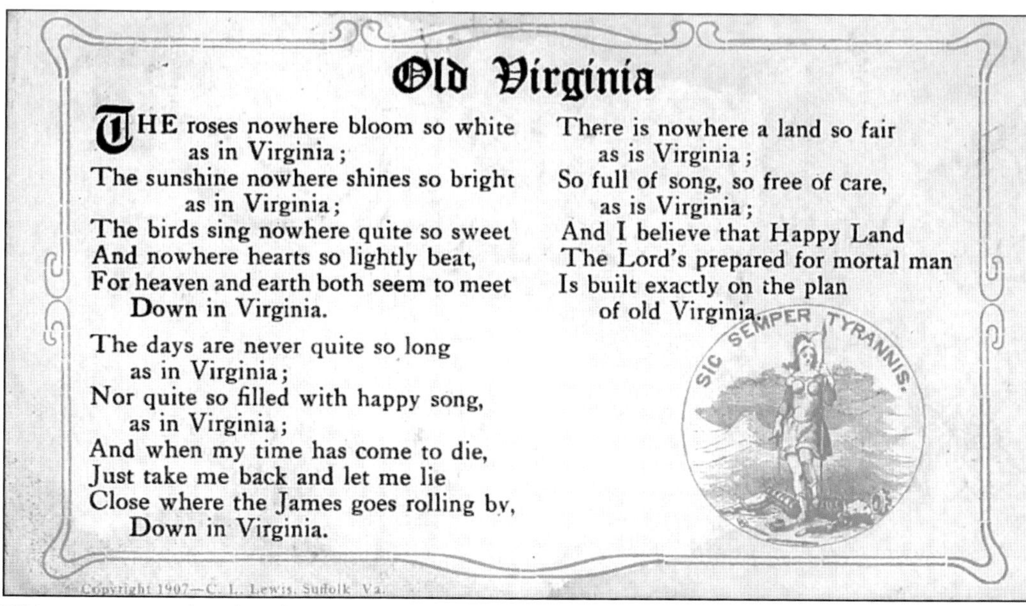

Old Virginia

THE roses nowhere bloom so white
as in Virginia;
The sunshine nowhere shines so bright
as in Virginia;
The birds sing nowhere quite so sweet
And nowhere hearts so lightly beat,
For heaven and earth both seem to meet
Down in Virginia.

The days are never quite so long
as in Virginia;
Nor quite so filled with happy song,
as in Virginia;
And when my time has come to die,
Just take me back and let me lie
Close where the James goes rolling by,
Down in Virginia.

There is nowhere a land so fair
as is Virginia;
So full of song, so free of care,
as is Virginia;
And I believe that Happy Land
The Lord's prepared for mortal man
Is built exactly on the plan
of old Virginia.

Copyright 1907—C. L. Lewis, Suffolk, Va.

This poem may also date from the Jamestown Exposition like the map above.

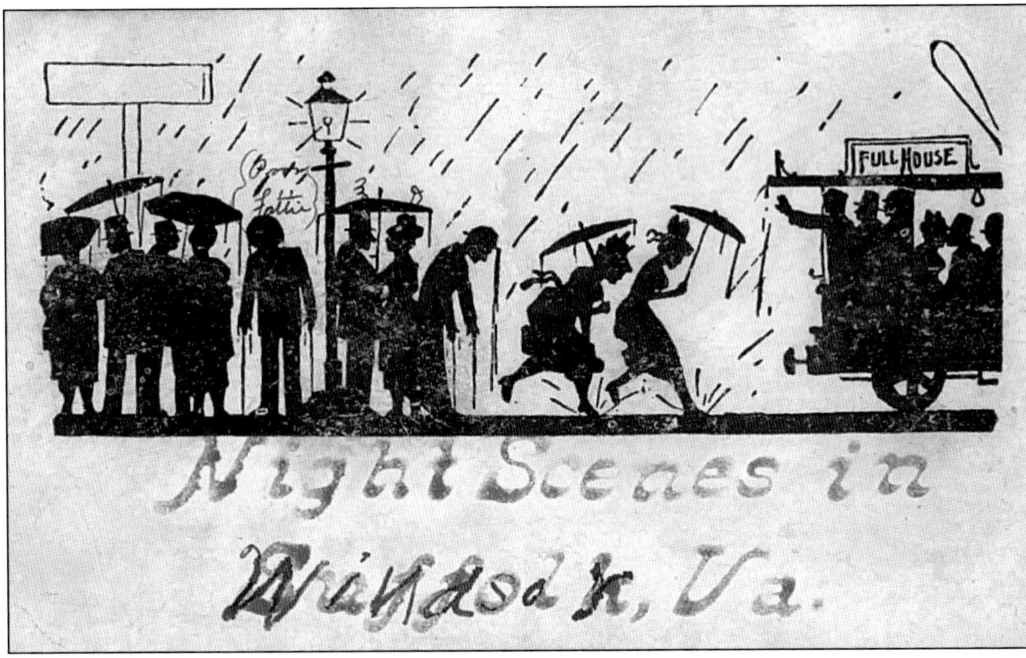

Though this card originally said "Night Scenes in Suffolk, Va.," someone changed the word "Suffolk" to "Windsor," the name of a small town about 10 miles away.

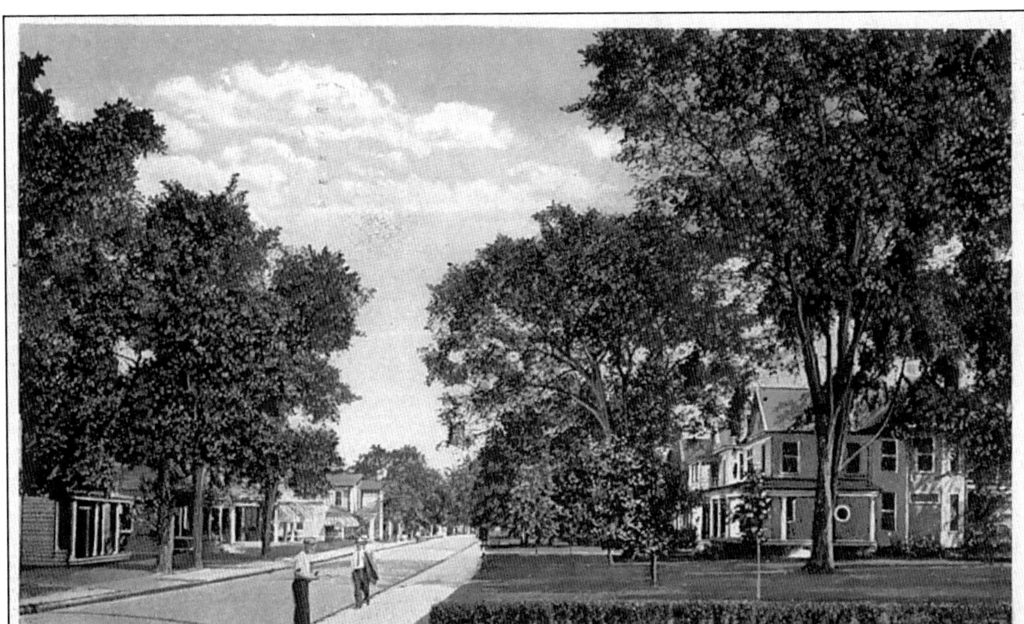

No matter where we wander, no matter where we roam, at the end of the day, thoughts turn toward home.